access to history

Russia and its Rulers 1855–1964

Andrew Holland

Series editor: Geoff Woodward

HODDER
EDUCATION
AN HACHETTE UK COMPANY

The Publishers would like to thank the following for permission to reproduce copyright material:

Photo credits: p.4 © Chris Hellier/CORBIS; **pp.5, 6** © CORBIS; **p.9** © Library of Congress – digital ve/Science Faction/Corbis; **pp.11, 13** © Bettmann/CORBIS; **p.88** *t* © Marc Garanger/CORBIS, *b* © Thomas Johnson/Sygma/CORBIS.

Acknowledgements: p.61 M. Lynch, *Reaction and Revolution: Russia 1881–1924*, Hodder Education (2004); **p.110** A. Nove, *An Economic History of the U.S.S.R.*, Allen Lane (1969); **p.112** J.N. Westwood, *Endurance and Endeavour: Russian History 1812–2001*, Oxford University Press (2002).

Every effort has been made to trace all copyright holders, but if any have been inadvertently overlooked the Publishers will be pleased to make the necessary arrangements at the first opportunity.

Although every effort has been made to ensure that website addresses are correct at time of going to press, Hodder Education cannot be held responsible for the content of any website mentioned in this book. It is sometimes possible to find a relocated web page by typing in the address of the home page for a website in the URL window of your browser.

Hachette UK's policy is to use papers that are natural, renewable and recyclable products and made from wood grown in sustainable forests. The logging and manufacturing processes are expected to conform to the environmental regulations of the country of origin.

Orders: please contact Bookpoint Ltd, 130 Milton Park, Abingdon, Oxon OX14 4SB. Telephone: (44) 01235 827720. Fax: (44) 01235 400454. Lines are open 9.00–5.00, Monday to Saturday, with a 24-hour message answering service. Visit our website at www.hoddereducation.co.uk

© Andrew Holland 2010
First published in 2010 by
Hodder Education,
An Hachette UK company
338 Euston Road
London NW1 3BH

Impression number   5
Year   2014 2013 2012

Cover photo: Russian World War I Poster Exhorting Citizens to Arms © Swim Ink 2, LLC/CORBIS
Typeset in 10/12pt Baskerville and produced by Gray Publishing, Tunbridge Wells
Printed in Great Britain by CPI Group (UK) Ltd, Croydon, CR0 4YY

A catalogue record for this title is available from the British Library.

ISBN: 978 0340 983706

Contents

Chronology of Key Events

Introduction

About this book

This book covers the period from 1865 to 1964 in Russian history, from the ascension of the **Tsar** Alexander II to the end of the rule of communist leader Nikita Khrushchev. It focuses on the nature of Russian government and its impact on the Russian people and society. In particular, emphasis is placed on the degree of change and continuity between the **autocratic** rule of the tsars and the communist dictatorships that followed.

In order to discern patterns of change and continuity over the period in question, it is important to consider the similarities and differences between each ruler and not just before and after the 1917 Revolution. At the same time, getting too embroiled in the details of particular events and developments will mask the trends in change and continuity. Most people will know something about Rasputin, the murder of Nicholas II and his family, the 1917 Revolution, the atrocities committed by Stalin and the Cold War. However, the purpose of this book is to encourage the reader to synthesise such particular knowledge so that judgements can be made about more general patterns of change and continuity. This is all especially important when studying this period of Russian history. It is easy to simply assume that the events of 1917 acted as a major turning point in the development of Russian government. A more thoughtful analysis of the history, though, will reveal that there is a case for arguing that there was more continuity than change in the way Russia was ruled.

Each chapter deals with a particular theme:

- Chapter 1 deals not only with the different ideologies used by governments to rule but also with the changing structures that were adopted. The latter are often overlooked by students but are crucial to understand if one is to make sense of developments in Russian government and politics.
- Chapter 2 looks at the extent and effectiveness of opposition to rulers and how this was dealt with. Readers should think carefully about how the success of opposition groups is best measured and the relative importance of factors that influenced that success.
- Chapter 3 focuses on the domestic policies implemented by rulers and what impact they had on economic and social change. There is particular emphasis on how peasants and workers were affected; readers should remember that there were distinct differences between these groups.
- In Chapter 4, the causes, course and consequences of a number of wars are assessed. Students should concentrate on how wars influenced the development of Russian government as this is the war-related area that examination questions focus on.

Chronology

To be able to think conceptually about a period in history, it is necessary to know initially about the chronology and narrative of that time. With this in mind, you should at first familiarise yourself with the chronology of events on page iv and link this with the short outlines of the administration of each ruler presented on pages 4–14. A study of the more detailed themes will then prove easier as each ruler can be placed in context.

Synoptic understanding

While forming a chronological framework is essential, so too is understanding how events may be connected, in both the short and long term. To achieve this, it is important at the end of studying a particular ruler to consider what has changed and what has remained the same, and to practise cross-referencing developments. Sometimes these links highlight points of similarity and continuity; sometimes they emphasise differences and change. When a key event has been analysed and tied to another event to show change and continuity, then ideas and concepts will have been synthesised. In this way the skills of synthesis may be used to achieve a synoptic understanding of the period and theme. Of course, any synthesis requires specific examples to support and evaluate an assertion. In accumulating a body of knowledge, students should ask themselves how this evidence might be useful when constructing an argument. Being able to use knowledge flexibly is a key skill and one that students should regularly practise.

A **synoptic** approach to history demands that the historian uses all of his or her knowledge, understanding and skill to study a given period. Although the main focus of this book is to encourage the reader to uncover patterns of change and continuity and similarity and difference, other concepts need to be considered. This is especially true when examining the importance of particular events such as the many wars that occurred between 1855 and 1964. An assessment of their importance would be meaningless without attention to causation and consequence. Equally, students will need to use their powers of critical thinking when analysing and evaluating evidence. For example, and as a generalisation, 'right-wing' historians such as Robert Conquest have been far more critical of the Russian communist regimes than have those historians of the 'left', such as Eric Hobsbawm.

Synoptic
A general view or a summary of the whole picture.

Key term

Note making

Before you begin to make notes, read through the introductory section of each chapter to get an overview of the main themes and familiarise yourself with any notes you already have on a particular topic. You will not need to make notes on every part of each section since some of the material will be known to you. Use the headings and sub-headings as starting points for the principal arguments in each section. Decide how many examples are needed to back them up and use the ideas and examples to complement existing notes and knowledge. Be selective, but use at least two examples, ensuring that you can explain, in some detail, their historical significance. Use the summary diagrams in a similar way to help condense your notes and structure your ideas.

Essays

A-level questions have been set at the end of each chapter, together with two contrasting answers of a very good and average standard. Each essay has been assessed and a mark and grade awarded according to official mark schemes. The commentary in each of the margins of the sample essays is a descriptive analysis of each paragraph and is used by the examiner to make the summative comments at the end of the essay on which the level and final mark are based. Each essay is meant to show how students might improve their own standard of work with the prime aim of achieving a high grade. Students approach A-level essays in different ways and there is no model approach. Nevertheless, some techniques clearly work better than others and, by comparing essay plans, approaches, styles, and how students use their knowledge synoptically, it should be possible to see why one answer has merited a higher mark.

As a general rule of thumb, the very best answers will be organised thematically. For example, the answer to a question that demands explanation of why some rulers were more effective than others in governing Russia could be organised by comparing the following: personal qualities, strategies and tactics employed, access to resources, contextual factors, extent and organisation of opposition. Each of these factors would form the themes for separate paragraphs. What needs to be avoided is a purely narrative and chronological approach which may implicitly provide an answer to a problem posed but which drifts away from the exact demands of the essay question. Students should also steer clear of what examiners call 'aerial bombardment' answers. This is where essays are full of facts which are only very loosely applied to the exact question set. Such responses are unlikely to get marks above the middling levels.

When comparing a grade C with a grade A answer, ask yourself which features in the C-grade essay prevented it from gaining a higher mark. And how much of a grade A essay do you need to read before you feel it has the making of a top-class answer? A point worth remembering is that the best students are not always the most knowledgeable but they do know how to make best use of their knowledge.

If, as a result of reading this book and incorporating some of the ideas and skills contained within it, students deepen their knowledge and develop a synoptic understanding of the topic, then it will have fulfilled its purpose.

Russian rulers

Alexander II 1855–81

Profile: Alexander II (1818–81)

1818 – Born into the Romanov dynasty

1855 – Became tsar as a result of the death of his father Nicholas I

1856 – Made peace with enemies in Crimean War. Announced shortly after that 'it is better to begin abolishing serfdom from above than to wait for it to begin to abolish itself from below'

1857 – Created the Secret Committee on Peasant Affairs which was designed to plan for the emancipation of the serfs (freeing serfs from control by their 'owners')

1861 – Introduced the Great Emancipation Statute

1863 – Reformed the education system by allowing the existence of private schools, by making alterations to the curriculum and by establishing an inspectorate

1864 – Formed the *Zemstva* (regional councils) to improve local government. Changes to legal structures and processes were also made in the same year

1865 – Issued new guidelines for publishers and writers which allowed for greater freedom to express new and challenging ideas

1866 – Ended reform programme after first serious attempt on his life

1877 – Organised the 'Trial of the 50', the trial of key political opponents

1881 – Assassinated by the members of political terrorist group called the 'People's Will'

The Russian people seemed to welcome Alexander II to the throne and were generally happy with his reforms. However, the radicals were not impressed as Russia continued to be governed through autocracy. Ironically, Alexander was about to sign an agreement just before his death that would probably have resulted in a more democratic government.

Problems

Before Alexander II came to the throne, serious social unrest over living and working conditions had been mounting. The effects of the Crimean War added to this discontent (see Chapter 4 for details about the causes, course and consequences of the war). Among the higher echelons of Russian society, there was also concern that Russia was falling behind Western Europe and would soon become a second-rate power.

Emancipation of the serfs
An announcement in 1861 that peasants would be freed from being owned, like any other property, by wealthy landowners and the state.

Domestic policies

The Tsar implemented a package of reforms, the majority of which naturally stemmed from the **emancipation of the serfs** in 1861. Changes were made to local government, the military, the legal system, education and the economy which seemed to constitute the start of a more liberal age. But this did not prevent Alexander II from resorting to repression to keep opponents in line. One of the ironies of this period was that as the people became more liberated, they showed an inclination to threaten the security of the ruling élite and were subsequently clamped down on again.

Alexander III 1881–94

Profile: Alexander III (1845–94)

1845 – Born into the Romanov dynasty
1881 – Became tsar as a result of the assassination of his father. Immediately passed the Statute Concerning measures for the Production of State Security and the Social Order. The Russification programme was also launched in the same year, starting with pogroms against Jews
1883 – Established the Peasant Land Bank to provide cheap loans for the purchase of land
1884 – Made further adjustments to the provision of education
1887 – Ordered the execution of Lenin's brother (see profile on Lenin) and four others who plotted to execute the Tsar
1889 – Land Captains were appointed to monitor and control the behaviour of peasants
1891 – Forced to deal with terrible famine
1894 – Died of nephritis (a kidney disorder) at the age of 49

Alexander III was a military man who believed strongly in autocracy. His period of rule is often seen as one of reaction and repression in response to the more relaxed liberal period of governance under his father. He was intent on returning stability to Russia and on ensuring that social unrest and opposition to tsarism did not get out of hand. His reign did prove to be relatively peaceful and some very positive economic reforms were carried out.

Problems

The assassination of Alexander II illustrated the degree of opposition that had mounted during his reign and that threatened autocracy. Alexander III also had to deal with land ownership issues that resulted from the emancipation of the serfs and clamours for more rapid industrialisation.

Domestic policies

A 'reaction' to the liberal policies of Alexander II occurred. Many of the reforms prior to 1881 were reversed or altered. Of particular note was the 1881 Statute of State Security which sanctioned greater use of repression. **Russification** was also

Russification
A policy aimed at transforming the different peoples of the Russian empire into 'pure' Rus (the supposedly original inhabitants of Russia).

introduced to control the discontent among national minority groups. All of this was a marked departure from the freedoms granted by the previous ruler. On a more positive note, the Tsar appointed Sergei Witte as Finance Minister to modernise the Russian economy. However, Alexander never lived to witness the full impact of Witte's efforts as he died prematurely from kidney disease in 1894.

Nicholas II 1894–1917

Profile: Nicholas II (1868–1918)

1868 – Born into the Romanov dynasty

1894 – Took over as tsar on the death of his father, Alexander III. In the same year he married the Princess Alexandra, the German granddaughter of Queen Victoria

1905 – Announced the October Manifesto and new constitution

1906 – Introduced the first *Duma*

1913 – Organised the tercentenary celebrations of Romanov family rule

1914 – Took Russia into the First World War by signing the general mobilisation order

1915 – Ordered Russian armed forces to be placed under the personal command of the Tsar

1917 – Return to Petrograd halted by rebels. Senior military officials and members of the *Duma* advised Nicholas to stand down. Abdicated to 'save' Russia

1918 – Murdered, along with his family, in Ekaterinburg

Although Nicholas II attempted political reforms to appease opposition his mishandling of Russia's involvement in the First World War led to his downfall and the end of the Romanov dynasty. Nicholas seemed to lack the political knowledge, understanding and skill of his father. If he had worked more cooperatively with the opposition groups in the *Duma* he may have survived. But his stubborn attitude resulted in strict adherence to autocracy which proved unacceptable to other prominent members of Russian government.

Problems

Unlike his father and grandfather, Nicholas did not have the personal qualities required to be a successful ruler. Opposition to his rule proliferated and became more organised in the form of the **radicals** (Social Democratic Workers' Party – the SDs – and the Socialist Revolutionary Party – the SRs) and the **liberals** (Kadets and Octobrists – see Chapter 2 for more details about these groups). The Bolsheviks, a division of the SDs, went on to seize power from the Provisional Government and to murder Nicholas and his family. To distract the attention of the people from growing economic problems, Nicholas engaged in a disastrous war with Japan (1904–5). The consequences of this fuelled the so-called revolution of 1905 (see Chapters 2 and 4 for more details about the war and the link with revolution). Nicholas

Key terms

Radicals
Those who wanted a complete overhaul of the political system including the abolition of the monarchy.

Liberals
Those who wanted changes to the political system but with the monarchy kept in place.

Key figure

P.A. Stolypin 1862–1911
Russian Prime Minister from 1906 to 1911. He was best known for his economic policies and land reforms as well as the rather repressive methods he advocated to achieve his aims.

Key terms

Duma
An elected imperial parliament but with a restricted franchise (only a narrow range of people could vote representatives on to the *Duma*).

Constitutional monarchy
A government that is organised and administered according to a set of written or unwritten rules (a constitution) but one that retains a monarch as a figurehead. In such a government, the monarch would relinquish autocratic power but would retain the right to veto legislation and policies deemed to be inappropriate.

Petrograd Soviet
The Petrograd workers' council set up to campaign for workers' rights.

also committed Russia to fight in the First World War although initially this was welcomed by the bulk of the population. However, he never got to grips with the enormous challenges this posed. With hindsight, it would appear that his decision to take personal control of the armed forces, thus leaving his wife (and Rasputin) in charge of domestic affairs, was a huge mistake. In 1917 he was forced to abdicate and his regime was replaced by the Provisional Government (see Chapter 1 for more details on this event).

Domestic policies

- *Economic reforms.* Nicholas encouraged Witte to continue with his plan to modernise the Russian economy with a particular emphasis on the expansion of heavy industries and the railways. Agricultural issues were addressed mainly through the efforts of **Stolypin** and his land reforms.
- *Political reforms.* As a result of the serious popular unrest of 1905, Nicholas ordered the setting up of a representative political chamber called the *Duma*. Although this appeared to be a step on the road to a **constitutional monarchy**, Nicholas came to distrust the *Duma* to the extent that he severely restricted its composition and powers.
- *Social reforms.* In the field of social reform, there was some reversion to the ideas espoused by Alexander II. Education was expanded and there was a relaxation in censorship. Nevertheless, Nicholas showed little intention of diverting from autocracy and his general attitude towards the Russian people did not marry well with their changing wants and needs.

The Provisional Government (March–October 1917)

- 2 March: a Provisional (temporary) Government was set up to take over from Nicholas II who had abdicated. The government was meant to last until a Constituent Assembly could be elected. The Provisional Government consisted of politicians that had been elected to the *Duma* in 1912. One of the problems they faced was that they were associated with the 'old' regime.
- 12 March–4 April: opposition mounted as a result of leading Bolsheviks and other revolutionaries returning from exile.
- 20–21 April: faced with demonstrations against Russia's involvement in the war, Prince Lvov, Prime Minister of the Provisional Government, formed a coalition government with members of the **Petrograd Soviet**.
- June: the Minister of War, Kerensky, launched a new offensive against Germany to boost the morale of the population and to increase support for the government.
- July: demonstrations against the war gathered momentum and a fresh campaign to repress revolutionaries was launched. Kerensky was appointed Prime Minister.
- August: the new Commander-in-Chief of the Army, General Kornilov, plotted to overthrow the Provisional Government.

The attempted coup was successfully dealt with by Kerensky in cooperation with the Petrograd Soviet.

- September: the Provisional Government failed to prevent the domination of the Petrograd Soviet by the Bolsheviks.
- October: the Provisional Government was arrested. Kerensky escaped and formed a personal army to fight the Bolsheviks. Kerensky's forces were eventually defeated at Pulkovo.

Problems

Although the Provisional Government was only ever intended to be a temporary arrangement, it could not disguise the fact that it was unelected, unrepresentative and essentially the 'old guard' in disguise. From the beginning it was also pushed into accepting a power share with the Petrograd Soviet. This meant that the Provisional Government had to rely on members of the Soviet to provide support if reforms were to be pushed through. The two biggest problems it faced were demands for fairer land distribution and Russia's war performance. Neither was tackled with any confidence which led to the opposition gaining momentum and eventually taking over.

Domestic policies

The Provisional Government attempted to halt social unrest by imposing a number of liberal measures:

- The police department was disbanded and all policing was to be carried out by local militias.
- Old-style regional governors and officials were replaced with a new wave of administrators.
- Many political prisoners (for example, Trotsky) were released or given an amnesty to return to Russia.
- Newspapers, books and pamphlets increased in circulation. The net effect was to allow Russian people to voice their opinions more strongly about how they wanted their country to be run in the future.
- From the beginning the Provisional Government had promised and planned for the creation of a democratically elected **Constituent Assembly**. In the end their promises did little to appease agitators and the new liberal climate simply allowed dissent to mount.

The inherent weaknesses of the government plus the context it was operating in provided an opportunity for the Bolsheviks to take over.

Constituent Assembly
An assembly of politicians that would be elected by the 'people'.

Key term

Lenin, the Bolsheviks and the one-party state (October 1917–24)

Profile: V. I. Lenin (1870–1924)

1870	– Born as Vladimir Ilyich Ulyanov in Simbirsk, in the Urals. His father was a member of the lesser nobility and worked as a schools' inspector
1887	– The execution of his brother strengthened Lenin's will to change the way Russia was ruled
1891	– Graduated from university with a law degree
1895	– Liaised with Plekhanov, a prominent revolutionary who had been exiled
1897	– Was exiled to Siberia. Adopted the name of Lenin (after the River Lena in Siberia) as an alias
1898	– Married N. Krupskaya
1900	– Joined the Social Democratic Party (SDs) and went into a self-imposed exile abroad
1902	– Published *What is to be Done?* (a collection of ideas about how Russia should be ruled)
1903	– Led the Bolsheviks as a breakaway group in the SDs. From 1900 to 1903 he edited the main newspaper of the revolutionary movement (*Iskra* or *The Spark*)
1905	– Returned to Russia to witness the 'revolution' but was not actively involved
1906–17	– In exile overseas once more
1917	– Returned to Russia after the Russian Revolution (February). Went on to lead Bolsheviks in displacement of the Provisional Government
1917–20	– Strengthened Bolshevik rule and played an important role in ensuring the defeat of opposition during the Civil War
1921	– Replaced War Communism with the New Economic Policy (see Chapters 3 and 4)
1922–3	– Immobilised after a number of strokes
1924	– Died

Although Lenin was often in exile he was a great influence on the revolutionary movement through his writings and actions. He was instrumental in the Bolshevik seizure of power and the establishment of communist rule in Russia. Some historians believe that Lenin laid a firm foundation for future communist leaders to build on. Thus, Stalin and Khrushchev are seen to continue with Leninist ideas and policies rather than to introduce their own brand of communism. Not all agree with this and point to the highly repressive nature of Stalin's rule and the destalinisation under Khrushchev as evidence that there was significant change in the way Russia was ruled by the communists.

s

ed two immediate problems after he seized power. First,
ne had to confront opposition. Second, he needed to tackle
Russia's involvement in the First World War. After he dealt with
these issues he then had to move on to consolidate Bolshevik
power and win acceptance of the new regime from the rest of the
world.

Domestic policies

Lenin solved the war problem by authorising the signing of the
Treaty of Brest-Litovsk in March 1918. This was essentially a
peace treaty with Germany and the terms for Russia were harsh.
Bolshevik authority was quickly established through the setting
up of the Soviet of People's Commissars or *Sovnarkom*. This élite
cabinet set out its stall by issuing a number of decrees. A number
of these focused on banning opposition and were to be enforced
through the use of a new secret police force, the *Cheka*. But
opposition either went underground or was difficult to control
because of the geographical size of Russia.

The strength and spread of opposition resulted in a Civil War
which the Bolsheviks won by using the **Red Army**, the *Cheka* and
the policy of **War Communism** (see Chapter 4 for more details
about the war including the nature and extent of opposition to
the Bolsheviks). The latter was despised and, when the war was
over, it was replaced with the **New Economic Policy** (NEP). The
NEP was the main plank in Lenin's strategy to stabilise Russia
and modernise the economy. After Lenin died, a power struggle
ensued. One of the issues debated was the viability and efficacy of
the NEP. The right wanted it to continue whereas the left wanted
it to be replaced. When Stalin emerged victorious from the
struggle he quickly imposed a personalised style of rule and a raft
of economic and social policies that mirrored his brand of
communism.

Red Army
The communist
army that originally
recruited mainly
from the soviets
and factory
committees.

War Communism
A set of economic
policies involving
the centralised
control of industry
and commerce
(nationalisation) by
the communist
government.
Surpluses of goods,
especially food,
were requisitioned
and redistributed
among the
population. It was
considered to be a
harsh but necessary
measure to ensure
that the people
supporting the Reds
were adequately fed,
clothed and
sheltered during a
time of national
crisis (the Civil
War).

New Economic Policy
An economic policy
that liberalised, to
an extent, the
operation of the
Russian economy
and one aimed to
counter the adverse
impact of War
Communism. Thus,
individuals were
once more allowed
to produce goods
(including food)
purely to make a
profit.

Key terms

Stalin and totalitarianism (1928–53)

Profile: I.V. Stalin (1879–1953)

1879	–	Born as Iosif Vissarionovich Dzhugashvili in Georgia
1899	–	Expelled from Tbilisi Seminary (college for those training to be priests) for political views
1905	–	Started to represent local branches of Bolshevik Party (Georgia and South Russia) at conferences
1912	–	Elected to the Central Committee of the Bolsheviks
1913	–	Exiled to North Siberia
1917	–	Returned to Russia and became close ally of Lenin
1917–22	–	Became specialist in national minorities' issues (appointed Commissar for Nationalities in first Soviet government). Active as a commander during the Civil War
1922	–	Appointed as General Secretary of the Communist Party
1923–7	–	Involved in a dispute with Trotsky, Kamenev and Zinoviev over who was to lead Russia after Lenin's death (see Chapter 1)
1927	–	Controlled Party Congress and expelled main rivals from the party
1928–33	–	Introduced the planned economy and the police state
1928	–	Adopted the first Five-Year Plan (see Chapter 3 for details)
1929	–	Started collectivisation programme
1933–4	–	Allowed a 'thaw' in levels of control and repression
1936–8	–	Instigated the Great Terror and show trials
1939	–	Appointed Beria as head of the secret police. Also allowed the signing of the Nazi–Soviet Pact (see Chapter 4 for details)
1939–45	–	Led Russia in a war against Nazi Germany and successfully repelled German invasion
1945–53	–	Implemented internal reconstruction programme and devised strategies to cope with the initial stages of the Cold War
1953	–	Died (some historians have suggested he was murdered)

Stalin is usually associated with a level of repression that was unprecedented in Russian history. He is also accredited with industrialising Russia and ensuring that the Russian people were able to defeat Nazi Germany. However, there is much debate over the Stalinist era with a number of historians claiming that Stalin's personal role in key developments has been exaggerated.

Problems

Stalin had to deal with the legacy of Lenin, who had been revered, and the fact that there were those in the party who mistrusted Stalin's intentions. There were also the ongoing problems related to agriculture, industry and **national minorities**. From 1939 to 1945, Russia became involved in the Second World War and was invaded by Nazi Germany. Before his death in 1953, he had yet another war to confront – the Cold War. However, the most challenging aspects of the Cold War had to be dealt with by Khrushchev who took over from Stalin.

Domestic policies

There was clear continuity in the way that Stalin dealt with opposition. He used the secret police (NKVD) to arrest people who ended up being jailed, exiled or executed. Such arrests happened in waves and were known as purges. **Show trials** and other forms of propaganda were used to control the behaviour of the people. The scale of repression was far greater than under any other leader but the importance of it lay in the terror that it created. The fear of the Stalinist regime was of a magnitude that meant that Stalin had absolute control of people's lives.

The problem of agriculture was tackled through the imposition of **collectivisation** and **dekulakisation** which was also intertwined with repression. Agricultural policies were geared towards aiding the development of heavy industry; those employed in growing numbers in factories, mines and industrial plants relied totally on peasants for their food.

Stalin's industrial policy focused on centralised planning (Five-Year Plans) and a move away from any semblance of the **free market**. This too was integrated with repression; workers who did not reach targets were usually punished severely. Whether these policies were the main factor in helping Russia repel the Nazis during the Second World War is a matter for debate. What is fairly clear is that after the war Stalin was seen as a hero and he strengthened his position as a prominent world leader.

Khrushchev and destalinisation (1956–64)

Problems

Although Stalin had become a hero of the Russian people he was still associated with the Great Terror and years of unprecedented repression. Khrushchev therefore had to stamp his own personality on Russian government and change the image of Russia created by Stalin. The latter was especially important given the nature of international relations in the post-war era. Agriculture was still considered to be in something of a mess but heavy industry had progressed, albeit to the detriment of living standards. From Khrushchev's perspective one of the most important problems facing politicians was a deterioration in working and living conditions. The last thing he wanted was mass social unrest.

Profile: Nikita Khrushchev (1894–1971)

1894	– Born in the Ukraine, son of a peasant
1899–1917	– Employed as an industrial worker in Donbas region. Elected to local workers' council (soviet) in 1917
1918	– Appointed as commissar (official) in the Red Army
1922–9	– Very active as party member in the Ukraine
1929	– Enrolled as a student at the Moscow Industrial Academy
1935–8	– Successful as the First Secretary of the Moscow Party. Responsible for the planning and building of the Moscow metro system
1938	– Moved on to become First Secretary of the Ukraine Party
1941	– During the war, operated as key political commissar with special responsibility for Stalingrad
1944	– Gained position as Prime Minister of the Ukraine
1949	– Became First Secretary of Moscow Party again but also Secretary to the Central Committee
1953–6	– Started to dominate the party and won struggle for power against Malenkov and Beria. The Virgin Land campaign was started (see Chapter 3 for details)
1956	– Launched a verbal attack on Stalinism during the 20th Party Congress. This marked the start of what has been called destalinisation. Also, Russian troops were ordered to crush an uprising in Hungary
1957	– Moved towards decentralising the control of the Russian economy. Ordered the launching of the first Russian spacecraft called *Sputnik I*
1961–4	– Faced with major Cold War crises (construction of Berlin Wall, Cuban Missile Crisis, nuclear arms race, space race)
1964	– Removed from power
1971	– Died

Khrushchev was a staunch believer in the communist ideal and was intent on proving that Stalinism was an unfortunate blip on the road to a much better life for all Russian peoples. Thus, he promised a raft of economic and social reforms designed to raise living standards to levels not previously experienced.

Unfortunately, he struggled, against the backdrop of the financially crippling Cold War, to find the money to carry out his plans. He also suffered as a result of what some rivals saw as a liberal attitude and the image he portrayed as a man of the people. In the end it was relatively easy for his opponents to launch a campaign that secured his dismissal.

Domestic policies

Although Stalin was acclaimed as a war hero, he had gained support through fear and high-level repression. The non-communist world took advantage of this by proclaiming Russia to be the great enemy of the 'free' world. Khrushchev attempted to deal with this by denouncing the rule of his predecessor (destalinisation).

Nevertheless, he carried on with the centralised planning of the economy but with more focus on the enhancement of **light and consumer industries**. The mainstay of his agricultural policy was the **Virgin Land campaign** which was aimed at increasing the amount of land under the plough. A number of important social improvement programmes were put into operation especially in the field of housing. However, the Khrushchev era continued to witness the use of repression to maintain law and order. Political prisoners were released and the *Gulag* was mostly made redundant but Russian citizens were still subject to rule through autocracy.

Key terms

Light and consumer industries
Those industries that produced goods from primary products (coal, iron ore, other raw materials) to be consumed by the bulk of the population.

Virgin Land campaign
Khrushchev's plan to exploit the 'virgin' soils of Kazakhstan and Western Siberia.

Gulag
A labour camp that was used mainly to house political dissidents and those suspected of being anti-communist.

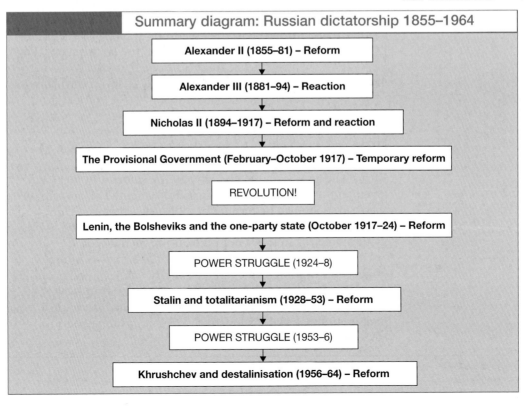

Summary diagram: Russian dictatorship 1855–1964

Alexander II (1855–81) – Reform

↓

Alexander III (1881–94) – Reaction

↓

Nicholas II (1894–1917) – Reform and reaction

↓

The Provisional Government (February–October 1917) – Temporary reform

↓

REVOLUTION!

↓

Lenin, the Bolsheviks and the one-party state (October 1917–24) – Reform

↓

POWER STRUGGLE (1924–8)

↓

Stalin and totalitarianism (1928–53) – Reform

↓

POWER STRUGGLE (1953–6)

↓

Khrushchev and destalinisation (1956–64) – Reform

1 The Nature of Russian Government

OVERVIEW

This chapter focuses on the main characteristics of Russian government from 1855 to 1964, which can be categorised under the following headings:

- ideologies
- government structures and institutions

Note that reforms and repression were tools which rulers used to govern Russia. Questions on the changing nature of Russian government usually need to be answered by making reference to the ideologies, structure, organisation *and* tools of governments. Thus, there is inevitably an overlap between the material in this chapter and that contained in Chapters 2 and 3.

In the main, political, economic and social reforms were used by the tsars and communists to appease the population or as a way of directly controlling behaviour. Generally, the tsars preferred appeasement whereas the communists opted for control. Details of political reforms can be found in early parts of this chapter and those of economic and social reforms in Chapter 3. The tsars and the communists also used repression as a tool of government (see Chapter 2 for details). All Russian governments used the secret police, the army, censorship and propaganda to keep those who opposed the ruling élites in check. The main difference was that the communists took the use of repression to a new height through purges, show trials and the instigation of 'terror'.

The main aim of this chapter is to provide a clear picture of how the nature and structure of Russian government changed from 1855 to 1964. Linked with this is the debate over the extent to which the basic ideas that underpinned Russian government also changed. Some believe that the communists were just as autocratic as the tsars if not more so. In this sense there was more continuity than change with respect to the ideologies adopted by different political regimes.

Note making
This chapter is concerned with the changing nature of Russian government. Read a section to get an overview of the main themes before you begin to make any notes. You are expected to be able to analyse characteristics so as to discern patterns of similarity and difference, and change and continuity over time, so you need to decide what are the principal arguments and which examples are required to back them up.

1 | Ideologies

Autocracy

From 1855 to March 1917, Russia was governed as an autocracy. Tsars had absolute power which was said to be ordained by God. This was not simply a theoretical concept; in practice, all Russians had to obey the will of the Tsar or suffer punishment, including the wrath of God.

The historian J.N. Westwood has indicated that there were actually three strands to tsarist autocracy:

- The 'tsar expected willing and total submission of his subjects … just as God expected the tsar's willing and total submission'. This was a system based on religious faith and therefore did not require the Tsar to be made accountable to the people through elections (or, more broadly, **constitutional government**).
- The Tsar was obliged to act as a kind of 'moral judge' on behalf of God. The righteous, as defined by the Tsar, would flourish and be 'saved' whereas the wicked would be condemned and punished. This was seen as a way of controlling the behaviour of the Russian people for their own good and, thus, for the good of the nation as a whole. In this sense the Tsar had a **paternalistic** duty to perform which successive tsars seemed to find burdensome. The welfare of all Russians depended totally on the actions of the Tsar although he was, of course, supported greatly by the **Russian Orthodox Church**.
- Autocracy was viewed as a practical necessity. The Russian Empire was so vast and diverse that it was better if only one person had total control over imperial affairs. Shared power would have resulted in chaos and inefficiency as far as the tsarist regime was concerned. For many, such as Konstantin Pobedonostsev (see profile on page 17), **liberal democracy** and constitutional government would have been disastrous for Russia as it would have led to too many people demanding too many different policies, most of which would have been unsuitable or impractical. Besides, as the vast majority of the population were illiterate peasants, democracy would have resulted in the governance of Russia by those who lacked the intellect of the aristocracy and 'the ability to reason'.

Key question
How far could all Russian governments from 1855 to 1964 be described as autocratic?

Key terms

Constitutional government
A government that is organised and administered according to a set of written or unwritten rules.

Paternalistic
Protecting the people.

Russian Orthodox Church
A branch of Christianity that was very traditional and that was independent from outside authorities such as the papacy. It was used to teach the people to obey the Tsar as he was said to be anointed by God.

Profile: Konstantin Pobedonostsev (1827–1907)

1864 – Helped prepare set of judicial reforms

1865 – Given task of tutoring Alexander II's son (to be Alexander III) and, later, Nicholas, son of Alexander III

1880 – Appointed Chief Procurator of the Holy Synod under Alexander II. This position allowed Pobedonostsev to advise the Tsar on religious matters but also to have influence in the church and over educational and social issues. It gave him ministerial status and therefore access to the Committee of Ministers

Pobedonostsev claimed that democracy was 'the biggest lie of our time' and was generally against any reforms that gave Russian people greater freedoms and rights. He was also an advocate of the idea that all peoples of the Empire should be Orthodox Christians. He considered the non-Orthodox, for example Jews, to be treacherous and not to be trusted.

Key terms

Liberal democracy
A political ideology that promotes the right of the people to be able to be free to choose. This would include freedom to speak what one believed in and the freedom to choose a representative in government.

'Orthodoxy, Autocracy and Nationality'
The slogan used by the tsars and Pobedonostsev to justify and explain the conservative nature of tsarist rule.

Fundamental Laws
Basic laws that reinforced the ideology underpinning tsarist rule.

Nicholas I

Although there was variation in how autocratic power was used by the tsars throughout the period, the significance of autocracy was continuously enforced through manifestos, speeches and policies. Before Alexander II ascended the throne in 1855, his father, Nicholas I, had reinforced the importance of autocratic rule through the use of propaganda and legislation. The slogan **'Orthodoxy, Autocracy and Nationality'** was used to promote the essence of tsarism and illustrated the reasons behind government aims and policies. This was reinforced with the passing of the **Fundamental Laws** of 1832, whose introduction stated:

> The emperor of all the Russias is an autocratic and unlimited monarch: God himself ordains that all must bow to his supreme power, not only out of fear but also out of conscience.

Alexander II

Alexander II did not waver from this sentiment despite showing a tendency towards being a reformer. Indeed, after the first assassination attempt on him in 1866, he adhered very strongly to the concept of autocracy and was as controlling and repressive as any tsar that preceded or followed him.

Alexander III

Alexander III, on succeeding to the throne in 1881 after Alexander II's eventual assassination, felt obliged once more to make a clear, bold statement about the necessity for the Tsar to have total and unquestionable control over the lives of Russian people. In his manifesto of 1881, he stated:

> We trust that the fervent prayers of our devoted people, known throughout the whole world for their love and devotion to their

sovereigns, will draw God's blessing upon us and the labour of government to which we have been appointed. Consecrating ourselves to Our great service, We call upon our faithful subjects to serve us and the state in fidelity and truth, for the eradication of the vile sedition disgracing the Russian land, for the strengthening of faith and morality, for the proper upbringing of children, for the extermination of falsehood and theft, and for the introduction of truth and good order in the operations of the institutions given to Russia by her benefactor, Our beloved father.

Nicholas II

Alexander III was obviously influenced by the nature of his father's death which he claimed was due partly to a move towards a more 'liberal' Russian society. Similarly, after 'liberal' concessions made by Nicholas II in 1905, another set of Fundamental Laws (1906) reiterated the need for the preservation of autocracy. The 1906 legislation stated that:

> The All-Russian Emperor possesses the supreme autocratic power. Not only fear and conscience, but God himself, commands obedience to his authority. The person of Sovereign Emperor is sacred and inviolable. The Russian Empire is governed by firmly established laws that have been properly enacted. No new law can be enacted without the approval of the State Council and the State *Duma*, and it shall not be legally binding without the approval of the Sovereign Emperor.

Thus, all of the tsars were consistent in the way in which they promoted and justified autocracy. Even when reforms were enacted, there was never any question that ultimate power and control, as sanctioned by God, rested in the hands of the Tsar.

Alexander II

Nevertheless, there were differences in the way in which the tsars performed their autocratic role. Influenced by Russia's dismal performance in the Crimean War (1854–6) against more advanced, industrialised enemies, Alexander II went for a reform programme with the aim of enhancing Russia's status as a major world power. The main plank of this was the emancipation of the serfs (1861) from which stemmed other reforms to local government, the judicial system and education.

Freeing serfs from both private and state ownership was highly controversial and provoked much opposition from the landed classes. Despite this, the Tsar pushed the changes forward knowing that his absolute authority would be respected. He was canny enough to realise, though, that a measure as dramatic as the Emancipation Edict had to be 'sold' to those who had most to lose. With this in mind he announced to his nobles, in 1856, that it was better to abolish serfdom from above rather than from below and the final legislation of 1861 contained a stipulation that serf owners would be compensated for their losses. Although this did not satisfy all parties, it did appease the most vocal critics. It was done in such a way that allowed dissenters to express themselves but with the knowledge that the Tsar's decision would still be final.

Alexander III

Alexander III believed that his father had played a dangerous reform game which ultimately cost him his life and he quickly resorted to a more repressive form of autocracy. Opposition, especially the **People's Will**, was ruthlessly suppressed and many of the changes instigated by the previous Tsar were reversed. This change in approach has been labelled the **'Reaction'** but, interestingly, was not entirely the creation of Alexander III. A major influence behind the Reaction was Pobedonostsev who proclaimed what some historians consider to be an autocratic ideology. His philosophy was built on the following principles:

* 'inertness and laziness are generally characteristics of the **Slavonic** nature'
* only a small minority, needless to say the aristocracy, had the ability to think problems through to arrive at intelligent solutions
* the rest of humanity were mainly influenced by 'the forces of the unconscious, land and history'.

This led to the belief that constitutional government or 'Parliamentarianism' was not possible as the 'people' did not possess the mental attributes to make it work. Liberal democracy was to be avoided at all costs and was to be repelled through the maintenance of autocracy. As personal tutor to Alexander III and Nicholas II when they were young, Pobedonostsev undoubtedly had a strong influence on how they later formulated and exercised their autocratic power.

Nicholas II

It is not surprising that Nicholas II continued in the same vein as his father. The constitutional reforms of 1905 are seen by some historians as a blip in that they were forced on the Tsar as a result of economic crisis and the disastrous consequences of the Russo-Japanese War (1904–5) (see the section on government structures and institutions on pages 30–3 for details of the reforms including the introduction of the *Duma*). This line of argument is supported by the fact that the **Fundamental Laws of 1906** watered down the effect of the reforms and by 1917 the *Duma* was little more than a talking shop frequented by politicians who possessed commitment to autocracy. Some disagree with this view and believe that without the interruption of the First World War, Russia would have continued on the path towards constitutional reform. However, the weight of evidence suggests that Nicholas made concessions only to keep opposition temporarily at bay and that his aim was always 'to uphold the principle of autocracy as firmly and unflinchingly as did my ever lamented father'.

Key terms

People's Will
A terrorist group consisting of members of the educated classes who were upset by Alexander II's refusal to continue with his reform programme after the mid-1860s.

'Reaction'
Alexander III reacted to the liberal reforms put together by his father by reversing them and introducing more repressive measures.

Slavonic
Belonging to the Slav peoples. These peoples consisted mainly of Great Russians (Muscovites), Ukrainians and Cossacks, all of whom spoke the same Indo-European language.

Fundamental Laws of 1906
Regulations that reinforced the position of the Tsar. Law 5, for example, stated that 'Supreme Autocratic power belongs to the Emperor of all Russia'.

Thus, the tsars used their autocratic power differently according to their differing circumstances. The key point to make, though, is that political, economic and social reforms were never made with the intention of the Tsar relinquishing any degree of control. Others in society might have become more empowered but they were always going to be subject to the ultimate authority of the Tsar.

> **Essay focus**
>
> The introduction, paragraph one, in Essay 1 on page 48 is a good example of how a key term, such as autocracy, should be defined. It signals to the examiner that the candidate has a good grasp of the key concept around which the answer to the question will revolve.

Dictatorship

Marxism

The Russian concept of **dictatorship** was partly derived from the writings of Karl Marx and Frederick Engels. By the late 1840s their work was known among a minority of Russian radicals but it was not until the 1880s that their ideas had really taken root within the Russian intelligentsia. There were three aspects of Marxism that seemed especially relevant to those who opposed autocracy.

Marx and the idea of superstructure

Marx believed that at any one point in time the foundation or base of society was maintained and established by a ruling élite; this base quite obviously benefited the élite to the detriment of others. In tsarist Russia the foundation was serfdom and agriculture with a bit of industrialisation thrown in. It was this arrangement which served mainly the interests of the landowning ruling élite. To maintain this, a superstructure of institutions was needed by the ruling class to establish order. Marx believed that this kind of system was unfair and was bound to lead to conflict. In his eyes the only way to prevent this was to destroy the base. Russian intellectuals took this to mean that serfdom and capitalism should be replaced by a more egalitarian society that revolved around cooperation.

Marx and the Labour Theory of Value

Marx adopted the 'Labour Theory of Value' which claimed that under a **capitalist economy** the **proletariat** would never gain the full value of their efforts. A disproportionate amount of wages would be taken away to provide capitalists with profits far in excess of what was needed to maintain industrialisation. Marx believed this was inevitable as the sole purpose of the capitalist was to make a profit. However, it would eventually prove unacceptable to workers as they increasingly realised that they were being exploited. Marx predicted that the result would be a worker uprising to overthrow the system, i.e. a revolution. Unsurprisingly, it was expected that this transformation would

Key question
How did the ideology of the dictatorship of the proletariat differ from autocracy and totalitarianism?

Key terms

Dictatorship
Absolute rule, usually by one person, with no legal, political, economic or social restrictions.

Capitalist economy
An economy based on making as much profit as possible from industrial and commercial activity.

Proletariat
A term used to describe those who worked in industry and lived in urban areas.

Profile: Karl Marx (1818–83)

1818	– Born in Trier, Germany
1841	– Became a journalist after graduating in law
1845	– Expelled from Paris after spreading revolutionary ideas
1848–9	– Supported the revolutions in Germany and wrote the *Communist Manifesto* (1848) which set out his own ideas about revolution and the nature of communism
1849	– Moved to Britain and wrote *Das Kapital*, a book which outlined the 'evils' associated with capitalist economies (those based solely on the profit-making motive)
1883	– Died in London while still in exile

Profile: Frederick Engels (1820–95)

1820	– Born in Barmen, Germany, the son of a wealthy factory owner
1844	– Met Karl Marx in Paris
1845–6	– Set out his political ideas (similar to Karl Marx) in a book called *The German Ideology*. This was co-written with Karl Marx
1848–83	– Helped Marx write and publish further books. He also provided financial help to Marx and his family especially when Marx experienced bouts of ill-health
1895	– Died

Key terms

Communist
A form of rule which allowed for the control, by the 'people', of the means of production, distribution and exchange.

Dictatorship of the proletariat
In theory, rule over the bourgeoisie by the workers. Lenin argued that before this could happen, workers would have to be ordered what to do by the Bolsheviks as they did not have the knowledge, understanding and skill to take full control of governing Russia.

begin in the advanced industrialised European nations such as Germany and Britain. This was an issue that Russian radicals had to square with what was happening in their homeland; Russia was largely rural and 'backward' and, according to Marx, not the kind of place where a revolution would happen. Thus, Russian radicals did not operate, in theory, under conditions that were helpful in allowing them to achieve their aims.

Marx and the dictatorship of the proletariat

Marx referred to the likely conflict between capitalists and workers as a class struggle. In fact, he argued that it was the final part of what had been an ongoing series of struggles throughout history between different social groups. The conflict between capitalists and workers would be the ultimate stage of the process as workers would destroy the base and seize control of the means of production, distribution and exchange. But Marx also stated that there would need to be a transitory period before the workers could govern effectively. This in turn needed an intellectual élite to manage the transition and instruct the masses about how to implement a truly **communist** form of rule. Furthermore, a period of the **dictatorship of the proletariat** would occur. In other words, the proletariat would have to be dictated to before they could dictate how Russia was to be ruled.

The Bolsheviks under Lenin, followed by Stalin, adhered to these guidelines but made their own modifications to suit the circumstances they found themselves in. Hence, by the end of the **Civil War** (1917–21) the governance of Russia was based on **Marxism–Leninism** and then, from 1927 to 1953, by **Marxism–Leninism–Stalinism**.

Marxism–Leninism

By the early 1890s, the young Lenin had fully embraced Marxism. At this time Marxists were largely tolerated by the authorities as they did not appear to be as radical as other groups. Indeed, the early Russian Marxists seemed to be content to discuss how Marxism could be interpreted in the context of the changing Russian economy and seemed to struggle to put across their message to the proletariat.

By the mid-1890s, Lenin, along with **Martov**, started to advocate the need to support workers in their attempts to gain higher wages and better working conditions. Help was given to organise strikes in St Petersburg (1895, 1896, 1897), which certainly had a significant impact as the authorities quickly reacted by exiling the ringleaders. Despite an attempt to unite all of those interested in Marxism, through the formation of the Russian Social Democratic Workers' Party (RSDLP) in 1898, Lenin and others argued that there were two ways in which Marxists could progress their cause and only one would be effective. For Lenin, supporting workers to gain concessions within the capitalist system was the wrong path to take. The authorities' reaction to the St Petersburg strikes proved to Lenin that the 'superstructure' would always prevail to keep workers in their place. The alternative was to move straight to attacking the 'base' to overthrow the existing ruling order.

An intense debate between Marxists ensued over which route to take. Lenin set out his 'revised' version of Marxism in a pamphlet entitled *What is to be Done?* (1902). In this he argued that the **dialectical** phase of Marxism could be speeded up when applied to Russia. He believed that there was no need for a democratically elected constitutional assembly which would eventually be controlled by the masses. Instead he argued for a leap to a Party Central Committee led by professionals who would govern in the interest of workers until the latter were ready to take control themselves. This was Lenin's interpretation of Marx's road to the dictatorship of the proletariat (that is, the core of Marxism–Leninism). Lenin's move towards this approach caused uproar within the RSDLP and, by 1903, a deep split had emerged between, what Lenin labelled, the **Bolsheviks** (Marxist–Leninists) and the **Mensheviks** (other Marxists).

After the October Revolution of 1917 (see pages 37 and 166–7 for details of the revolution), Lenin went about fully implementing Marxism–Leninism. Opposition to Bolshevik ideology and rule resulted in the Russian Civil War. One school of thought is that Lenin welcomed the war as it was an

Key terms

Civil War
A war within a state between civilians holding opposing ideals.

Marxism–Leninism
Lenin's interpretation of Marxism which argued that the move to worker control of the means of production, distribution and exchange could be speeded up.

Marxism–Leninism–Stalinism
Stalin's version of Marxism–Leninism.

Dialectical
The ongoing changes in society from one stage to another.

Bolsheviks
A breakaway RSDLP group who were the 'majority' (as labelled by Lenin).

Mensheviks
A breakaway RSDLP group who were the 'minority' (as labelled by Lenin).

Key figure

Y.O. Martov 1873–1923
Initially, friend Lenin and co-editor of the radical newspaper *Iskra*. However, the two eventually fell out over what tactics to use to achieve their political aims.

Key terms

Reds
A general term for those who actively supported the Bolsheviks during the Civil War.

Whites
A general term for those who actively opposed the Bolsheviks during the Civil War.

Command economy
An economy that is controlled totally by the state.

Key figure

Leon Trotsky 1879–1940
A revolutionary best known for his leading role in securing Bolshevik success during the Russian Civil War.

Key question
To what extent did Stalin simply build on the ideologies and policies of other Russian leaders, especially Lenin?

Key terms

Five-Year Plans
These involved the setting of production targets to be achieved on a five-yearly cycle.

Cult of personality
The use of propaganda to build a positive image of a leader so that the population offer total obedience to that leader.

opportunity to eradicate the bourgeoisie from Russian soil forever. Although the Bolshevik **Reds** defeated the **Whites** this did not mean that Marxism–Leninism was 'safe'. Within the party there was continuation of debate over how the Bolsheviks should progress. Lenin's toleration of the 'moderates' was evident when he replaced War Communism with the New Economic Policy (NEP). War Communism was viewed as too harsh and was associated with causing famine whereas the NEP was more liberal and gave the people freedom to produce goods and services without restriction (see Chapter 3 for more details on these policies). More radical members of the party saw this as bowing down to bourgeois elements and demanded more central control. Others, such as **Trotsky**, went further still and pushed for a move towards a 'Permanent Revolution' which entailed spreading communism throughout the world and not just Russia.

Trotsky's views caused a reaction from Stalin and his supporters who stressed that the most sensible and appropriate policy was to establish 'socialism in one country'. Stalin argued that the Communist Party could not influence the growth of communism elsewhere until it was firmly established and agreed to within the Soviet Union. What these developments illustrate is that Lenin, just like the tsars, adjusted his ideology and policies to stave off opposition but had no intention of veering away from his main short-term goal of ruling, with the help of the party, as a dictator. Again, in comparison with the tsars, a policy of appeasement did not fully resolve the issue of opposition within the ruling élite. It took a far more radical approach to do this.

Totalitarianism
Marxism–Leninism–Stalinism

The death of Lenin in 1924 resulted in a power struggle and a general heightening of tension within the party over how Russia was to be governed in the future. By 1927, through skilful manipulation of different individuals and factions, Stalin gained leadership of the Soviet Union. He quickly went about promoting his redefined version of Marxism–Leninism. There were two parts to Marxism–Leninism–Stalinism:

- Stalin argued that the 'base' of society could only be permanently changed by utilising a particular type of 'superstructure'. He went on to implement this through a **command economy** centred on **Five-Year Plans** and collectivisation (see Chapter 3 for details of these policies).
- The superstructure had to be highly personalised and under the total control of one individual, that is Stalin. This was considered to be absolutely necessary in the short run to prevent the damaging infighting that had occurred in the recent past. If disagreement with this was to arise then it would be labelled bourgeois and dealt with quickly and efficiently. The creative and persistent use of propaganda (centring on the development of the **cult of personality**) and implementation of repressive measures on a scale never

witnessed before would ensure that the whole population would adhere to Stalin's ideology.

Historians have explained this shift from a Lenin-style dictatorship to **totalitarianism** in a number of different ways:

- One argument is that Stalin simply took the opportunity to exploit the circumstances he found himself in to implement an ideology that provided a practical solution to the Soviet Union's problems. Stalin is seen as having a sincere belief that, to make the Soviet Union a great and prosperous place to live in, the only workable approach was for the strict implementation of Five-Year Plans and collectivisation.
- Others believe that Stalin manipulated and distorted Marxism–Leninism to serve his own **megalomania**. This is evidenced especially through the years of the power struggle after Lenin's death and was further reinforced by the use of repression in the form of show trials, the purges and the imposition of the cult of personality once Stalin had taken control (see Chapter 2 for details about the power struggle).
- A recent view is that Stalin built on the foundations laid by Lenin. In a sense Lenin, through the Party Central Committee and other institutions, had already moved towards destroying the base through using the superstructure (see section on Marx and the idea of superstructure for further explanation of this). Lenin had also used the *Cheka* to instigate a frightening level of force to repel opposition and to stabilise central control of the economy. Thus, Lenin had already made the most significant and decisive reinterpretation of Marxism. Stalin then took Marxism–Leninism and imposed it in a way that he thought Lenin would have done if he had lived longer.

Although it is difficult to be clear about Stalin's motives, it is evident that his version of absolute and total rule was taken to a new level. The result was wide-scale terror, destruction and death that masked any positive achievements that came out of the Stalinist era. This is highlighted by the fact that even though Stalin could be given much credit for defeating Nazi Germany during the **Great Patriotic War**, his successor, Khrushchev, vilified him and proceeded to 'destalinise' the Soviet Union.

Destalinisation

After Stalin's death, in 1953, a power struggle ensued. This gathered momentum after an emergency meeting of the **Council of Ministers**, the party **Central Committee** and the **Supreme Soviet of the USSR**. A rationalisation of Stalin's **Presidium** was agreed along with a clarification of the roles of leading communists. From this, four rivals emerged:

- *Malenkov*. He became chairman of the Council of Ministers and head of government. These positions were to be held

---

Key terms

Totalitarianism
A centralised form of dictatorial government that controls every aspect of the behaviour of the citizens of the state.

Megalomania
An individual's belief that they are very powerful and important.

Great Patriotic War
The war against Nazi Germany from 1941 to 1945.

Council of Ministers
Senior politicians who drafted domestic policies.

Central Committee
The chief decision-making group of the Russian Communist Party.

Supreme Soviet of the USSR
The main law-making body in Soviet government.

Key question
Did destalinisation create a new Russian political ideology?

Presidium
A small group of ministers rather like the Cabinet in the UK political system.

Key term

**First secretary of
the party**
The most important
administrative
officer in the
Communist Party.

Duopoly
Power in the hands
of two people.

**Collective
leadership**
Rule by a group
whereby
responsibilities are
equally shared out.

alongside his role as **first secretary of the party**. However, due
to Malenkov appearing to collude with Beria to form a
duopoly of power, he was demoted from party secretary just
two weeks after Stalin's death. This post was passed on to
Khrushchev.

- *Beria*. He was appointed Minister of Internal Affairs (MVD), an
office which absorbed the previously titled Ministry of State
Security. Many considered Beria a dangerous influence and
some believed he was involved in the murder of Stalin. It was
not long before he was denounced as a traitor, arrested and
executed. After he was shot in 1953, the MVD was placed
under the control of the party rather than one individual. This
was something of a break from the past as state security had
nearly always been the responsibility of a particular individual
and usually someone with a nasty streak.
- *Khrushchev*. He gained the post of Secretary of the Party
Central Committee from Malenkov. On paper, this was not the
most significant job but in practice it meant Khrushchev was in
touch with the real desires and needs of party members. It
therefore gave him a very useful power base to work from,
which he did to great effect.
- *Vorishilov*. He was appointed President of the USSR and was to
act mainly as a figurehead.

Almost immediately after Stalin's death there were moves to
change the make-up of political personnel from top to bottom.
The Presidium was reduced to 10 members and by 1956 a third
of the Party Central Committee was new. A similar process
happened in the republic and local party committees where a half
of the secretaries were replaced. This was all part of the process
of bringing in new blood and getting rid of those who were the
closest sympathisers of the Stalinist regime.

Collective leadership
Underlying the revamp of the composition of government was
the notion that power should be devolved and placed in the
hands of a collection of individuals resulting in what was called
collective leadership. Initially, differences between Malenkov
and Khrushchev over which direction the USSR should head
meant collective leadership was difficult to achieve. Malenkov
wanted a move towards more consumerism and Westernisation
(similar to the demands of liberal reformers under the tsars and
to Lenin's NEP). Opponents of this argued it was only a reflection
of the desires of the administration and not the people of Russia.

Khrushchev's response
Khrushchev offered an alternative, which was his Virgin Land
campaign (see Chapter 3 for details), believing that this would
deal with problems that were the most pressing and which would
lead to greater internal wealth and stability. Supporters of
Khrushchev, and there were many, argued this was what the
majority of party members wanted and was more in line with

what Russians considered to be a priority. By 1955, under pressure from Khrushchev and his supporters, Malenkov was forced to resign as prime minister and was moved to the lesser position of minister for power stations. He was replaced by Bulganin, a character who was far more sympathetic towards Khrushchev's train of thought.

The move to destalinisation

The execution of Beria and forced demise of Malenkov did not mean that Khrushchev was safe or that he was simply becoming another dictator in the mould of Lenin and Stalin. Khrushchev was keen to progress with the idea of collective leadership and to move Russia away from governance based on extreme repression. In his view this had greatly tarnished the USSR's image overseas which was not helpful at a time of increasing international tension. He was also very aware that although there were still many Stalinists, Stalin's death had led to something of a reawakening among the people; there was a likelihood that citizens would come to a realisation that there was an alternative to the overly repressive nature of Stalinist rule and would demand change.

With the legacy of Stalinism in mind, Khrushchev launched a scathing attack on the deceased Stalin which became integral to what was called **destalinisation**. The denunciations started formally at the 20th Party Congress in 1956. Khrushchev made a speech on 'The Cult of the Individual and its Consequences'. The contents of the speech were never published (hence, it was 'secret') but the key points were leaked to Communist Party organisations so that they would be familiar with the line that Khrushchev was to take as the new leader of Russia. The following criticisms were made of Stalin:

> **Key term**
>
> **Destalinisation**
> The denunciation, by Khrushchev, of the policies of Stalin.

- He had never been accepted by Lenin as a potential leader as was clearly stated in Lenin's 'Testament'.
- Stalin had created a state that was totally unprepared for military conflict in 1941. As a result, millions of Russians suffered unnecessarily.
- He had committed a range of crimes against the people that were unforgivable. Parts of the speech talked about Stalin's demand for absolute submission of the will of the people, the creation of fear and insecurity among the population and, most importantly, the fact that anyone who disagreed with Stalinism 'was doomed to moral and physical annihilation'.
- He also committed misdemeanours against 'outsiders' who should have been embraced by the Soviet leadership. For example, Stalin ordered the assassination of the Hungarian revolutionary leader, Bela Kun.

The impact of the 'Secret Speech'

Although the contents of the 'Secret Speech' were not officially disclosed until 1961 it still caused an outcry among senior party members. The cult of personality had resulted in a society that had been immersed in rhetoric that declared that everything that Stalin did was for the good of the nation and the people. To have him suddenly denounced as a traitor and murderer came as a great shock. It took very little time for opposition to formulate against Khrushchev.

The role of the Anti-Party Group

The 'Anti-Party Group' (those who opposed Khrushchev), as they were labelled, gained a loose agreement from the Presidium to get rid of the post of first secretary of the party, which would have resulted in the destruction of Khrushchev's power base. The chief protagonists, Molotov, Kagonovich and Malenkov, were quickly and easily dealt with by Khrushchev. The latter pointed out that only the party Central Committee could change the organisation of the party structure and, therefore, his opponents' actions were unlawful. The three opponents were swiftly removed from the Presidium which left Khrushchev free to progress with destalinisation.

Other features of destalinisation

The key features of destalinisation, other than the verbal denunciation by Khrushchev, consisted of the following:

* A release of political prisoners from labour camps. This started soon after Stalin's death but gathered momentum from the time of the Secret Speech.
* A relaxation of censorship resulting in the publication of articles, novels and plays that criticised Stalin. Good examples were the works written by Ehrenburg, Pasternak, Solzhenitsyn and Yevtushenko. However, writers and artists did not have total freedom to produce what they wanted which resulted in some 'emigrating'.
* The legacy of the cult of personality was chipped away at. Pictures and statues of Stalin were removed from public places. Stalingrad was renamed Volgograd. The ultimate insult to Stalin happened at the 22nd Party Congress in 1961 when it was ordered that Stalin's body should be taken from the Lenin mausoleum and buried in a concrete-filled hole beneath the wall of the Kremlin.

The reaction to destalinisation

Once the initial shock engendered by the Secret Speech was over, the reaction to destalinisation bore a striking resemblance to that which occurred when Alexander II introduced his reforms. There were strikes (which included newly released prisoners from the *Gulags*), riots and protests for even greater freedoms (especially from the satellite states such as Yugoslavia, Poland and Hungary). But Khrushchev was determined not to return to the Stalinist past and resisted using violence to deal with unrest. Order was maintained through the MVD which remained under the control of the party and Khrushchev showed a keenness to promote the notion that a 'thaw' in the use of repression had happened. This did not stop him dismissing popular politicians at will (e.g. Zhukov, Bulganin) when they seemed to stray from the party line and using physical force when deemed necessary (e.g. tanks were sent into Hungary in 1956 to suppress the Nagy regime). Thus, Khrushchev, like Alexander II, did not intend to move too far from authoritarian rule and the one-party, one-leader state was to remain intact until the fall of the Soviet Union in 1991.

Summary diagram: Ideologies

Similarities
- Belief in the need for absolute control
- Personalised power
- The use of repression to maintain control
- The use of reform to maintain control
- Reluctance to allow openness and proliferation of freedoms

Differences
- Justifications for autocratic rule; tsars (God), communists (nature of the proletariat and historical inevitability)
- Views on human nature; tsars (weaknesses inherent), communists (determined by social class and therefore environment)
- Views on reform; tsars (not welcomed as they led to challenges to government), communists (not welcomed as they maintained the bourgeois system)
- Views on representative government; tsars (threat because of dilution of power), communists (threat because parliaments were bourgeois)

2 | Government structures and institutions

Government under the tsars 1855–1917

When Alexander II came to the throne he was left with a central government structure that dated back to the beginning of the nineteenth century. In the eyes of the new Tsar, there was little need to change the organisation of government despite 'failures' highlighted by the Crimean War. From 1855 to 1905 the format and institutions of central government remained largely the same with only one significant, but temporary, addition made in 1861 (see Figure 1.1).

This system appeared to function effectively but economic and social change gave rise to the emergence of a number of political groups that clamoured for more representation through a constitutional form of government (see Chapter 2 for a fuller discussion of opposition groups). More radical elements wanted a complete overthrow of the system and its replacement with a form of rule based on communist principles.

Pressure for change

The pressure for change started to accelerate during the disastrous Russo-Japanese War of 1904–5. The year 1905 is often called one of revolution, although it is very debatable whether there was a degree of change that completely altered the way in which Russia was run. The period was certainly one of great turmoil; there were assassinations of key political figures, a massacre of a group of workers by state troops (**Bloody Sunday**), strikes, a naval mutiny (*Potemkin*) and various other incidents of social unrest.

Key question
Did the basic structure of Russian government remain the same throughout the period from 1855 to 1917?

Key terms

Bloody Sunday
On 9 January 1905 a group of demonstrators marching on the Winter Palace, and led by Father Gapon, were shot at by soldiers. Over 200 people were killed and about 800 injured.

Potemkin
A battleship on which a mutiny occurred. The incident was later made famous through the silent film *Battleship Potemkin* (1928).

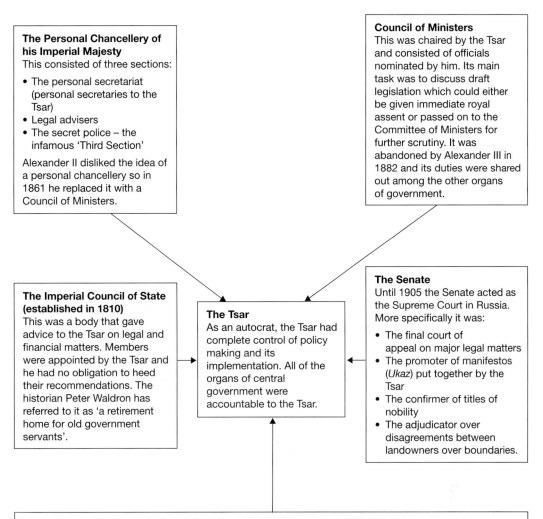

The Personal Chancellery of his Imperial Majesty
This consisted of three sections:

- The personal secretariat (personal secretaries to the Tsar)
- Legal advisers
- The secret police – the infamous 'Third Section'

Alexander II disliked the idea of a personal chancellery so in 1861 he replaced it with a Council of Ministers.

Council of Ministers
This was chaired by the Tsar and consisted of officials nominated by him. Its main task was to discuss draft legislation which could either be given immediate royal assent or passed on to the Committee of Ministers for further scrutiny. It was abandoned by Alexander III in 1882 and its duties were shared out among the other organs of government.

The Imperial Council of State (established in 1810)
This was a body that gave advice to the Tsar on legal and financial matters. Members were appointed by the Tsar and he had no obligation to heed their recommendations. The historian Peter Waldron has referred to it as 'a retirement home for old government servants'.

The Tsar
As an autocrat, the Tsar had complete control of policy making and its implementation. All of the organs of central government were accountable to the Tsar.

The Senate
Until 1905 the Senate acted as the Supreme Court in Russia. More specifically it was:

- The final court of appeal on major legal matters
- The promoter of manifestos (*Ukaz*) put together by the Tsar
- The confirmer of titles of nobility
- The adjudicator over disagreements between landowners over boundaries.

The Committee of Ministers (established in 1861)
There were initially 13 ministers (10 by the 1890s) who each had a responsibility for a particular aspect of the administration of Russian affairs. Each ministry was connected to departments that had very specific responsibilities, e.g. state horse breeding. Four of the ministerial posts were considered more important than the others:

- Minister for the Interior – responsible for domestic affairs particularly those concerning law and order
- Minister for War
- Minister for Finance
- Over Procurator of the Holy Synod – responsible for all religious affairs.

Ministers had a purely administrative role. They did not formulate policies and were always answerable to the Tsar. With hindsight, a major weakness of the Committee was that members seldom consulted each other and often pursued policies that conflicted. This was especially problematic when the Minister of Finance wanted to implement tighter budgetary control while other ministers planned to spend large amounts on reforms. The Committee was abolished in 1906. Its work was shared out between a newly formulated Council of Ministers, the *Duma* and the State Council (see Figure 1.2, page 30).

Figure 1.1: Central government institutions 1855–1905.

The response to the events of 1905

The most important response from Nicholas II came in the form of the **October Manifesto** which confirmed that a more representative form of government would be installed that centred around a kind of parliament called the *Duma*. This, along with the Fundamental Laws, created a structure that in theory was markedly different from that which had been in place for many decades.

October Manifesto
Nicholas II's blueprint for a new form of elective government that revolved around the *Duma*.

Key term

The Tsar
Despite the introduction of a democratically elected *Duma*, the Tsar continued to rule as an autocrat. His position was actually reinforced by the passing of the Fundamental Laws of 1906.

↓

The Council of Ministers
This became the main law-making and administrative body. It was chaired by a Prime Minister (the first was Witte) who was selected by the Tsar. It was like a parliamentary cabinet found in Western liberal democratic systems of government. Its membership consisted of officials similar to those who had served as ministers in the Committee of Ministers. It provided material for the upper and lower houses to debate. In theory, the results of such discussions would then be reported back to the Tsar who would then make a decision as to whether the Council of Ministers should implement a new law or policy. The Fundamental Laws (Article 87) allowed ministers to report directly to the Tsar when the two houses were in recess. Thus, in reality, the Tsar could bypass the State Council and *Duma* if he believed that they might try to prevent certain measures from being enacted. The two chambers would have found it impossible to undo any legislation once the Tsar had given it his stamp of approval.

↓

The State Council (the nominated and elected upper chamber)
The main task of this body, previously the Imperial Council of State, was to act as a check on the activity of the *Dumas*. The latter had to agree with the State Council over the nature of possible reforms before they could be considered for approval by the Tsar. Members of the council were either nominated by the Tsar as under the old system, or elected as representatives of towns, the church, guilds, universities, *Zemstva* (local government councils) and the nobility.

↓

The *Duma* (the elected lower chamber)
The *Duma* was to be an assembly of people elected from a variety of social groups who would meet to debate the affairs of state. Although it was not given the authority to pass laws it could block proposed legislation. The election process was made deliberately complex. It involved voting for 'others' who would then choose representatives from political parties to sit in the chamber. This 'electoral college' system was designed in a way that favoured those with property and discriminated against workers and peasants. However, as the first *Duma* proved, there was no guarantee that the result of elections would create a *Duma* that was in total support of the ruling élite. Elections to the *Duma* were to occur every five years, but the Tsar had the authority to disband the *Duma*, which he did in 1906, 1907 and 1917.

↓

The Senate
The make-up and role of the senate was pretty much as it was before the issuing of the Fundamental Laws.

Figure 1.2: The new government's structure after 1905.

Dumas from 1906 to 1917

Between 1906 and 1917, four *Dumas* were elected, whose composition, duration and impact varied considerably. The progress of each is outlined below.

The First *Duma*, April–July 1906

Members of the first assembly participated in some rigorous debate over matters of the Empire. This included the **Polish question** and the rights of religious dissenters and Jews. However, the most important discussions were over the issue of land distribution. The government made a statement that compulsory redistribution was not an option. This angered the First *Duma* and it put forward its own, more radical solution to the rural crisis. The proposals gained press coverage with the prospect of inciting public rage. Nicholas II deemed the actions of the lower chamber to be illegal and disbanded it after only two months.

Between the sitting of the First and Second *Dumas*, a rather sinister development arose concerning the treatment of civilian protesters. After the arrest, trial and imprisonment of key Kadet and Labourist Party members for stirring up trouble in Finland by signing the **Vyborg Manifesto**, a new approach to dealing with such dissidents was adopted. The new Chairman of the Council of Ministers, **Stolypin**, thought that the approach to dealing with rebels was too slow, cumbersome and 'soft'. He therefore ordered a speeding up of the trial system for civilian rioters by introducing field court-martials. The result was a series of very quick trials and executions which gained the inglorious label of 'Stolypin's neckties'.

The Second *Duma*, February–June 1907

The composition and feelings of the Second *Duma* were greatly affected by Stolypin's policies. There was a decline in representation from the **Kadets** and **Labourists** but an increase from the Social Democrats (SDs), Socialist Revolutionaries (SRs), **Octobrists** and the far right (see Chapter 2 for more detail on the nature and extent of political groups). In many ways this was irrelevant as the Tsar and Stolypin continued to show mistrust of the work of the *Duma*s over the land reform issue again but also concern over protests about the management of the Russian army. It was not long before tsarist supporters demanded once more that the *Duma* should be disbanded. This was achieved by a sneaky police tactic which involved framing a social Democrat member of the *Duma* to make it appear that he was arranging a mutiny of soldiers. The Tsar then proceeded to proclaim that the *Duma* was subversive and had to be dissolved. It also provided an excuse for an overhaul of the election system which was blamed for giving rise to a representative body that was undermining the government.

Key terms

Polish question
The question as to whether the Poles would be allowed self-rule.

Vyborg Manifesto
A set of demands from militant *Duma* MPs asking the people of Finland not to pay taxes or serve in the armed forces until the *Duma* was restored.

Kadets
The Constitutional Democrats, a liberal political group, founded in 1905.

Labourists
Those who were specifically interested in improving the working conditions of the proletariat.

Octobrists
Supporters of the Tsar and, in particular, his proposals made in the October Manifesto.

Key figure

Pyotr Stolypin 1862–1911
Russian prime minister from 1906 to 1911.

The Third *Duma*, November 1907–June 1912

As a result of the election reforms, the Third *Duma*, unsurprisingly, was made up of a majority of people who were loyal to the crown; that is, wealthy property owners from the countryside and cities. There was also a significant reduction in nationalist members from non-Russian parts of the empire. However, as historian J.N. Westwood has pointed out, 'an unrepresentative *Duma* was not necessarily an ineffective *Duma*'. During the period of this *Duma*, there were major reforms that strengthened the army and navy. The judicial system was further improved with the reinstatement of **Justices of the Peace** and the abolition of **Land Captains**. For the first time, state-run insurance schemes for workers were introduced. All of this came about as a result of Nicholas II and ministers showing more trust in the lower chamber. Even though Stolypin did his best to destabilise the *Duma* by manipulating **Article 87** to create an even greater bias towards autocracy, the lower chamber served its full term of office.

The Fourth *Duma*, November 1912–February 1917

The final *Duma* was dominated once more by politicians from the far right. Its rule coincided with heightened and brutal repression of civil disorder. This was characterised by state police killing striking miners at the Lena Goldfields (1912). The murders outraged many *Duma* members who viewed this as a retrograde step by the government in its attempt to deal with Russia's economic and social problems. Guchkov, leader of the moderate Octobrists, warned the Tsar and ministers that the Russian people had become revolutionised by the actions of the government and that they had lost faith in its leaders. In 1914 the *Duma* made the following proclamation and prophecy of doom:

> The Ministry of the Interior systematically scorns public opinion and ignores the repeated wishes of the new legislature. The *Duma* considered it pointless to express any new wishes in regard to internal policy. The Ministry's activities arouse dissatisfaction among the broad masses that have hitherto been peaceful. Such a situation threatens Russia with untold dangers.

The final *Duma* became infamous for eventually putting pressure on the Tsar to abdicate and went on to form the backbone of the short-lived Provisional Government. However, despite its criticisms of government rule, it remained an institution that was dominated by the 'old guard'.

Overall, it is clear that the *Duma* was not simply a gesture towards representative government. It was an institution that did play an important role in instigating political, economic and social changes that had a beneficial impact on many sectors of Russian society. Nevertheless, as historian Peter Waldron has argued, collectively, the *Dumas* and the Council of Ministers 'made very little difference to the underlying nature of the

Key terms

Justices of the Peace
Landowners appointed as officials to maintain law and order at a local level. They worked in conjunction with the police.

Land Captains
Landowners who were appointed, from 1889 onwards, mainly to supervise the work of the regional councils or *Zemstva* that had been introduced by Alexander II.

Article 87
A section of the 1906 Fundamental Laws that allowed for proposed legislation to be submitted directly to the Tsar for his approval.

Russian state'. *Duma* politicians on the left were largely ignored by the government and the majority in the lower chamber remained loyal to the principle of autocracy.

> ### Essay focus
>
> Figures 1.1 and 1.2 (on pages 29 and 30) reveal how complicated the structure of Russian government was. In Essay 1 (page 48), paragraph 4, a very clear synopsis of organisational and administrative structures is made and linked to an evaluation of changes made by Nicholas II. This is a good example of condensing complex material to support an argument.

Key question
To what extent did the failure of the Provisional Government illustrate the strength of autocracy throughout the period from 1855 to 1917?

Key terms

Progressive Bloc
A group within the Fourth *Duma* consisting of members of the Kadets, Octobrists, Nationalists and Party of Progressives, who challenged the authority of Nicholas II.

Real wages
Wages after the impact of inflation is taken into account.

Key figure

Grigori Rasputin 1869–1916
The religious mystic who gave counsel to Nicholas II and his family.

The First World War and the Provisional Government

The emergence of the Progressive Bloc

The progress of the fourth *Duma* was interrupted by the outbreak of the First World War in 1914. The *Duma* met a week after the start of the war and its work was immediately disrupted by a group of socialist members walking out in protest at Nicholas II's decision to commit Russia to a war that they did not think could be won. By 1915, there was further discord with the emergence of the '**Progressive Bloc**', a majority of *Duma* representatives who demanded a National Government to take charge of the war effort. In August 1915, Nicholas responded to the challenge to his authority by suspending the *Duma* and personally taking charge of the armed forces. This is further evidence of how little authority the *Duma* had and how Nicholas had no intention of relinquishing power, especially during a time of national crisis.

The changing economic and social context

The actions of Nicholas further alienated a majority of those in the *Duma* and their supporters. The *Duma* reopened in November 1916 but with the Progressive Bloc still prominent. By this time, economic and social conditions in Russia had deteriorated. **Real wages** had plummeted, food prices had rocketed upwards and fuel supplies had diminished, mainly as a result of an inadequate transport system. There was also increasing concern over the role of the Tsarina in the governance of the empire, especially while her husband was absent from St Petersburg. Not only was she mistrusted due to her Germanic background but she was also maligned as a result of her 'friendship' with the holy mystic, **Rasputin**. These conditions and developments provided the backdrop to a series of events that quickly and dramatically resulted in the abdication of the Tsar and the end of Romanov rule. The key events were as follows:

- 9 January 1917 – about 150,000 workers took to the streets of St Petersburg to celebrate the anniversary of Bloody Sunday.
- 18 February 1917 – a strike occurred at the Putilov Steel Works.
- 19 February 1917 – bread rationing was introduced.

- 23 February 1917 – marchers celebrating International Women's Day and workers from the Putilov plant combined to protest about poor working and living conditions.
- 25 February 1917 – a general strike took place with workers being fired on by troops. Rodzianko, president of the *Duma*, urged the Tsar to 'change' his attitude towards governing.
- 26 February 1917 – the *Duma* defied the Tsar's instruction to disband. A major turning point was the decision by troops (about half of the **Petrograd** Garrison) to join the protesters.
- 27 February 1917 – the Petrograd Soviet was formed alongside the Provisional *Duma* Committee. This was the foundation of governance through a dual authority and clear indication that the Tsar was considered unfit to rule by a majority of senior politicians.
- 1 March 1917 – Soviet Order No. 1 was passed which gave the Petrograd Soviet total control over the whole of the Russian military.
- 2 March 1917 – under pressure from close advisers and family members, Nicholas II decided to abdicate. An official Provisional Government was formed to deal with the crisis until elections to a Constituent Assembly could be held.

Petrograd
St Petersburg was renamed Petrograd in August 1914.

Belligerent countries
Those countries that had been directly involved in the First World War.

Key terms

This sudden turn of events had not been expected and even the revolutionary elements in Russian society were taken by surprise. In theory, the abdication of Nicholas and the formation of the Provisional Government marked the end of autocracy in Russia. In practice, the move towards greater democracy was short-lived and, within a few years, the governance of Russia was dominated once again by the actions of one person, Lenin, supported by a closely knit set of advisers from the Bolshevik Party. Some historians have argued that the era of the Provisional Government was the only time that the Russian Empire was united. Others have pointed out that, although this is true, it was unlikely from the start that the new government would be able to sustain unity. It faced the following difficult challenges:

- The Provisional Government was self-appointed and not democratically elected. It consisted mainly of the 'old guard'; most were members who had previously served in the *Duma* of 1912 and who were very conservative in outlook. This was not a problem for the members of the assembly as their mission was to establish a system which would bring about a democratically elected government (that is, a Constituent Assembly).
- Authority was shared with the Petrograd Soviet who, from the start, opposed most of what the Provisional Government proposed.
- The first government established a set of eight principles by which it would rule. These were classically liberal in nature and included decrees on political amnesty, full freedom of speech, an end to all discrimination, an end to the death penalty and the setting up of an independent judiciary. Russia was said to have become 'the freest of the **belligerent countries**'.

However, the downside for the Provisional Government was that it allowed the proliferation of protest groups (as had happened when Alexander II 'reformed'), the most dangerous being the Bolsheviks.

- Economic issues such as runaway inflation, low real wages and the length of the working day proved very difficult to deal with.
- The peasant land issue dragged on throughout the Provisional Government's time in office. The best solution they could provide was to argue that, due to the nature of the land redistribution problem, only a properly elected assembly could deal with it. Thus, peasants would have to wait until the elections to the Constituent Assembly for their grievances to be met.
- There was continuous disagreement between the Provisional Government and the Petrograd Soviet over Russia's involvement in the war. The former wanted to push on for 'a decisive victory' while the latter demanded 'peace without annexations or indemnities' but also '**revolutionary defensism**'. This rift was never resolved and was a major reason for the eventual failure of the government.

Key terms

Revolutionary defensism
Defence and protection of everything achieved by the revolution of March 1917.

Kronstadt
A Baltic naval base.

An attempt to bridge the differences between the two competing authorities was made in May 1917 with the formation of a coalition government. This was led by Prince Lvov who invited six members of the Petrograd Soviet to join. But it did little to appease the more radical members of the Soviet and the problems faced by the ruling body continued. National elections to a Constituent Assembly were postponed, the land issue was ignored, workers committees were clamped down on and involvement in the war continued. All of this combined to produce a further decline in support for the Provisional Government and rising militancy within the Petrograd Soviet.

The demands of the Soviet
By June 1917, members of the Soviet were demanding even more involvement in the national government. Some supporters of the Soviet had adopted the slogan 'All Power to the Soviets' and this sentiment was strongly expressed during the sittings of the first All-Russian Congress of Soviets. This shift in stance appeared to be a significant threat to the continued existence of the government. In an attempt to rejuvenate support, the President of the Provisional Government, under the guidance of Kerensky, the Minister for War, launched a military 'offensive'. This failed with the Russian forces experiencing heavy losses and many soldiers deserting.

The 'July Days'
Protests against the war heightened and reached a disturbing peak in July when sailors at **Kronstadt** mutinied. At this point, there were many opponents of the government, most notably the Bolsheviks, who believed that the Soviet needed to seize power.

The Menshevik and SRs refused to support this idea and in the end troops loyal to Lvov saved the day by clearing the streets of Petrograd of the dissidents. Kerensky emerged from this with credit; despite the failures of the army in the war, troops had been organised successfully to quell internal rebellion. As a result, on 8 July he was appointed prime minister. Kerensky launched a 'reaction' against those involved in the **'July Days'** rising. The Bolsheviks became the target for repression; their newspaper, *Pravda*, was banned, leading members were either imprisoned or exiled and the party as a whole was branded as being treacherous.

The Bolsheviks and the land question

Kerensky seemed to have beaten off the Bolshevik threat but two developments quickly undermined his achievements. One was a shift in Bolshevik policy towards the peasant land question. Until the 'July Days', the Bolsheviks believed that a revolution could only be generated through the industrial proletariat. However, as an increasing number of peasants started to take land illegally, Lenin and other Bolshevik leaders realised that they could exploit this activity by claiming it was truly revolutionary. By promoting a **Land to the Peasants** campaign, the Bolsheviks quickly gained support from rural workers and seemed to promise a solution to the land question that the Provisional Government had failed to do.

The Kornilov affair

The second major challenge to Kerensky occurred in August when the military commander, **Kornilov**, marched with his troops to Petrograd with the intention of forcefully closing down the Soviet. Kerensky seemed to believe that Kornilov, having defeated the Soviet, would then move on to take over the Provisional Government and impose a military-style dictatorship. Kerensky, therefore, agreed to the Bolsheviks being given arms to defend Petrograd. In the end, a bloody conflict was averted. Railway workers refused to transport Kornilov's army. Kornilov also received advance warning of how quickly the Bolsheviks had mobilised their defences and decided that the proposed takeover had a good chance of ending in disaster. He therefore abandoned his plan and was arrested.

The Kornilov affair was significant for two reasons. First, the Bolsheviks were viewed as heroes for organising the protection of Petrograd. Second, it was evident that the Provisional Government was susceptible to being challenged by the military and therefore, others who might want to use force to seize power. After the affair, the Bolsheviks quickly gained more support so that by early September they had majorities in both the Petrograd and Moscow Soviets. By the end of October they had ousted the Provisional Government and taken control of Petrograd. The main events leading to the final takeover were as follows:

'July Days'
A month of protests and strikes against the war and the ineffectual policies of the Provisional Government.

Pravda
The key Bolshevik newspaper which was allowed to start publication again in 1917.

Land to the Peasants
A propaganda campaign that promised the land issue (a fairer distribution of land) would be resolved in favour of the peasants.

Lavr Kornilov 1870–1918
Appointed in July 1917 as the new commander-in-chief of the armed forces. After the attempted coup he was arrested and imprisoned but as soon as he was released he formed the anti-Bolshevik Volunteer Army. He died fighting in the early stages of the Civil War.

- 8 September: the Bolsheviks were in control of the Petrograd Soviet. By the middle of September they also controlled the Moscow Soviet.
- 7 October: Lenin returned from exile.
- 10 October: the Bolsheviks began planning for a revolution.
- 23 October: Kerensky closed *Pravda* and *Izvestiya* (Bolshevik newspapers); a round-up of leading Bolsheviks was attempted.
- 24 October: the Petrograd Soviet's Military Revolutionary Committee began to seize power under the command of Trotsky.
- 26 October: the members of the Provisional Government were arrested, except for Kerensky, who fled (later to settle in the USA).
- 27 October: the **All-Russian Congress of Soviets** (in sitting since 25 October) was informed by Lenin that the Bolsheviks had seized power.
- 2 November: the Bolsheviks had total control of Moscow.

The Russian Revolution was over and a complete change in the way Russia was to be governed seemed imminent.

Key term

All-Russian Congress of Soviets A meeting of delegates from soviets throughout Russia to decide on the policies to be adopted by the soviets.

Key question
How far did the Bolsheviks revolutionise the way Russia was governed?

Lenin and the Bolshevik government

The Bolsheviks did not introduce a new constitution for the governance of Russia until July 1918. From October 1917 to June 1918, there were a number of issues that they had to deal with to allow them to consolidate their position.

The Second All-Russian Congress of Soviets

The Second All-Russian Congress of Soviets met on 25 October. The Bolshevik leaders knew that they had to get the approval of the Congress to rule Russia if their proposed government was to have legitimacy. This proved quite easy as right-wing SRs and Mensheviks, who favoured a coalition government, walked out of the Congress in protest. This left the Bolsheviks with virtually no opposition and a clear mandate to rule.

The 'Petrograd revolution'

The October Revolution, in reality, was a Petrograd revolution. The Bolsheviks, therefore, had to spread their authority. They attempted to do this by encouraging the setting up of more soviets in towns and cities across Russia. This proved difficult due to opposition from the 'old guard' and it was not certain how long the new soviets would last. Resistance from whole regions in the empire was a major reason for the outbreak of a civil war that was to last until 1921.

The Constituent Assembly

The Bolsheviks knew that they had to allow the proposed elections to a Constituent Assembly in November to go ahead. Failure to do so would have resulted in a degree of opposition from other parties and the people that the Bolsheviks would have struggled to deal with. Unsurprisingly, the Bolsheviks failed to win a majority, coming second to the SRs. Lenin claimed that the Constituent Assembly was 'elected on the old register' and 'appeared as an expression of the old regime when the authority belonged to the bourgeoisie'. This was used by Lenin as justification for shutting the Assembly down after just one day. The fact that there was no popular demonstration against this move was testament to the power of persuasion that Lenin possessed. In January 1918, the Third All-Russian Congress of Soviets sanctioned the shutting down of the Constituent Assembly and also proclaimed the establishment of the Russian Soviet Federative Socialist Republic (RSFSR). The RSFSR was essentially the Great Russia of the old Empire but was now to be ruled without a monarch (hence the use of the term republic).

The Decree on Land

Shortly after taking control from the Provisional Government, the Bolsheviks issued the Decree on Land. This was their proposal to deal with the peasant land problem. It sanctioned the requisition of private land by peasants (something that was already happening) but stated that the division and distribution of it could only be carried out by village soviets. Some argued that this went against what Bolsheviks had previously opposed which was the creation of a 'petty bourgeois' type of peasantry. However, it was very similar to what rival SRs had proposed for years and therefore went some way to winning over the support of their opponents.

The issue of the war

To start to deal with the issue of a damaging war, the Bolsheviks issued another decree, the Decree on Peace. This called for an immediate truce and a peaceful settlement based on justice and fairness. It laid the foundation for an **armistice** that was signed on 2 December 1917. Despite the Decree, Germany insisted on some very harsh terms for a final settlement which disturbed patriotic Russians and divided the leadership of the Bolshevik Party. Lenin, contrary to the wishes of other leading Bolsheviks, especially Trotsky, argued strongly for an acceptance of a treaty; not signing up to it would have meant a 'death sentence for the Soviet government'. On 3 March 1918, the Soviet representative, Sokolnikov, signed the Treaty of Brest-Litovsk which ceded a huge portion of territory, amounting to about a third of European Russia, to Germany. Most importantly, this included the Ukraine, Russia's most important grain-producing region. Russia also agreed to pay **reparations** of three billion roubles. It was no wonder that Trotsky called the treaty a *diktat*.

The end of the war

By August 1918, Lenin's gamble had paid off. Germany's campaign on the Western Front collapsed and it was not long before they withdrew from Russia completely. The Brest-Litovsk agreement became meaningless and Lenin now had the chance to rid the party of those who had continued to doubt his judgement.

The organisation of the Bolshevik government

The organisation of the Bolshevik government took shape quickly after the Second All-Russian Congress of Soviets had disbanded. The Congress had given the Bolsheviks a mandate to rule Russia based on the assumption that a Bolshevik government was a Soviet government in the truest sense. If this had been the case, the new regime would have constituted a major break with the tsarist past as genuine Soviet rule would have revolved around the freedoms and liberties gained as a result of the revolts of February 1917. But as the historian J.N. Westwood has stated, 'the Bolsheviks abandoned many of the aims which had been professed by generations of Russian Revolutionaries, including themselves, and they reintroduced, often in a more repressive form, long-reviled tsarist policies which had been abolished after the February revolution'.

Box 1.1 shows the new Bolshevik structure of government.

The All-Russian Congress of Soviets and the Central Executive Committee

The Congress and its organising committee (Executive Committee) were meant to be the mainstay of the new government. In theory, the commissars (see below) were answerable to the Executive Committee although the reality was different. When, in the summer of 1918, Mensheviks and SRs were expelled from the Executive Committee, it became dominated by Bolsheviks. Many of these were also 'people's commissars' and Russia was not far off being ruled as a 'one-party state'.

The Council of People's Commissars (*Sovnarkom*)

This consisted of 'people's commissars' (ministers) who had specific governmental responsibilities. Trotsky, for example, was placed in charge of foreign affairs and Stalin had to deal with nationalities. The chairman (prime minister) was Lenin. To begin with the Council also consisted of left-wing SRs.

The *Cheka*

In December 1917, the All-Russian Extraordinary Commission for Fighting Counter-revolution was introduced (abbreviated to *Cheka*). It was headed by Dzerzhinski, a Polish communist. The main aim of the *Cheka* was to prevent the emergence and growth of counter-revolutionary movements. It therefore acted as a tool, rather than an organ, of government. It was disbanded in 1922 and replaced by the Main Political Administration (GPU/OGPU).

Box 1.1: The new Bolshevik structure of government.

This new 'system' appeared to be democratic insofar as members of *Sovnarkom* were the product of a chain of elections:

* village soviets chose representatives for district soviets
* district soviets then elected members for the provincial soviets
* provincial soviets provided the membership of *Sovnarkom*.

But the soviets were dominated by Bolsheviks and it is no coincidence that the new organisation of government was very similar to the way in which the Bolshevik Party was structured:

- At local level, the party consisted of cells of a handful of members who would organise meetings (political workshops) to encourage grassroots support.
- Cell members were elected to town or district committees.
- Committees then provided representatives to the annual party congress.
- The congress chose members to form the party Central Executive Committee (consisting of about a tenth of congress members). In turn, the Central Executive Committee was responsible for the administration and operation of three political offices:
  - the Politburo: this was a small, élite group of Bolsheviks that was responsible for formulating policies. The Politburo came to dominate the Central Committee and, hence, the running of the party
  - the Orgburo: this office organised party affairs
  - the Ogburo: this body was responsible for maintaining order and dealing with opposition.

The Bolsheviks promoted the party as one that was working to create a more egalitarian society based on the principle of **democratic centralism**. Quite simply, central control of Russian affairs would be in the hands of politicians who had, for the first time, been elected by the Russian people (that is, the people of the RSFSR). Central control was justified partly by the need to create stability after the Civil War. This was all very misleading especially as the soviets, and subsequently *Sovnarkom*, were dominated by Bolsheviks.

Once the government was elected all of the key posts were held by senior Bolsheviks and all other levels of administration were swamped with what were called '**leading cadres**', drawn from the Bolshevik Party. This had been purposefully manufactured during the Civil War years with the help of the *Cheka*; any opposition to the Bolshevik move towards a one-party state was quickly eradicated. This, of course, included other political parties. Anyone wanting to be actively involved in politics had to get permission to join the Bolshevik Party or become part of an opposition movement in exile.

As the party essentially became the government, membership to the former was increasingly seen as a privilege and a way to become more socially mobile. Thus, membership numbers grew significantly during the immediate post-Civil War period. In 1921, there were around 730,000 members but by 1928, this had increased to about a million. Many found new careers and opportunities as part of the *Nomenklatura* but much depended on the socio-economic background of members as to what role they would play. By the time of Stalin's accession to power, the party had become very hierarchical:

- By the early 1930s, nearly 10 per cent of the party were made up of *apparatchiki* (full-time, paid party organisers). These were educated members of society who served mainly as party secretaries.

Key terms

Democratic centralism
Under the Bolsheviks, the people would agree to being led by a cadre (group of key personnel) based in Moscow, until a genuine workers' government could be put in place.

Leading cadres
The 'top' members of the Communist Party responsible for organising and educating the masses.

Nomenklatura
'Approved' officers, administrators and managers in the communist regime who possessed specialist skills.

- About 30 per cent of the party were employed as 'other' administrators in the party and, hence, the government. These too were educated people who, under the tsarist regime, had largely been part of the growing middle class.
- The rest of the party consisted of workers and/or peasants who, in their spare time, operated as party activists.

As the party and government became more hierarchical and centralised (and, interestingly, nepotistic) the political regime became even less democratic. Officials became more detached from grassroots affairs and workers showed less interest in politics. This was reinforced by the changing nature of the proletariat. More industrial workers were recruited from the ranks of the peasantry who were notorious for being apathetic towards party affairs. Some attempt was made to address this issue through recruitment campaigns such as the **Lenin Enrolment** but this had minimal effect on the general composition of the party. When Lenin died in 1924, it was apparent that the highly centralised, bureaucratic and authoritarian nature of Bolshevik rule bore a striking resemblance to the form of government that had existed during the tsarist era.

Key term

Lenin Enrolment
A campaign aimed to encourage peasants to officially join the Bolshevik Party.

Key question
To what extent did Stalin govern Russia in a more ruthlessly autocratic manner compared with other Russian leaders?

Stalin and the USSR

Under Stalin, the basic structure and organisation of government remained the same although it is reasonable to say that the nature of rule changed. Stalin wished to continue with democratic centralism as this was essential to the implementation of his economic policies and to dealing with internal enemies. The epitome of Stalin's attempt to further stabilise government was the creation in 1936 of a new constitution. This built on the earlier constitutions of 1918 and 1924 (see below) but also suggested that democratic centralism would be balanced in the future by increased freedom for the peoples of the USSR. The differences between the constitutions were as follows (see map on page 74 to locate the different republics):

- 1918 – a constitution which created the RSFSR (that is, Russia, but also including parts of central Asia, most notably Kazakhstan, Uzbekistan and Turkmenia).
- 1924 – a new constitution formally created the Federal Union of Soviet Socialist Republics (USSR). By this time, via a treaty of 1922, the Republics of the Ukraine, Belorussia and Transcaucasia (Azerbaijan, Armenia, Georgia) had joined with the RSFSR (see page 38 for further details). Each republic was allowed its own government and other symbols of sovereignty such as national flags. However, such governments were still answerable to *Sovnarkom*.
- 1936 – the 'Stalin' constitution added Kirghizia and Tajikstan to the list of states given full republic status. It also created a system that appeared to allow greater representation of the interests of separate nation states in the centralised government of the USSR. Figure 1.3, page 42 shows the newly created structure.

Supreme Soviet of the USSR
This elected the Council of People's Commissars (*Sovnarkom*), was headed by a presidium and was given the sole power to make laws for the whole of the union. It was divided into two houses, partly to give the impression that a genuine federal form of government had been created.

Soviet of the Union
- Members were to be elected by electoral districts – one member per 30,000 people
- Elections were to take place every four years
- The Soviet of the Union therefore contained representatives of the peoples of the whole of the USSR.

Soviet of Nationalities
Membership consisted of:

- 25 members per union republic
- 11 members per autonomous republic
- five members per autonomous region
- one member per national area

These regional categories simply reflected the different importance given to particular national groups.

Figure 1.3: The structure of the USSR.

The Supreme Soviet met twice every year. Delegates were given the opportunity to gain knowledge and understanding of government policies, to debate their implications and then to give them a stamp of approval. Coupled with this improved representation were other concessions such as the right of republics to administer their own education systems and the power to break away from the Soviet Union.

The role of the Communist Party of the Soviet Union (CPSU)

But the new constitution did not alter the fact that the Communist Party dominated both the union and republican governments; dissent from the party line was never going to be tolerated and, in this sense, the 'Stalin' constitution created a political system that differed very little from that which had been in existence since the 1918 constitution. In fact, this was made fairly clear in Article 126 of the Stalin Constitution which stated that the party was the 'nucleus of all the public and state organisations of the working people'.

Further additions to the USSR

Estonia, Latvia, Lithuania and Moldova were joined to the USSR from 1939 to 1940. However, the next important change to the constitution of the USSR was in 1977. Thus, even with destalinisation, the organisation and structure of central government remained virtually the same during the period up to 1964. This was also true of the way in which the party was run. What did alter was the way in which the tools of government were utilised.

Key question
How important were changes to local government in altering the nature and scope of autocratic rule in the period from 1855 to 1964?

Key term

Mir
A group of elders who were responsible for governing the behaviour of members of rural communities or villages.

Local government

Before 1861, provinces were largely under the jurisdiction of noble landowners. Village issues were discussed by the **mir** and representations, if necessary and appropriate, were made to local nobles who might then voice peasant concerns to an appropriate government minister. In this way, local nobility acted as a bridge between central government and the outreaches of the Empire. This all changed with the emancipation of the serfs. The nobility, with a significant reduction in land holdings and the obligations that went with serfdom, no longer had a political role to play. Peasants became isolated from the rest of society, with no outlet to express their grievances. The management of local affairs was, by default, left in the hands of local police constables appointed by the Interior Ministry. Peasants seemed to resent this as the police were hardly the best people to feedback peasant grievances to the authorities.

To help overcome the gap created by the Emancipation Edict, in 1864 Alexander II introduced the institution of the *Zemstvos* (*Zemstva* in plural) or regional council. This was characterised by the following:

- An elected membership voted in by a mixture of landowners, urban dwellers and peasants. Electors were selected mainly by property qualification. The result was that the vast majority of *Zemstva* were dominated by the nobility and professional classes (and this was partly intended as a way of giving back some authority and status to nobles).
- Located only in areas considered to be part of Great Russia. Hence, *Zemstva* were not found in Poland, the Baltic region and the Caucasus. Also, for numerous reasons, not all of the provinces eligible for representation were covered by *Zemstva*; by 1917 there were still 37 without one.

In 1870 an urban equivalent was introduced called the *Duma*. The entry qualification to this body was even tougher than for the *Zemstvos* which meant the exclusion of the urban proletariat.

The Third Element

Until October 1917 both the *Zemstva* and *Duma* flourished. They provided important services especially in the fields of education, public health and transport. They were particularly valued by local people due to the way in which *Zemstva* members used intimate, detailed knowledge of local affairs to pressure central government to carry out reforms that might benefit living standards. Central government, however, increasingly found *Zemstva* members irritating. By the end of the nineteenth century, the councils in some provinces had come to be dominated by local intelligentsia consisting of teachers, lawyers and doctors. Such people were vociferous in demanding that central government should be re-modelled on the lines of the *Zemstva* and *Duma*. This liberal voice against autocracy was named the

'Third Element'. The other elements were those directly employed in the 'administration' (government) and those who 'represented the social estates' (nobility).

The monitoring of the Third Element

The behaviour of those involved in local politics was monitored closely from 1889 by Land Captains. However, this did not stop the Third Element becoming a very important driving force within the liberal movement and one which Nicholas II took seriously. Although the Tsar dismissed *Zemstva* demands for their members to be represented in central government as 'senseless dreamings', he did allow them to hold their own national congress and, in the aftermath of Bloody Sunday, to hold a special meeting with *Zemstva* representatives to discuss political reforms.

Conclusion

Although the provincial governments were perceived to be successful, their progress was somewhat undermined by the emergence of rural and, more importantly, urban soviets. After 1917, both the *Zemstva* and *Duma* (being labelled bourgeois and counter-revolutionary) were made redundant. Local government was then dominated by soviets who became an integral part of what was called democratic centralism (see page 40 for details). This situation remained until the end of the period.

Soviets

The first workers' council or soviet emerged in St Petersburg at the time of the publication of the October Manifesto. Its aim was to coordinate strikes and protect the work of factory workers. Fairly quickly, SRs and SDs looked to gain representation on the executive committee and had most influence over how the council was run. In 1917 the council was officially referred to as the Petrograd Soviet of Workers' Deputies and the executive committee had come to be dominated specifically by the Bolsheviks.

The power of the Soviets

From March to October 1917, the Soviet wielded much power. Some historians have gone as far to say that it was the Soviet that actually controlled Russia rather than the Provisional Government. The Soviet dictated when, where and how strikes would occur. Essential services, especially those connected with transport, were largely in the hands of the Soviet. Also military members had the authority to approve or veto the use of the armed forces.

Soviet Order No. 1

The issuing of Petrograd Soviet Order No. 1 took military control a step further by making officers submissive to soldier representatives' commands. From April 1917 onwards Lenin called for 'All Power to the Soviets' although this slogan was little used after the failure of the July Days. The call for the councils to take power rose again in October, by which time the Bolsheviks dominated the soviet movement.

Trotsky and the Petrograd Soviet

Trotsky became chairman of the Petrograd Soviet in October and some Bolsheviks urged for the Soviet to displace the Provisional Government; for many this would have been a true workers' revolution. However, Lenin demanded that, to prevent the need for a power-sharing arrangement, the Bolsheviks should seize power before the All-Russian Congress of Soviets was due to meet on 25 October. When the Congress found out about the overthrow of the Provisional Government, the SRs walked out leaving the Bolsheviks in total control. Thus, the Bolshevik takeover was now synonymous with a Soviet coup and there was little need then for the formal existence of the Soviet.

Judicial changes

The judiciary was obviously an important organ of government. However, despite some reforms, the Russian legal system remained archaic compared with that of the West. The main changes were as follows:

- 1864 legal reforms: these resulted in the introduction of a jury system for criminal cases; the creation of a hierarchy of courts to cater for different types of case; better pay for judges (lessening the chances of corruption); public attendance at courts was allowed.
- 1877: following an assassination attempt on Alexander II's life, a new department of the Senate was set up to try political cases. The **Vera Zasulich case** and the eventual murder of the Tsar in 1881 indicated that the new policies of the Senate failed.
- 1881: Alexander III moved away from the 'liberal' approach to law and order adopted by his father. The police were centralised under the Minster for the Interior, special courts were designed for political cases and Justices of the Peace were abolished and replaced by Land Captains.
- 1917 onwards: the period of communist rule was dominated by the idea of 'revolutionary justice'. This was epitomised by the new criminal code of 1921 that legalised the use of terror to deter crime (i.e. all anti-revolutionary behaviour). The whole judicial system rested on this principle to the end of the period in question. Stalin took the use of terror to an extreme level but Khrushchev moved back to a softer approach through destalinisation.

Key term

Vera Zasulich case
Zasulich was a revolutionary who shot and wounded the governor of St Petersburg, General Trepov, in 1878. Trepov was considered to be a tyrant of the highest order who thought nothing of flogging political prisoners for no good reason. Zasulich was put on trial but the jury found her not guilty as her actions were considered to be just. Many believed that was clear indication that the legal reforms of 1864 had created a climate that would allow revolutionary activity to flourish.

Summary diagram: Government structures and institutions

The Tsars
- Autocratic – officials and organs of government were answerable to the tsars
- Hierarchical
- Many organs – the Council of Ministers, the Imperial Council of State, the Committee of Ministers, the Senate
- Reform – a nod to democracy with the introduction of the *Duma*
- Local government – the *mir*, the *Zemstva*, the *Duma*
- Judiciary – liberalisation but with 'checks', for example Land Captains

CHANGE

The Provisional Government
- Democratic rather than autocratic replaced tsarism but unelected (the 'old guard')
- Hierarchical but shared power with the Petrograd Soviet – the Dual Authority
- Two organs (Provisional Government and the Petrograd Soviet)
- Reform – early changes provided greater freedoms to the people
- Judiciary – liberalisation; political prisoners freed (although exiled or reimprisoned later). Key cause of downfall (overthrown by Bolsheviks)

CHANGE or CONTINUITY?

The Communists
- Autocratic and dictatorial – all officials and organs of government were answerable to the 'leader' (Lenin, Stalin, Khrushchev)
- Hierarchical
- Many organs – All-Russian Congress of Soviets, the Central Executive Committee (Politburo, Orgburo, Ogburo), the Council of People's Commissars (*Sovnarkom*)
- Reform – a nod to democracy with the introduction of the Supreme Soviet (Soviet of the Union, Soviet of Nationalities)
- Local government – soviets abandoned; localities governed by party cells and hierarchy of local party officials
- Judiciary – dominated by 'revolutionary justice'

3 | Conclusion

In the sense that autocracy means a government headed by a ruler with unlimited power, there was little change in the way Russia was run between 1855 and 1964. Some may argue that the dictatorship established under Lenin was different from the tsarist autocracy in that the use of force to impose the will of the leadership was greater and more persistent. There was another twist to the story when Stalin came to power; his highly personalised approach to rule coupled with the 'Terror' resulted in an obedience from the people that was symptomatic of totalitarianism. One decision the reader needs to make on this issue is whether autocracy, dictatorship and totalitarianism amounted to the same kind of rule over the Russian people. Some might claim that ideological differences between regimes were great enough to create profound and significant ways in how governance occurred.

Key question
How far did the nature of Russian government change from 1855 to 1964?

Something else that seemed to remain pretty much the same was the structure of government. It was always hierarchical, dominated by one person and lacking representation of the bulk of the population. The only part-exception was the Provisional Government but this did not last very long. There were times when there were attempts to develop a more democratic structure, for instance in 1905, but these efforts were largely disingenuous. Another common feature of regimes was the high level of bureaucratisation, established in the main to provide work for those who aspired to some level of power and responsibility but who were unlikely to make it to the very top of government. As many bureaucrats were educated, in theory they were potential leaders of subversive groups. Encouragement to become a government official took away the incentive to become a rebel and was a way of lessening the chances of opposition gaining momentum. Generally, to have a post as a civil servant was considered fortuitous and prestigious.

Essay focus

Essay 1, paragraph 8 (see page 48), discusses the importance of propaganda and censorship as a tool of government. How important was this compared with the other tools of government in maintaining order in Russia from 1855 to 1964? (See Chapter 2 for details on propaganda and censorship.)

Further questions for debate

1 How far was there more change than continuity in the way Russia was ruled in the period from 1855 to 1964?

2 'There was very little difference between tsarist autocracy, Lenin's dictatorship and Stalin's totalitarianism.' How far do you agree with this statement?

3 To what extent did the 1917 October Revolution completely change the nature and function of Russian government?

4 'Without the interruption of the First World War, Russia would have moved towards a permanent democratic system of government.' How far do you agree with this statement?

5 How far was Stalin's government the most autocratic of any of the rulers of Russia in the period from 1855 to 1964?

Choose two of the above questions and write plans in the form of notes and/or diagrams. Your plans should outline your main arguments, any relevant supporting evidence and how key ideas are linked synoptically.

Advice on answering essay questions on similarity and difference

The following essays constitute answers to a question that focuses on the concept of similarity and difference over time. Note that the question is presented with a quotation and then a command stem tagged on. Quotations can be very useful as they provide a ready framework for an essay answer. However, care needs to be taken when unpacking the content of the quotation. You should remember to take careful note of the topic (Russian governments, 1855–1964) and key words that may need defining or clarifying ('autocracy' and 'simply exchanged'). Furthermore, it is important to note that the command statement (How far do you agree ... ?) requests a balanced response. You may or may not agree with the assertion posed by the quotation but it is important to consider a variety of different perspectives before coming to a judgement. Thus, a comparison of different political regimes over an extended period of time is always likely to reveal a mixture of similarities and differences.

Two important points need to be noted about the content required to answer this question. First, information on the tools that governments used to rule Russia (reform and repression) can be found in Chapters 2 and 3. You will probably need to read these chapters before using the essays at the end of this chapter. Remember that one of the key objectives of the OCR Themes paper is to get students to think synoptically. In other words, you should be able to draw on your knowledge and understanding of *all* of the different sections in the OCR Themes specification for Russia and its Rulers 1855–1964 to answer any *one* particular question.

Second, some of the examples used in the essays to support key points will not necessarily be found in this book. This has been purposefully done to remind students of the need to read widely so that they can accumulate a range of different material that they can use as 'evidence'. To this end students would do well to consult a number of the texts mentioned on the reading list at the end of this book. Also, remember that the Themes paper is about writing synoptically to cover a 100-year period and applying historical concepts to historical problems (change/continuity, similarity/difference and cause/consequence). The learning and use of facts is only important insofar as it will prevent the student from providing overgeneralisation and assertion in essays.

Read each of the following essays carefully. Each essay was written in one hour and without the use of notes. Note any strengths and weaknesses and compare your views with those of the assessor. Marks should be awarded for each of the two assessment objectives described in the tables at the end of the book (see pages 192–3).

Essay 1: 'A study of Russian governments in the period from 1855 to 1964 suggests that Russia simply exchanged one form of autocracy for another after 1917.' How far do you agree with this statement?

1 The tsarist and communist governments that dominated this period were all autocratic insofar as they believed in absolute power, i.e. that all political power should be in the hands of one or a few individuals. However, governments differed with respect to why they believed in autocracy and how it was implemented. It is also important to note that there were times when there were moves away from autocracy most notably in 1905 and in February 1917. Thus, it would be an exaggeration to claim that Russia simply exchanged one form of autocracy for another after 1917.

1 A solid start that gives a good indication that both similarities and differences between the two types of political regime are going to be discussed.

2 This is a well-synthesised section on the nature of tsarist autocracy. It clearly draws out the continued importance of autocracy to the tsars but also indicates that there were some subtle changes in the way it was implemented.

2 The tsars adhered closely to the ideology of autocracy up to 1917. They justified their authoritarian position by claiming that it was by the divine right of God that they had been placed on earth to rule over the Russian people. Although Alexander II was a reformer (the 'Tsar Liberator') he emphasised that his mission was to strengthen and perfect Russia's internal well-being 'with the help of divine Providence'. When his reforms ironically created a surge in opposition, he felt totally justified in using force to deal with it. Alexander III, in the wake of his father's assassination in 1881, did not hesitate to reverse his father's reforms and used much repression against political agitators. He also ignored the Loris–Melikov proposals for representative government. He introduced Land Captains to control rural unrest, employed the policy of Russification to unite the empire and deployed the secret police to clamp down on revolutionaries. This strengthening of autocracy and 'reaction' to the liberalism of Alexander II was again based on the will of providence and the idea that it was for the good of the Russian people. According to Alexander III, the people were 'known throughout the whole world for their love and devotion to their sovereigns'. When Nicholas II came to the throne in 1894, he stated in his manifesto that he would 'adhere unswervingly, as my father, to the principle of autocracy'. The October Manifesto of 1905 and the creation of the *Duma* suggested that there might be some deviation from a full autocracy but the Fundamental Laws of 1906 ensured that the tsar retained his absolute powers.

3 A skilful analysis of similarities and differences is in evidence here. The theme of changing ideology is developed further and is linked to how the new communist ideology was put into operation.

3 Lenin was an autocrat similar to the tsars in that through his leadership of the Bolshevik Party, he demanded total loyalty and agreement with his policies. Those who disagreed with the Bolshevik ideal were branded bourgeois and/or anti-revolutionary. Such opposition was dealt with mercilessly through imprisonment, exile or execution. Stalin continued with this dictatorial approach but in a way that meant that every aspect of a citizen's life was under the total control of the state. In particular, collectivisation and the Five-Year Plans, implemented with the help of the NKVD, ensured the development of a form of totalitarianism that Russian people found almost impossible to oppose. Although the communists maintained autocratic rule there were differences in the way in which they justified their ideologies. Lenin's interpretation of Marxism was founded on the idea that workers (and peasants) were not politically educated enough to take responsibility for running Russia. They had to be dictated to by Lenin and a cadre of Bolsheviks before there could be a genuine Dictatorship of the Proletariat. Stalin built on this but took Marxism–Leninism to another level of autocracy by claiming the need to eradicate all of those who were potential wreckers of the new order. Thus, one form of autocracy was not simply replaced by another as the reasons for the use of absolute control differed.

4 A continuation in autocratic rule could also be seen in the way that different governments used similar organisational and administrative structures. The tsars and communists adopted very hierarchical, 'top-down' structures to rule. Under Alexander II and Alexander III the Committee of Ministers, the body responsible for the day-to-day administration of Russia, was directly responsible to the tsar. This was also true of the Supreme Court, or Senate. In both cases, members were appointed by the tsar under the guidance of advisors. During the reign of Nicholas II, the disturbances of 1905 resulted in a change, in theory, to a more democratic system. The Committee of Ministers disappeared and was replaced by a Council of Ministers headed by a prime minister. In addition, an elected lower chamber, the *Duma*, was introduced which was designed to allow for the open discussion of affairs of state. In practice, the new system was not truly democratic as the tsar could ignore the recommendations of the *Duma*. When the latter became critical of tsarist rule, Nicholas passed legislation that restricted the type of person that could sit in the *Duma*.

> **4** The answer has moved on to another theme; that of structure of government and administration. This is an area that candidates often overlook.

5 Under the communists there was also centralised organisation and administration. *Sovnarkom* was a bit like the *Duma* in that it was democratically elected by the people. But, in reality, *Sovnarkom* had little authority as it was dominated by Bolshevik Party members who, in turn, were obliged to show total obedience to the party leadership. Under Stalin, some amendments to organisation were made under the 1936 constitution but this attempt to provide a federal system of government disguised the fact that the newly created Soviet of the Union and Soviet of the Nationalities were both dominated by Communist Party members. This continued throughout the rule of Khrushchev despite the process of destalinisation. Thus, as Russia had become a one-party state under the communists, and party members dominated the organs of government, so-called democratic centralisation was a cover-up for a political structure that was highly autocratic in nature.

> **5** Similarities and differences continue to be highlighted. Khrushchev is mentioned for the first time although the comment on his contribution to Russian government is a bit thin.

6 The tsars and communists used similar tools to govern Russia autocratically. The tsars used economic, social and political reforms partly with a genuine concern to modernise Russia. This was especially true of the emancipation of the serfs, Witte's Great Spurt and Stolypin's land reforms. However, reforms were also used to appease the population and to avert social unrest. A good example of this would be the introduction of the *Duma* in 1906. The communists also used reforms to drive Russia forwards as could be seen with Stalin's Five-Year Plans and Collectivisation and Khrushchev's Virgin Land campaign. The communists also used reform to quieten the population as was seen with the New Economic Policy but a major departure from the tsars was that communist reforms took social control to a much higher level. The Stalinist reforms instilled a degree of fear and terror into the population never witnessed before.

> **6** A decent section on reforms that gives some indication of how and why autocracy was used differently. Some comments could do with a bit more support.

7 Again, some very useful comments made here about the tools of autocracy but slightly more supporting evidence is needed.

7 Where reforms did not appease grievances or where new freedoms actually led to an increase in opposition to the ruling élites, then both tsars and communists turned to repression. Throughout the period all regimes made use of the secret police to arrest, trial and exile, imprison or execute enemies of the state. The tsars used the Third Section and the *Okhrana* to target individual dissidents whereas the *Cheka* under Lenin was used more generally to get rid of groups that caused trouble. Under Stalin, the NKVD helped organise the show trials and implemented the purges that resulted in the deaths of millions of Russians. Thus, although the ruling élites all used repression, the communists appeared to take such measures to new heights; it was not simply an exchange of one form of autocracy for another.

8 This is another example of a theme of autocracy that is given scant attention by the majority of candidates. Details on the use of censorship and propaganda can be found in Chapter 2.

8 Censorship and propaganda were also used as tools to maintain autocratic rule by the communists and the tsars. From 1865 to 1881 there was some relaxation of censorship rules but under Alexander III there was a return to a clamping down on newspapers, journals and educational institutions. Change occurred again under Nicholas II with a return to *glasnost* (the policy of openness); the number of periodicals increased threefold and working-class newspapers appeared for the first time such as *Gazeta Kopeika* (*The Penny Paper*). The Bolsheviks abolished press freedoms as there could be no questioning of the value of the revolution; all written criticism would have been considered counter-revolutionary. This was reinforced by the setting up of the Association of Proletarian Writers and, from 1932, the Union of Soviet Writers. Both of these organisations controlled who was allowed to officially be a writer and what was allowed to be published. This largely remained the same for the rest of the period. Propaganda went hand in hand with censorship. Freedom of speech was allowed under all regimes as long as it resulted in a strengthening of autocracy. Under the tsars citizens were manipulated to talk favourably of the Little Father and the Romanov dynasty. Later, the Cult of Personality emerged resulting in hero worship of Lenin and Stalin. As long as commentators spoke in support of the ruling élites they were tolerated. In this sense autocratic rule remained the same throughout the period even though there were times when there was a relaxation of control over the printing presses and other forms of the media.

9 The conclusion is to the point and follows on from the main part of the essay. A clear judgement is made which shows a good understanding of the exact demands of the question.

9 In conclusion, there is no doubt that all Russian governments were autocratic to a greater or lesser degree. However, it is a gross generalisation to claim that one type of autocracy was simply replaced by another. There were significant differences in the justification for (and hence the nature of) autocracy and also the way in which it was implemented. On balance, the communists were more autocratic than the tsars, taking centralised rule and degrees of repression to levels never seen before.

Assessment for Essay 1

A decent range of evidence is used to support comments about a number of key themes. Historical terminology is used appropriately and confidently. The writing is clear, coherent and mostly cogent. **[Level 1B: 17 out of 20 marks]**

The response is consistently analytical, focusing on the discussion of a number of themes to identify patterns of similarity and difference. There is very good synthesis and synoptic assessment of the whole period although some sections are fuller than others. **[Level IB: 35 out of 40 marks]**

The overall mark is 52 which is a solid A grade. It is just on the cusp of a high Level I response. The concept of similarity and difference over time is handled well but some of the supporting material is a bit patchy, especially that relating to the rule of Khrushchev.

Essay 2: 'A study of Russian governments in the period from 1855 to 1964 suggests that Russia simply exchanged one form of autocracy for another after 1917.' How far do you agree with this statement?

1 It would be fair to say that the regimes of the tsars and communists had much in common with respect to the ideology and methods used to rule Russia. They were both autocratic and used repression to enforce their policies. But there were also important differences in the way they ruled.

> 1 A fairly general introduction although there is indication that similarities and differences are going to be discussed.

2 The control over their respective populations differed greatly. It would be fair to say that before 1917, Russia was an authoritarian state. The people were governed very strictly and had to obey the commands of the tsar. Under Lenin and Stalin Russia was far more of a totalitarian dictatorship that infiltrated all areas of people's lives. Stalin had the means to influence the lives of everyone in his country and did so to great effect. The cult of personality was inflicted on all of those who lived during the Stalinist era. Internal passports were introduced and everyone effectively became a slave to Stalin. The tsars maintained overall control during most of their reign but did not dominate people's lives as pro-actively as Lenin and Stalin. Their power came from the weakness of opposition whereas Lenin and Stalin forcibly imposed their regimes on the Russian people. Estimates suggest that up to 20 million people became the victims of Stalin's brutality. In this sense the autocracy of the tsars compares favourably to communism as it was not as total and with less harsh consequences for all of the Russian people.

> 2 A fair attempt is made here to synthesise and to analyse the nature of autocratic rule. The differences between autocracy, dictatorship and totalitarianism could have been explored more carefully.

3 The regimes were similar in some respects, however. Political representation was effectively non-existent during the time of the tsars and the communists. This similarity is not unsurprising, however. The idea of a democratic state was alien to many as can be seen by the failure of the Provisional Government. The tsars and communists maintained centralised government structures without democratically elected constituent assemblies as this was in line with maintaining strong rule. Although there was a *Duma* and later *Sovnarkom*, these were not democratic and were always under the control of Russian leaders. Also, the importance placed on economic

> 3 There is a consistent focus on the link between reforms and the nature of autocratic rule. However, some of the comments are rather vague; more examples to support key observations are needed.

improvements was regarded as crucial by both the tsars and the Bolsheviks as a way of governing. But economic reforms are policies most rulers would aim to pursue as a way of keeping the people happy and to control their behaviour. Thus, Alexander III and Nicholas II started to industrialise Russia in the hope this would improve the standard of living of most Russians. Lenin's New Economic Plan and Stalin's Five-Year Plans were also attempts to increase Russian prosperity. These policies were also enforced in such an autocratic way that they had the added bonus of keeping the workers in their place. This was also similar to the provision of social welfare. All the regimes made at least some improvements to education, health provision and housing. Nevertheless, these improvements were often carried out to keep peasants and workers happy and not simply because governments were concerned about the welfare of the people.

Despite these similarities in how reforms were used to govern Russia, there were also significant differences. The fact is that the two regimes were directed by contradictory ideology which meant that motives behind economic and social reforms were different. The tsars were determined to maintain power and if social improvements could also be made then this was done. However, Tsarist Russia was generally economically and socially stagnant for most of the period and only showed real growth under Nicholas II. The communist period saw much more significant economic and social change. There was a radical economic upheaval but noticeable growth. The social structure under the communists also altered dramatically, with the move from an agricultural based society to an industrial one. Thus, autocracy remained but reasons for it changed resulting in different levels of economic and social change.

4 This section makes some sound comments about the similarities and differences over the use of repression. As with the other sections, there is no mention of the post-Stalinist period.

4 Both regimes made use of secret police to secure their positions and to keep the country as ordered and as stable as possible. The *Okhrana*, the tool of the tsars, was responsible for much of the backlash after terrorist activities carried out by groups such as the People's Will. The tsars used their police as a way of preventing change whereas under communism oppression was a means of forcing through their intended reforms. Lenin had up to 50,000 bourgeois killed to suppress opposition during the period when his position was most unstable. Similarly, Stalin used this idea, albeit on an unbelievable scale, to force through changes. The huge feats of industrialisation were achieved due to the NKVD arresting huge numbers of people to be used as slave labour. Although various types of police were used throughout the period, their purpose differed greatly. Tsarist Russia used its police to prevent change and in no way to actively oppress and kill innocent people as in post-1917 Russia.

5 The two regimes were similar in ideology but not in their intentions, actions or results. Perhaps serfdom was the least tenuous link. Far from freeing the working class, Stalin created a country of urban serfs. The problems of Russia remained despite the complete revolution in Russian life. Russia remained inferior to the West and its superpower status was forged out of a lack of strong opposition in Europe. The land crisis was only solved because of the countless millions who died from war and the purges. However, Russia went from a bleak, miserable and stagnant place to a totalitarian state that worked against its people. In this sense, one form of autocracy was replaced by another but the change wasn't simple.

5 A bit of a flowery ending but at least the assertion in the quote is addressed and questioned. A firmer judgement was needed to take this response to a higher level.

Assessment for Essay 2

Where evidence is used it is accurate and relevant. The response is mostly well organised and written in a clear, legible manner. **[Level III: 13 out of 20 marks]**

There is a decent attempt to provide a balanced, analytical response but some of the explanation is a bit uneven. Also, some of the support provided is a bit thin and general. **[Level III: 25 out of 40 marks]**

The overall mark is 38 which is a middling C grade. The candidate has made a fairly good attempt to deal with the concept of similarity and difference and to remain focused on the exact demands of the question. But there is a lack of some supporting material and some comments needed explaining more fully. Of particular note was the lack of comment about the post-Stalinist era.

2 The Opposition to Regimes

Note making

Carefully read through each section of the chapter before attempting to take notes. When taking notes on the different types of opposition, especially the groups that emerged under the tsars, you may find it useful to construct a table to allow for comparative analysis. You could arrange your notes under sub-headings such as aims of the group, nature of leadership, strategies and tactics and level of success. Another table could be constructed to compare the nature and level of response to opposition that emerged during different periods of rule. Make sure you provide an appropriate selection of examples to support the more general points.

1 | The changing nature of opposition

The opposition to regimes from political parties

This section deals mainly with opposition from outside the ruling élite. The official history of political parties in Russia was relatively short. Parties were made legal in 1905 but then banned by the Bolsheviks during their 10th Party Congress in 1921. Before 1905 political groups did exist, although illegally, and were tolerated as long as their behaviour remained respectable. The period before 1905 was characterised by the emergence of several groups considered below.

The Populists (*Narodniks*)

The Populists consisted mainly of Russian intellectuals who, ironically, were given greater freedom to express their disquiet about tsarist rules as a result of the reforms of Alexander II (see pages 4–5). The chief proponents of the populist cause were Nikolai Chernyshevsky and Pyotr Lavrov. Both were influenced by the writings of Karl Marx (see pages 21–3) and used such ideas to formulate their own brand of popular socialism.

Chernyshevsky's views were first made explicit in 1863 with the publication of *What is to be Done?* This was significant in that, despite relaying a fairly simplistic message about how poor Russians could be released from their misery, it seemed at a later date to have a profound impact on Lenin.

Lavrov took a more pragmatic approach than Chernyshevsky by organising a campaign from 1873 to 1874 called 'Going to the People'. This involved about 4000 university students dispersing into the Russian countryside with the aim of politically educating the peasants. The movement became more organised with the formation in 1876 of the group **Land and Liberty**. In general, though, Russian rural folk resented attempts to be won over and the scheme to politically educate them failed. Land and Liberty was soon in disarray especially when the leadership could not decide on what strategy to adopt to take the movement forward. Some favoured direct action (including violence) while others preached a more peaceful approach based on the concept of **Black Repartition**.

Key question
How far did the nature and extent of opposition from political parties change from 1855 to 1964?

Key terms

Land and Liberty
A pressure group consisting of intellectuals who believed it was important to live among peasants so as to get to understand their plight.

Black Repartition
A vision held by peasants of a time when all land would be shared out equally.

'The People's Will'

A sinister branch of populism emerged from the Land and Liberty movement. This was the terrorist group known as 'The People's Will'. Formed in 1879, they turned to 'the propaganda of the deed' (violence) as a means to spark revolution. In particular, their objective was to assassinate the Tsar; four attempts were made on Alexander II's life before he was killed by the People's Will in 1881. In this sense, populist opposition was successful, although the assassination did not prompt a complete overthrow of tsarism. Probably of more significance was the inspiration that the People's Will provided to future revolutionaries.

The Socialist Revolutionaries (SRs)

The Socialist Revolutionaries (SRs) emerged from the populist movement and continued to focus on improving the living conditions of the poorest people in society. The difference from early populists was that the SRs showed greater awareness of the needs of the growing urban proletariat. What remained the same was the methods by which the SRs intended to achieve their aims.

The Socialist Revolutionary Party was formed in 1901, led by the socialist intellectual Victor Chernov, but by 1905, the group had split into the more radical left-wing SRs and the moderate right-wing SRs. The left carried on the tradition of direct action, established by the People's Will; from 1901 to 1905 they were said to be responsible for over 2000 political killings, including **Grand Duke Sergei** and **Vyacheslav Plehve**. The right established a pattern of working with other parties and groups and gathered much support and momentum after the 1905 revolution (see pages 28–9). The right were of particular appeal to peasants, as they promised to deal with the ongoing peasant land issue. This only exacerbated the rift within the Socialist Revolutionary movement, as the left made claims that the plight of workers was ignored by the right.

Despite the divisions, the SRs remained the party with most support and were the biggest threat to tsarist rule up to the time of the October 1917 revolution. They certainly seemed to be a more effective opposition than earlier populists, although this was likely to have been due to changing economic and social conditions that, by the 1890s, were more conducive to a radical populist movement looking to gain support.

The Social Democrats (SDs)

In 1898 the All-Russian Social Democratic Workers' Party was founded in Minsk. The group was based generally on Marxist principles but more specifically on the interpretation of Marx's work made by **George Plekhanov**. The rapid industrialisation of the 1890s and the subsequent rise of **working-class consciousness** increased the appeal of Marxism. Plekhanov emphasised the need to educate workers in Marxist principles, but as one historian has stated:

Key figures

Grand Duke Sergei 1864–1905
Brother of Alexander III and Governor General of Moscow at the beginning of the twentieth century.

Vyacheslav Plehve 1846–1904
The much hated Minister of the Interior who served from 1902 to 1904.

George Plekhanov 1856–1918
A highly respected Populist and member of Black Repartition who was one of the first to be converted to Marxism (known as the 'father of Russian Marxism').

Key term

Working-class consciousness
An awareness among workers that they were experiencing similar living and working conditions and therefore belonged to a single class of worker.

Few working men had the time and inclination to master Marxist theory, and there was a wide cultural gap between them and their instructors.

This caused some SD supporters, especially Julius Martov and Vladimir Ulyanov (Lenin) to look for a more active, pragmatic way of implementing Marxism. Initially, they focused on looking to support workers to improve pay and lower working hours. However, Lenin was uncomfortable with this as it appeared to have a limited effect on changing a 'system' that was the cause of worker impoverishment in the first place. He therefore turned to preach the need for a revolution to be supported by workers, but to be led by a professional **vanguard** (that is, the intelligentsia). This was spelt out in Lenin's own version of *What is to be Done?* published in 1901.

By 1905, the SDs, similar to the SRs, revealed divisions in their ranks. The second congress of the party witnessed the emergence of a more formal split between the Bolsheviks (majority) led by Lenin and the Mensheviks (minority). The Bolsheviks, of course, went on to seize power from the Provisional Government in October 1917 and start the process towards a one-party state after the closing of the Constituent Assembly of January 1918. In this sense, they became the most effective of all of the political parties. Such a remarkable achievement is further underlined by the fact that the Bolsheviks, despite their name, were a minority faction within a party. They also lacked the level of numerical support found with the other parties.

The Liberals

Something of a liberal trend was apparent at the start of the period, with those who regarded themselves as '**Westernisers**' (as opposed to **Slavophiles**) wanting to move Russia towards being governed in a similar way to Western European democracies such as Britain. The development of liberal thinking was enhanced with the emergence of the *Zemstva* (see Chapter 1) and the mid-1890s revival of the concept of a *Zemstvo* union. In 1904, **Pyotr Struve** founded the Union of Liberation which demanded greater freedoms and justice for all Russians. In particular, the Union wanted fairer and more land distribution for peasants, a representative Constituent Assembly and improved conditions for industrial workers. The group appeared to have some effect on advisors to Nicholas II, although a fully elected Constituent Assembly was not properly considered until the upheaval of 1905 (see pages 29–30).

The Kadets and Octobrists

After the so-called revolution of 1905 the clamour for a constitutional monarchy gathered pace with the formation of the Constitutional Democrats (Kadets). Led by **Paul Milyukov**, this was the intellectual arm of the liberal movement, and went on to play a very important role as opposition within the first *Duma*. A more moderate liberal group also emerged at this time called the

Key terms

Vanguard
In this context a leading group of people whose mission was to lay the base for a proletarian takeover of the governance of Russia.

Westernisers
Those who wanted to modernise Russia in the same way as Western Europe.

Slavophiles
Those who believed that Orthodox Slavs were superior to Western Europeans.

Key figures

Pyotr Struve 1870–1944
Started his political career as a Legal Marxist (that is, one who preached an acceptable form of Marxism in the eyes of the authorities). He later changed to become a Kadet and then a White during the Civil War.

Paul Milyukov 1859–1943
An historian and leader of the Kadets. He was also Foreign Minister in 1917.

Key figures

Alexander Guchkov 1862–1936
Leader of the Octobrist Party. He was also War Minister in 1917.

Mikhail Rodzianko 1859–1924
A prominent Octobrist Party member and President of the Third and Fourth *Dumas*.

Octobrists. These were individuals, such as **Alexander Guchkov** and **Mikhail Rodzianko**, who displayed loyalty to the Tsar but who wanted changes to be made to the system of government. The two groups were supporters of Nicholas II's October Manifesto (see page 30) and were therefore much maligned by other organisations of a more revolutionary nature. But this should not detract from the fact that the Octobrists, like the Kadets, spoke out against more conservative elements of the *Dumas* and their leaders went on to become key members of the Provisional Government.

The success of opposition before 1917

Generally speaking, opposition to tsarism before February 1917 was divided between those that wanted change within the tsarist system and those that wanted to overthrow it completely. When measured by these broad aims, opposition was relatively unsuccessful. The major political changes promised by the October Manifesto were largely cancelled out by the Fundamental Laws of 1906 and the Romanov dynasty remained intact until Nicholas II found it impossible to cope with the effects of the First World War. The lack of effective opposition before 1917 was due partly to the control exerted by successive tsars, but also to the lack of unity within and even between opposition groups.

The creation of the Dual Authority

On 26 February 1917 the *Duma* refused to disband at the command of the Tsar. This would not have been too much of a problem for Nicholas II if the army had remained loyal, but it did not. Troops sided with striking workers and other protesters and on 27 February the *Duma* was further boosted by the creation of the Petrograd Soviet of Workers (see pages 30–1). Between them, the *Duma* and Soviet created a 'dual authority'. The *Duma* was to form the core of a Provisional Government that would engender 'legal changes' before a fully representative, democratically elected Constituent Assembly could be put in place. The Soviet was to cooperate by keeping a check on the behaviour of workers and soldiers to ensure they supported the new but temporary regime.

Domination of opposition by the Bolsheviks

Despite climate of collaboration that appeared to have been created, the Provisional Government faced a similar degree of opposition to that experienced by the tsars. This came mainly from the Soviet, especially after September 1917 when it was totally dominated by the Bolshevik Party. The Bolsheviks came to dominate the opposition for the following reasons:

- The majority of members of other parties wanted a short-term government based on consensus, with the main aim of creating a Constituent Assembly. The leading Bolsheviks rejected this as such an arrangement would continue to favour 'old interests' to the detriment of workers and peasants.

- The initial changes made by the Provisional Government allowed for the revitalisation and expansion of political groups. This especially favoured the Bolsheviks whose leaders had been in exile for some time but who returned with a vengeance. Stalin moved back to Petrograd from exile in Siberia in March 1917 and Lenin from Switzerland in April. Lenin moved quickly to publish his **April Theses** in which he condemned the Provisional Government for being bourgeois and called for a seizure of power by the Soviet.
- Bolshevik leaders cleverly used propaganda to appeal for support from both workers and peasants. The slogan 'All Power to the Soviets' promised workers (including soldiers and sailors) control of the political system. This was coupled with the slogan 'Bread, Peace and Land', which targeted peasants. Lenin changed his mind about peasant support. Originally, he saw peasants as a hindrance to any potential revolution as he thought they were apathetic and stupid. But their proactive approach to appropriating land illegally had displayed a certain revolutionary zeal, which Marx and Lenin had not predicted. Lenin therefore decided peasant support was worth having. The actions of the peasants contributed partly to Lenin's adaptation of Marxism to create Marxism–Leninism (see pages 8–9).
- The Provisional Government, both under Prince Lvov and Kerensky, struggled to deal with the Bolsheviks. Although leading Bolsheviks were exiled or imprisoned after the disturbances of the July Days (see pages 35–6), Kerensky inadvertently strengthened their position by indirectly involving them in the resolution of the Kornilov affair (see page 36). On the 7 October, Lenin returned once more to Petrograd to plan for a revolution. Kerensky waited until the 23 October to order another round-up and deportation of Bolsheviks but it was too late. The next day, the establishment of the Petrograd Soviet's Military Revolutionary Committee (MRC) was announced. By the end of October, Lenin and the MRC (headed by Trotsky) had disbanded the Provisional Government, exiled Kerensky and announced to the Congress of Soviets that the Bolsheviks had seized power.

April Theses
Lenin's outline of policies to be followed by the Bolsheviks after his return from exile in April 1917.

De facto
Rule as a matter of fact or circumstance rather than rule gained by legal means.

Key terms

Elections to the Constituent Assembly

Although the Bolsheviks had claimed *de facto* rule, they knew they had to allow the elections to the planned Constituent Assembly to proceed. The Bolsheviks hoped they would win a clear majority to legitimise their position. When this did not materialise it created the same problem of how to deal with opposition for Lenin that had existed for the tsars and the Provisional Governments. The results of the election clearly showed that the degree of 'opposition' was substantial (see Table 2.1).

Table 2.1: Results of the election for the Constituent Assembly

Party	Votes	Seats
SRs	17,490,000	370
Bolsheviks	9,844,000	175
National minority groups	8,257,000	99
Left SRs (pro-Bolshevik)	2,861,000	40
Kadets	1,986,000	17
Mensheviks	1,248,000	16
Total	**41,686,000**	

Source: M. Lynch, *Reaction and Revolution: Russia 1881–1924*, Hodder Education (2004).

Lenin, quite obviously, believed that the Bolsheviks would not be able to achieve and consolidate power through future elections to the Assembly and therefore chose to use military force to end it. The official justification for such action was that the elections had been rigged, but also that conceding power to such an Assembly

> ... would again be compromising with the malignant bourgeoisie. The Russian soviets place the interests of the toiling masses far above the interests of treacherous compromise disguised in a new garb.

This, of course, did not put an end to opposition to the Bolsheviks. If anything, it increased it and also caused concerns to be expressed within the party over the methods adopted by Lenin. The reaction against Lenin was further strengthened by his desire to take Russia out of the First World War and strike a peace deal with Germany. The left SRs in particular saw Lenin as a traitor to the revolution and a German collaborator.

The impact of the Civil War

The leading Bolsheviks clearly knew that Russia was heading for a civil war. Some historians have gone as far as to say that Lenin willed such a conflict as it provided the opportunity for the Bolsheviks to eradicate their opponents forever. To an extent, the Civil War that ensued supports this thesis as the groups that made up the White armies (see page 23) were essentially the political opponents who had been represented in the Constituent Assembly.

However, the existence of the **Green armies** suggests that the nature of the war was not simply about party politics, but also concerned conflicts related to nationalities, regions and even individual families. Nevertheless, the victory by the Red Army in 1921 resulted in the Bolsheviks being in total control. At the 10th Party Congress in 1921, Lenin presented a paper entitled 'On Party Unity', which laid the base for making all other parties illegal and banning factionalism within the Bolshevik Party.

From 1921 to 1964 (and beyond) Russia remained a one-party state. But, this did not mean the end of opposition to communist rule. Those not affiliated to the party often displayed resistance

Key term

Green armies
Mainly peasant groups who opposed Bolshevik rule.

to the policies of the ruling élite. There was also a continuation of divisions within the communist party, which forced both Lenin and Stalin into using repression of an order not witnessed before.

Essay focus

Some historians like to argue that a key difference between the tsarist and communist eras when it came to effectiveness of opposition was that under the tsars opposition groups were allowed to flourish and pose a major threat. Essay 1, paragraph 7 on page 98, shows that this is a rather simplistic way of viewing opposition as its most obvious common characteristic was disunity.

Summary diagram: Opposition from parties

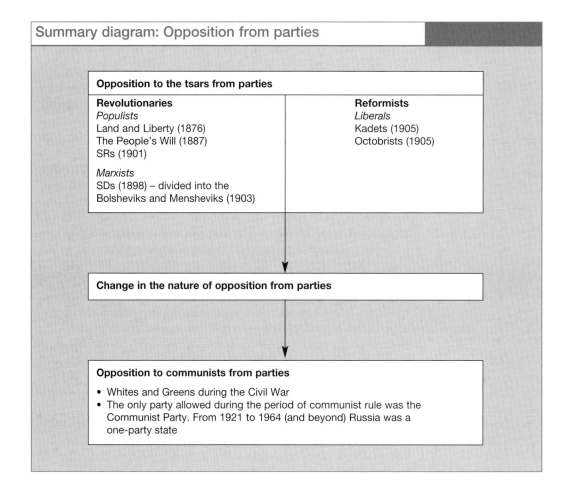

Opposition to the tsars from parties

Revolutionaries	**Reformists**
Populists	*Liberals*
Land and Liberty (1876)	Kadets (1905)
The People's Will (1887)	Octobrists (1905)
SRs (1901)	
Marxists	
SDs (1898) – divided into the	
Bolsheviks and Mensheviks (1903)	

Change in the nature of opposition from parties

Opposition to communists from parties
- Whites and Greens during the Civil War
- The only party allowed during the period of communist rule was the Communist Party. From 1921 to 1964 (and beyond) Russia was a one-party state

Key question
Did the tsars face more opposition from close advisers than the communist leaders?

Key term

Dissidents
Those who disagreed with the aims and procedures of the government.

Key figures

Lev Kamenev 1883–1936
Leading member of the Politburo from 1919 to 1925.

Grigory Zinoviev 1883–1936
Rose to prominence as chairman of the Petrograd Soviet (1917) and later became Chairman of Comintern (1919–26).

Alexey Rykov 1881–1938
Best known for serving as Prime Minister from 1924 to 1930.

The opposition to regimes from individuals and cliques

Both the tsarist and communist ruling élites experienced opposition from within. With the tsars, insider **dissidents** caused few problems. Expressions of discontent or actions that caused disapproval by the Tsar were usually dealt with by removing miscreants from their post. Those who suffered such indignities did not seem to hold a grudge and remained loyal to the autocracy. A good example was Sergei Witte who served as Finance Minister from 1892 to 1903 but was then unexpectedly demoted to Chairman of Ministers. This did not dissuade him from accepting the more important role of Prime Minister from 1905 to 1906.

'Inside' opposition during the rule of Lenin

With the communists, opposition from inside the party varied according to circumstance and who held the position of leader. During Lenin's stewardship, there were a number of occasions when internal disagreement threatened to derail the revolutionary movement:

- After the overthrow of the Provisional Government in 1917, a number of prominent Bolsheviks, including **Kamenev**, **Zinoviev** and **Rykov**, called for a coalition to be formed with other socialist groups. Although some left-wing SRs were allowed to join ranks, Lenin bullied his Bolshevik colleagues into accepting that compromise with opposing political groups was taboo.
- The signing of the Treaty of Brest-Litovsk was opposed by the left, especially Trotsky. Lenin fobbed off his opponents by claiming the war would soon be over and he was proved right.
- The adoption of War Communism (see page 10) during the Civil War and specifically, grain requisitioning, was considered harsh by some party members. Lenin conceded to pressure for change and introduced his New Economic Policy (NEP) (see page 10). This simply heightened tensions and widened divisions. Right Bolsheviks favoured this temporary concession towards capitalism while the left Bolsheviks saw it as a betrayal of the principles on which the 1917 revolution was founded.

The lead-up to the power struggle

Differences of opinion over which direction the party should take came to a head during the period from December 1922 to 1929. Lenin's failing health before 1924 started what has been commonly called a 'power struggle'. There were three key developments before Lenin's death in January 1924:

- A clique called the Triumvirate (*Troika*) was instigated within the Politburo, consisting of Zinoviev, Kamenev and Stalin. Its purpose was to combat the growing influence of Trotsky who Lenin seemed to favour as a successor.

- In December 1922, Lenin provided his Political Testament, a document which picked holes in the personal attributes and achievements of the majority of leading Bolsheviks. Stalin, in particular, received heavy criticism for his running of **Rabkrin** and his role in the 1921 **'Georgian Affair'**.
- By January 1924, Stalin had, by various means, already worked himself into a position of power through holding various political posts, including that of General Secretary (appointed in April 1922). As the historian Chris Ward has indicated, by the time Lenin's health started to deteriorate Stalin became

> … the only leader who was simultaneously a member of the Politburo, Orgburo, Secretariat and Central Committee. In addition, he could look back on almost seven years' experience of military commissions and jobs in the state's embryonic administrative apparatus.

This partly explains why Stalin took over the mantle from Lenin with relative ease.

Key terms

Rabkrin
The Workers' and Peasants' Inspectorate, a highly bureaucratic and overstaffed organisation.

'Georgian Affair'
The mishandling of Georgian nationalism by Ordjonikidze, the Commissar for National Affairs in Georgia. His actions were defended by Stalin.

The power struggle

After Lenin's death, a certain amount of manoeuvring for power occurred, which highlighted the factions that still existed within the party. Leading Bolsheviks disagreed over three key issues:

- First, there was much dispute between left and right Bolsheviks over whether there should be a continuation of the NEP.
- Second, the nature of rule was discussed, with many demanding that a more openly democratic form of government should be adopted.
- Finally, the link between ideology and the future of communism caused much consternation. The left, under the guidance of Trotsky, continued to press for a Permanent Revolution (see page 23), while the right emphasised the need for socialism in one country.

Stalin displayed skill in manipulating debates and individuals to consolidate his position, and thereby paving the way for a personal dictatorship. The past had shown that where opposition was divided, this invariably strengthened those who were ruling Russia.

The move towards Stalin becoming the dominant ruler went through a number of phases as considered below.

Stalin's pact with Zinoviev and Kamenev

In the year preceding Lenin's death, Stalin formed a pact with Zinoviev and Kamenev, with the aim of discrediting Trotsky. The latter's situation was not helped by the fact that he was absent from Lenin's funeral; this added to the charge that Trotsky was a traitor to the cause. In January 1925, Trotsky was replaced as Commissar for War.

Stalin's split with Zinoviev and Kamenev

By the end of 1925, it appeared that the left had largely been defeated. For prominent rightists this seemed to indicate that Stalin and his supporters were becoming too powerful. There was also particular concern about Stalin's plan for dealing with peasants and his proposed foreign policy. This caused Kamenev and Zinoviev to turn on Stalin but with little success; both were removed as secretaries of their local party. Also, the Politburo was simultaneously expanded (from six to eight members) and reinforced with Stalinists (Kuibyshev, Molotov, Rudzutak, Tomsky and Voroshilov).

The United Opposition group

Trotsky, Kamenev and Zinoviev responded by forming the United Opposition group. Their opposition to the NEP and demands for more 'free speech' were treated with contempt. All were excluded from the Politburo and by 1927 Trotsky was expelled from the party. Trotsky continued to provoke trouble and was considered responsible for organising, in October 1927, a threatening United Opposition demonstration in the Red Square in Moscow. He was quickly exiled to Kazakhstan and in January 1929 expelled from the USSR altogether. This clearly showed how easily internal threat to party unity could be dealt with.

The proposals for collectivisation

Stalin's proposals for collectivisation (see pages 117–20), including renewed grain requisitioning, were opposed by those on the right (especially Bukharin, Rykov and Tomsky). The right saw this as a retrograde step, as it seemed to resemble aspects of War Communism and pointed to the end of the NEP. Bukharin was particularly vocal in expressing his concerns and, as a result of joining forces with Kamenev, ended up being branded a **Factionalist**. This development played into Stalin's hands.

The removal of Bukharin

In 1929 Bukharin was ousted from his position as President of **Comintern**, editor of *Pravda*, and member of the Politburo. Tomsky and Rykov also suffered demotions. At this stage, it was enough for Stalin simply to get agreement among a core of loyal party members, to have 'critics' removed from positions of power. This was similar to how the tsars dealt with 'inside' opposition and it was adequate in enabling rulers to maintain autocracy. Thus, with both the left and the right removed from jobs where they could cause damage, Stalin was free to dominate proceedings. Both collectivisation and a series of Five-Year Plans (see pages 110–13) were implemented with a great deal of speed and effort.

Stalin's dominant position by the end of 1929 did not mean an end to criticism of the regime from within. However, this probably marks the point at which it is difficult to judge what

Key terms

Factionalist
One who went about pursuing his or her own interests to the detriment of party unity.

Comintern
The Communist International body was established in March 1918 with the aim of spreading communism overseas.

Stalin imagined to be a threat rather than what was a real and
serious challenge to his authority.

The purges

Throughout the 1930s there was a change from removing critics
from key political posts to purging groups from the party
altogether. According to the historian J.N. Westwood, purging
involved

> … thorough cleansing, and was used quite naturally to describe the
> periodic weeding out from party membership of those characters
> deemed unfit. From this small beginning the word came to
> describe a monstrous process of arbitrary arrests, fake trials, mass
> executions, and forced labour camps, which the weak and unlucky
> could not survive.

The purges of the 1930s were characterised by the following:

- By 1930, some party members, it was claimed, had taken a
  rather dilatory approach to implementing collectivisation at a
  local level. Others expressed distaste at Stalin's attempt to
  '**liquidate the *kulaks* as a class**'. Subsequently, such individuals
  lost their party card, reducing total membership by about a
  tenth.
- The mid-1930s witnessed a rise in both party and non-party
  members who were against the pace of collectivisation and
  industrialisation. Stalin dismissed these opponents as idle,
  selfish, moral degenerates, but it is difficult to discern how
  much of a threat they actually posed. Nevertheless, the party
  shed a further third of its members. It is worth noting at this
  point that reducing membership was not considered much of
  an issue, as it could easily be restored through recruitment
  drives (as was the case in 1931).
- The mid-1930s were also notable in that prominent Politburo
  members either were exiled or lost their lives after being
  accused of being **oppositionists**. By 1939 Kirov, Kossior,
  Ordhonikze, Kuibyshev and Rudzuki (full members of the
  Politburo) were all dead. This was on top of the 'show trial'
  and execution of older left (including Zinoviev and Kamenev)
  and right (including Bukharin and Rykov) oppositionists.
- By the beginning of the Second World War there was little left
  of the party to purge and Stalin's paranoia over those he
  believed to be challenging his authority receded. This was
  probably due mainly to Stalin's preoccupation with defending
  Russia during the war.

Clearly, any genuine and open opposition from within to Stalin
and his brand of communism was not tolerated and was
eliminated (not just displaced). In this sense, opposition from
within the ruling élite during the Stalinist era was the most
limited in scope and achievement relative to any other time in
the period from 1855 to 1964. During the rule of Khrushchev,

Key terms

Liquidate the *kulaks* as a class
Stalin's policy to
eliminate wealthier
peasants (*kulaks*) as
part of the class war
in the countryside.
Kulaks were
considered to be
bourgeois.

Oppositionists
Those who opposed
the communist
revolution.

destalinisation resulted in an end to purging and greater tolerance towards those who wanted to express disquiet at decisions made by leaders. This is reinforced by the fact that in 1959, there were only around 11,000 'counter-revolutionaries' being kept in labour camps, compared with about 5.5 million in 1953 (although not all of these people were party members).

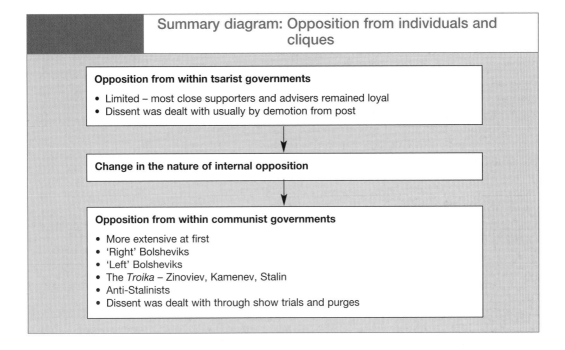

Summary diagram: Opposition from individuals and cliques

Opposition from within tsarist governments
- Limited – most close supporters and advisers remained loyal
- Dissent was dealt with usually by demotion from post

Change in the nature of internal opposition

Opposition from within communist governments
- More extensive at first
- 'Right' Bolsheviks
- 'Left' Bolsheviks
- The *Troika* – Zinoviev, Kamenev, Stalin
- Anti-Stalinists
- Dissent was dealt with through show trials and purges

Key question
Did the peasants pose more of a threat to the tsars or the communists?

The opposition to regimes from peasants
Role of peasants

It is important to avoid making generalisations about the role of peasants in Russian society throughout the period concerned. Although a majority remained largely ignorant and apathetic towards political change, a significant number were actively involved in opposing reforms that they felt led to a deterioration in living standards. Their level of commitment varied according to where they were located and to their status in rural society. Older, more educated peasants in poorer rural areas, for example, tended to be more politically active than others. Also worth noting is that peasants often acted independently against changes considered detrimental to their well-being. They seldom showed an allegience to political parties and were wary of those who claimed they would act in the best interests of rural folk.

Peasant unrest

Given that peasants constituted 70–80 per cent of the population of Russia at any point in time, any large-scale peasant uprising in any particular region was taken seriously. Peasant riots and protests were sometimes followed by significant reforms, although equally, a disturbance was just as likely to be dealt with by force.

Where and when riots did occur, they were often over one of two main issues: land distribution and access to food. Peasant opposition, ranging from mass demonstration to full-scale rioting, was prevalent from the time of Alexander II all the way through to Khrushchev. Before Alexander II came to the throne, peasants were involved in a 'normal frequency of small-scale revolts', the only major exception being the Pugachev rebellion against Catherine the Great.

The impact of the 1861 Emancipation Edict on peasant attitudes

Ironically, the 1861 Emancipation Edict (see page 5) unleashed a number of disturbances involving up to around 10,000 peasants at any one time, and, in one instance, the slaughter of about 200 by the military. This unrest was quietened until the 1890s, when further outbursts of revolt were quelled with the help of Land Captains. Peasant rebellions reached a new level during the period 1900–7, prompted by unsatisfactory attempts to deal with issues relating to **redemption payments**, land distribution and rising prices. Peasants became more inventive and politically intelligent in the methods they used to demand improvements. Often under the auspices of the *mir*, rural folk appropriated 'private' and state land (especially forest and grazing pasture), refused to pay taxes, robbed warehouses and stores, physically attacked landowners and resorted to **incendiary**.

The Black Earth region revolts

The revolts of 1906–7, especially in the **Black Earth region**s, proved very provocative to the extent that Stolypin, acting as Interior Minister and later Prime Minister, used a great deal of force to put down the unrest before also carrying out land reforms to appease peasant grievances. This is a good indication of the success that peasants had in employing direct action on a wider scale.

From 1908 to 1914, Stolypin's reforms seemed to pacify peasant leaders but the upheaval of the First World War ignited another phase of peasant revolt. From 1916, peasants were protesting at high food prices, but also the pressures they were submitted to as a result of rising demand for food from urban dwellers. This was exacerbated by the lack of provision of technology and materials (especially fertilisers) needed to improve productivity. Peasants were an integral part of the revolutionary events of 1917 (something that Lenin did not believe would happen), launching renewed attacks on landowners, particularly through the use of incendiary. This period witnessed a peasantry that was better organised, often with the aid of army deserters and more educated peasants who formed peasant soviets. They also showed a tendency to be more violent and adventurous tactically; public utilities in provincial towns were destroyed and some areas experienced **peasant vigilantism**.

Key terms

Redemption payments
The repayment of loans that had to be taken out to purchase land that was redistributed after 1861.

Incendiary
Setting fire to rural property, usually farm buildings and hayricks.

Black Earth regions
The area from the south-western borderlands into Asiatic Russia.

Peasant vigilantism
Rural people taking the matter of law and order into their own hands.

Key figure

Vasily Chapayev 1887–1919
A celebrated Russian soldier and Red Army Commander during the Civil War. He was 'the best known of the pro-Bolsheviks, being subsequently portrayed as a simple man capable of inspiring in unruly and illiterate soldiers to heights of endurance and heroism' (J.N. Westwood). He drowned in a river while attempting to escape from the Whites.

The impact of the Civil War on peasant attitudes

The Civil War was also a time when peasants turned to rioting in an attempt to better their position, although it is not clear as to what side peasants showed most allegiance. A number of quasi-independent peasant armies, led by heroes such as **Chapayev**, were established, that sympathised with the Bolsheviks. But peasants could also be found supporting the White armies, and by the end of the war, there was mounting resentment in general from peasants, against grain requisitioning, which was an integral part of the Bolsheviks' War Communism (see page 10). The murder of grain requisitioners and the threatening revolts at Tambov and Volga in 1920 were enough for Lenin to realise that the *Cheka* and the Red Army were not enough to keep peasants in line. Lenin had already been impressed by the fortitude and revolutionary zeal displayed by peasants and was increasingly willing to view them as a separate part of the proletariat that could take the revolution to its next phase. Thus, the NEP (see page 10) was introduced and used to appease peasants in a similar way that the 1861 Emancipation Edict and Stolypin's Land Reforms were utilised.

Collectivisation and peasant unrest

Stalin's collectivisation and dekulakisation programme once again ignited peasant unrest. Thousands of peasants died as a result of the first phase of collectivisation, but this did not prevent rebellion against the scale and speed of the reform. By March 1930 Stalin was prepared to make a concession to peasants that allowed them to opt out of collectivised farms. By June 1930 only 24 per cent of peasant holdings were collectivised. However, this proved temporary and Stalin launched a new drive towards collectivisation so that by the start of the Second World War over 90 per cent of agricultural land was worked by a collectivised or state farm. This new phase was disastrous for peasants, as they experienced a horrific 'Stalin-made' famine (1932–3) and the loss of the *mir* as an organising institution (dismantled in 1930). Once again, though, the peasants were not passive in their response. At the height of collectivisation significant numbers refused to cooperate and showed outright dissent by slaughtering large numbers of cattle and horses.

Khrushchev and stability in the countryside

During the Khrushchev era, there was very little rural unrest. J.N. Westwood has pointed out that 'for the first time since Peter the Great there was a genuine interchange between the tsar and people'. This was due to the fact that Khrushchev 'spent much of his time in the countryside, conferring with party secretaries, cajoling farm chairmen, and making promises to peasants in the kind of earthy language they could understand'. Despite this, Khrushchev's agricultural policies, especially the Virgin Land campaign, were not especially successful and by the end of his rule Russia once again faced food shortages (see page 121).

The opposition to regimes from workers
The nature of workers

Key question
How did the nature of worker opposition differ from other types of opposition?

The term worker is usually used to denote a person employed in any industry found in an urban setting (for example, a textile factory). It can also be used to refer to those employed in industries located away from the main cities (for example, miners). Relative to peasants, workers were numerically less significant, although the distinction between the two groups became somewhat blurred after the end of the Civil War as an increasing number of peasants were transformed into the urban proletariat.

The treatment of workers by tsars and communists

As the pace of industrialisation quickened, especially during and after Witte's 'Great Spurt', workers became an increasingly valuable asset to tsarist and Bolshevik regimes. Despite this, it took some time for rulers to realise that workers would not passively accept their lot in life simply because industrial employment offered more regular hours and better pay than work on the land. Thus, for example, there was no factory inspectorate until 1882, and a 10-hour working day for workers was not the norm until 1914 (well over 50 years after this was the case in Britain). Under the communists, treatment of workers was not much better, although in theory they were allowed legal representation through trade unions. It is not surprising therefore, that the whole of the period is littered with instances of workers protesting against employers and rulers about low wages, long working hours and poor working conditions in general.

Workers and politics

Whether worker protest can be interpreted as opposition based on political as well as economic grievances is more debatable. Having said this, both Lenin and Stalin believed that in line with orthodox Marxism, a true political revolution in Russia could only come as a result of workers becoming more conscious of their status and of the iniquities of the 'system' that governed their behaviour. The formation, growth and role of soviets in the final revolution of 1917 add weight to the argument that workers did play an important part in changing the nature of government in Russia.

Tactics used by workers

To achieve their aims, workers resorted mainly to striking and, occasionally, rioting. The strike tool was what differentiated between worker and peasant opposition. There are examples of both strikes and riots across the period. Strikes before the 1880s tended to be localised and small-scale affairs, but thereafter grew in size, and, subsequently, degree of threat. The strike in 1885 at the Morozov dye works, for example, involved over 8000 workers. Such events as this resulted in what was virtually a ban on striking, but this did not prevent a wave of sympathy strikes occurring after Bloody Sunday (January 1905). A more total, rigid ban occurred immediately after this, but workers were not fully deterred from taking direct action. The events of 1905 were echoed in 1912 when striking miners of the Lena goldfields were ruthlessly dealt with by the army, resulting in over 200 deaths. The police and army were also used to break up the St Petersburg strikes of July 1914, but this did not prevent workers from continuing to withdraw labour during the war period. In fact, given that the supply of labour was less than demand during this time, giving workers a strong bargaining hand, it is not surprising that striking intensified.

The strike at the Putilov works

The most famous strike during the war period started on 23 February 1917 at the **Putilov works** in St Petersburg. This event is often given credit as sparking the February revolution and subsequent fall of the Romanovs. The formation of workers' committees and the challenge to Bolshevik authority in 1917 by the railway workers were further examples of the urban proletariat becoming bolder in their attempts to challenge authority. The railwaymen's union demanded that they should be allowed to run the rail network independently from the Bolsheviks (after the October 1917 revolution). Their request was granted but only until March 1918 when the Bolsheviks took control of the transport system.

The Civil War as a turning point for workers

The Civil War was very much a turning point for workers. Many died in the fighting, which resulted in a shift of peasants from agricultural to industrial work. This created a factory workforce in the 1920s, considered by one historian to be '... ill educated, ill disciplined, and not particularly interested in the party'. This development, coupled with the emergence of the NEP, helps explain why workers appeared to be fairly docile throughout the 1920s and 1930s. When and where agitation occasionally appeared, it was efficiently and effectively dealt with. The purges under Stalin ensured that any trade union official who seemed to be getting 'too big for their boots' was ruthlessly dealt with. Workers also seemed to rather lamely accept the Five-Year Plans, although Stalin purposefully used this economic policy partly as a way of controlling worker behaviour. Interestingly, by the 1940s there had been a rise in the number of worker suicides which were associated with the pressures of not being able to meet production targets.

The impact of the Second World War on workers

During the Second World War, and in contrast to 1914–17, there were no strikes, although there were examples early on of a lack of patriotism and support for the conflict. Stability in industrial relations carried on under Khrushchev, although there were riots by workers over what were perceived to be falling living

Key term

Putilov works
The biggest private factory in Russia by the start of the twentieth century. It specialised in iron production and became very important during the First World War in providing artillery.

standards. In 1962 for example, workers at Novocherhassk protested against food shortages and rising food prices. As a result the authorities killed 20 workers, and a number of ringleaders were later executed. In this respect very little had changed since the time of the tsars.

The impact of worker opposition

Worker opposition was effective in the sense that:

- The average working day was reduced from 11½ hours in 1897 to seven hours in the 1960s.
- Official inspection and administration of working conditions was established.
- A change in the political system in 1917 promised a dictatorship of the proletariat that would merge to full worker control of the country.

However, full worker control of the means of production, distribution and exchange never occurred and workers were always likely to experience living standards that fell below their own expectations and those experienced by their counterparts in other parts of the industrialised world. On top of this, as with the peasants, workers were continuously repressed using both the law and the full force of the police and armed forces.

Summary diagram: Opposition to regimes from peasants and workers

	Peasants	Workers
Motives	• Fairer distribution of land • Improve living conditions • Eradicate food shortages brought on by grain requisitioning • Resist collectivisation	• Higher wages • Shorter working hours • Improve living and working conditions • Political representation
Strategies and tactics	• Rioting • Incendiary • Hoarding of food and seed • Slaughtering of livestock	• Rioting • Peaceful marches • Strikes • Formation of worker councils (soviets)
Success	• Emancipation of the serfs (1861) • Land reforms under Nicholas II • Acceptance of revolutionary potential by Lenin	• Reforms under Nicholas II • Petrograd Soviet • Support for 1917 Revolution • Productivity increases under Five-Year Plans
Failure	• Famines • Poor distribution of land despite reforms • Persecution of the *kulaks* • Effects of collectivisation • Effects of Virgin Land campaign	• Living and working conditions remained relatively poor • Limited political representation under any of the rulers

Key question
Why were some national minorities more successful than others in opposing tsarist and communist rule?

Great Russia
Also known as Muscovy, the old Russian principality that had Moscow at its centre.

Key term

The opposition to regimes from national minorities

The nature and extent of national minorities

'National minorities' refer to those who were not considered part of **Great Russia** and who did not originate from the Russian peoples. The main national minority groups were from Poland, Finland, the Caucasus and Central Asia and the Baltic Provinces (Estonia, Latvia and Lithuania). Russian Jews stand out as a rather unique national minority in that their geographical location was one that was artificially created and crossed the boundaries of other groups. According to the first Russian census of 1897, minorities made up about 55 per cent of the Empire's population in the Ukraine (see Figure 2.1 on page 74).

Not all national minorities opposed the ruling élites both during the tsarist and communist periods. As a generalisation, the Finns, Baltic Germans and Christian Armenians remained fairly loyal, whereas the Poles, Ukrainians and Tartars were a constant thorn in the side of Russian rulers. From the point of view of the tsars and communists, this did not seem to matter, as they were all treated roughly the same. All leaders, to a greater or lesser extent, aimed to Russify peoples of the Empire in what with hindsight proved to be a naïve and unrealistic attempt to create internal stability.

The main objective of the 'uncooperative' national minorities was, of course, to break away from central Russian rule and to gain independence. The experience of each national minority group in attempting to achieve autonomy varied according to time and place.

The Poles

Located on the western edge of the Empire, Poland had never 'obviously' been part of the Russian Empire and the Poles had a long history of attempting to break away from tsarist rule. After decades of repression, many Poles grew hopeful that Alexander II's reformist attitude would lead to an improvement in their position. The appointment of Aleksander Wielopolski as Prime Minister (1862–3), though, was greeted with suspicion, as he was considered to be a tsarist lapdog. In 1863, after reforms failed to materialise, Polish rebels attempted to seize control of the national government. The situation was only resolved when Wielopolski fled the country, with control of Poland placed in the hands of the War Minister Dmitry Milyutin. A revised Emancipation Statute was quickly introduced that provided fairer and more equitable distribution of land.

By the 1890s Poland had revealed its importance in fuelling Russian industrialisation. A Polish proletariat emerged that showed an interest and enthusiasm for Marxism and Socialism. In 1892, a Polish Socialist Party (PPS) was formed, closely followed in 1893 by the setting up of a Social Democratic Party. Also of prominence were nationalists who formed the National Democrats group. Polish politicians elected from these parties went on to make important contributions to the first and second

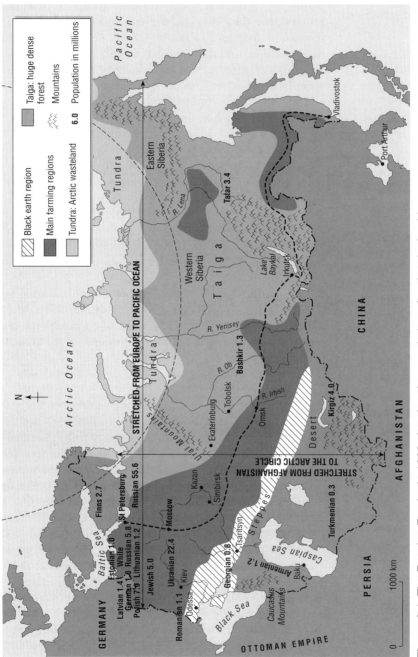

Figure 2.1: The Russian Empire in 1900 showing the population of national minorities.

Dumas (see pages 30–1), although along with other national minorities, their representation fell by 1914.

The First World War was a major turning point for Russian Poles. The signing of the Treaty of Brest-Litovsk in 1918 resulted in Poland gaining full independence. The Civil War created the prospect of Poland losing its newly found freedom but the Red Army suffered a major defeat in 1920 in its attempt to recapture Polish territory. The Poles retained their independence until the immediate post-Second World War period when, along with a number of other Eastern European states, Poland became a satellite state of the USSR until 1989.

The Ukrainians

The Ukrainians suffered similar treatment to the Poles during the rule of Alexander II. Although nationalism was not the same force as it was in Poland, the Ukrainians looked to build a separate cultural identity as reflected in literature and the arts in general. In response, Alexander II issued decrees (1863 and 1876) which forbade the publication and import of books written in Ukrainian. This early attempt at Russification was reinforced by Alexander III but, again, as with Poland, the peace treaty that ended Russia's involvement in the First World War also granted the Ukraine full independence. Unfortunately for the Ukrainians this was very short lived as they were not able to resist the might of the Red Army during the Civil War.

The Ukraine was a very important grain-producing area for Russia. Ukrainian peasants were fully aware of their importance to the Russian economy and were resistant to changes that they believed were unjust. In particular, Stalin's collectivisation programme was vehemently opposed. Stalin blamed such behaviour on the *kulaks*. The result was that Ukrainian peasants suffered more than any other regional group when it came to the purges.

In theory, the position of the Ukraine improved when, under the 1936 Constitution, it was included as part of the new federation of soviet states (see pages 41–2). But during and after the Second World War many Ukrainians were accused of being German collaborators. Those found guilty were either executed or transported to the far north.

The Caucasians

Those living in the Caucasus region of Russia were divided along religious lines. The Armenians and Georgians were Christians and the Azeris, Chechens, Ossetians and Abkhazians were Muslims. These divisions, coupled with the high level of illiteracy in the region, made Russification relatively easy. Nevertheless, populist movements arose to fight against repression. Of particular note were the Dashnaks and the Georgian Mensheviks who proved to be very antagonistic towards Nicholas II.

Georgia gained independence in 1920 but was 'retaken' by the Red Army in 1921. It was then suggested by some communists that Georgia should be amalgamated with Armenia and Azerbaizhan. Georgian communists opposed this arguing that they should be included in the Soviet Union on the same terms as other regions such as the Ukraine. Stalin, in his role as Commissar for National Minorities, ordered Ordjonikidze, his representative in Georgia, to bring the dissidents under control. Unfortunately, Ordjonikidze ended up physically attacking one of the Georgian communist leaders. The incident was made worse when Stalin attempted to defend the actions of Ordjonikidze. Lenin reacted by condemning the authoritarian approach adopted by Stalin, claiming that such actions would lead to further discontent not just in Georgia but throughout the Soviet Union. Ironically, the 1936 Constitution gave full republican status to Georgia although, as with the other republics, this was no guarantee of autonomy.

The Finns

The tsars before Nicholas II took a fairly liberal stance on Finland, conceding to demands for a separate Finnish Parliament (*Diet*) in 1863 and a constitution in 1865. The appointment by Nicholas II of Nikolei Bobrikov as Governor General marked a change in fortune for the Finns. Under Bobrikov Finland was fully integrated into the Russian Empire and Russified. Finland's separate army was disbanded, the Finnish State Secretariat was abolished, and Russian became the main language. Inevitably, this provoked much opposition mainly through a policy of passive non-cooperation, but it also led to the assassination of Bobrikov in 1904 by terrorists. In 1905 Finland was given full autonomy only to find the agreement was quickly reneged on by Stolypin in the same year. As with Poland, it was the treaty of Brest-Litovsk that enabled Finland to achieve lasting independence.

Peoples from the Baltic Provinces

The Baltic provinces consisted of Estonia, Latvia and Lithuania. At the start of the period, these provinces were strongly influenced by 'old' German rulers. The states were relatively stable and prosperous especially given the abundant supplies of raw materials that were essential to a range of industrial activities. The attraction of regular and better paid employment encouraged many native Russians to migrate to the area, with Riga (in Latvia), in particular, becoming a very important commercial and business centre. As the Russian economic influence increased Russification almost followed naturally. Thus, the use of Russian language became more widespread. This was illustrated, for example, by the renaming of various educational institutions.

German influence waned by the end of the century and this coincided with a rise in nationalism among native Estonians, Latvians and Lithuanians. However, this was never strong enough for independence to be achieved and in 1936 it was relatively easy for these states to be incorporated in the new federal system of Russian government. Under the 1936 Constitution all

Key terms

Pale of Settlement
This was the region within which Jews were allowed to settle. From 1835, it included Lithuania, Poland and the south-western provinces (including the Ukraine).

Ignatiev memorandum
Nicholas Pavolich Ignatiev (1832–1908) was Russia's ambassador to Constantinople. In 1876, he sent a note to Serbian leaders, without official approval, saying that they could rely on Russian help if they declared war on Turkey.

Pogrom
An organised massacre of Russian Jews.

Anti-Semitic
To be prejudiced against Jews.

Doctors' Plot
An announcement was made by the Stalinist regime in January 1953 concerning nine doctors who had worked alongside a US Jewish group to murder high-ranking Soviet officials. Seven of the doctors were Jews.

members of the new federation of states had the legal right to secede (that is, to break away from the USSR) but their behaviour was tightly controlled from Moscow. As in other regions, the authorities were not afraid to use severe repressive measures to maintain law and order. The Baltic provinces suffered especially badly during the later parts of the Second World War. There were mass deportations due mainly to a fear that there were many who were collaborating with the Nazis. After the war, the region became more stable and there were very few incidents of rebellion.

The Jews

Jews were a unique group in that they did not have a homeland in the Russian Empire. Before the time of Alexander II, an artificial place of settlement had been established (the **Pale of Settlement**) but this was restrictive for Jews. Alexander II therefore allowed members of the Pale to migrate to other regions. His father clamped down on this and generally the period up to the First World War was one during which Russian Jews were persecuted. Jews never seemed to pose much of an active opposition to Russian leaders; it was a perceived threat that resulted in them being treated so badly. Alexander III believed that Jews were behind the infamous **Ignatiev memorandum** along with all of the 'negative and insidious' influences from the West. Partly as a result of this, a mini-**pogrom**, called 'little thunder', occurred in the Pale prompted by an **anti-Semitic** group known as the Holy League. Other repressive measures from 1882 onwards included the following:

- the confinement of Jews once more to the Pale of Settlement
- the banning of Jews from trying to purchase land in prosperous rural areas
- restrictions on access to senior positions in the military or medicine
- removal from the electoral register of the *Zemstva*.

Nicholas II continued the anti-Jewish position taken by his father. They were accused of being 'revolutionaries' as some were affiliated to the SDs (and there was indeed a separate Jewish SD Party called the Bund). Despite Nicholas' dislike of Jews, he made some important concessions by allowing them to sit on the *Duma*.

The communists were just as repressive towards Jews. More 'special' settlements were established in the 1930s such as that at Khaburovsk. By the Second World War, more oppression took place with a ban being imposed on the Jewish religion, the closure of a range of Jewish institutions (for example, schools and societies) and a ban on specialist publications. This carried on after the war. Of particular note was the **Doctors' Plot** of August 1952 which ended in 15 Jewish leaders being tried and executed. The perceived threat of Jewish subversiveness and plotting was always apparent throughout the rule of Khrushchev, with a number of prominent Jewish technical specialists being executed for anti-communist activity.

> **Essay focus**
>
> Look at Essays 1 and 2 on pages 94–101. Notice that neither refers to national minorities as opposition. Although the methods used to deal with different types of opposition were similar throughout the period, national minorities posed unique problems to rulers. It would have been useful, therefore, if the essays had considered the implications for leaders of having to rule over a number of different ethnic groups.

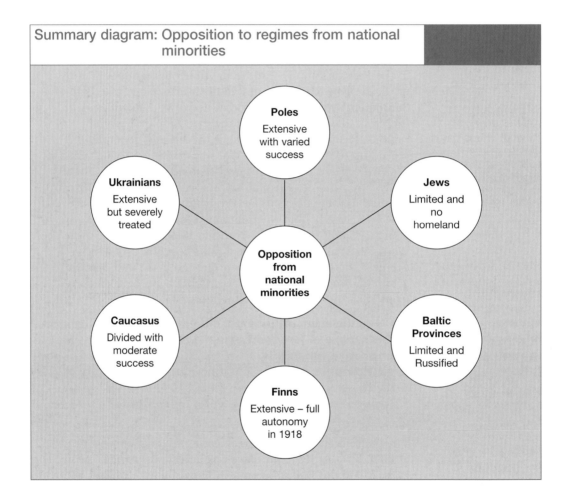

Summary diagram: Opposition to regimes from national minorities

2 | Methods of repression to control opposition

Repression means to control, restrain, prevent or inhibit the thoughts and actions of others. The use of repression by tsars and Bolsheviks presupposed that the thoughts and actions of others were so threatening that they needed challenging.

The use of repression was ongoing but there were times when extreme forms emerged. These 'epidemics' of extreme repression are referred to as 'terror' and were especially evident during communist rule. The main tools of repression used by all rulers were:

Key question
What were the most effective methods used by the tsars and communists to control opposition?

- The secret police – to investigate, arrest, imprison, execute and exile 'opposition'.
- The army – to deal with riots and unruly mob behaviour (including strikes).
- Propaganda – to manipulate the ideals, values, beliefs and attitudes of the people.
- Censorship – to control access to information that might share the ideals, values, beliefs and attitudes of the people.

These tools often coexisted, although there were times when one was more predominant than others. Also, they were used in conjunction with reforms; sometimes repression was used to enforce policies while at other times it existed to counter what some perceived as being liberal reforms that gave too much freedom to protest.

The secret police
The secret police was the institution that worked beyond the 'law' and was complementary to the regular police force. Russian leaders had a long tradition of using groups to inflict violence on others to control their behaviour.

The Third Section of the Imperial Chancellery
This was a form of secret police inherited by Alexander II. His forebear had used the Third Section mainly to exile opponents. In line with his reformist inclinations, Alexander II downgraded the role of the Third Section and abandoned it completely in 1880. It was replaced by the 'softer' Department of State Police (*Okhrana*), although the powers of this body were enhanced from the 1880s onwards with the growth of political pressure groups and parties.

The *Okhrana*
The *Okhrana* lasted until February 1917 when its headquarters was burnt to the ground by revolutionaries and the Provisional Government decided to disband it as part of a more relaxed policy towards political dissidents. Until that time, its role fluctuated according to circumstance. Alexander III fully utilised the *Okhrana* as a tool for spying on, arresting, imprisoning and/or exiling opposition. The relative stability of the 1890s led to the *Okhrana* taking a lower profile under the governance of Durnovo and Gromykin at the Ministry of Interior. *Okhrana* activity increased as the SRs and SDs took off, reaching something of a peak in 1905. Members of the *Okhrana* were used increasingly as infiltrating **agents provocateurs** (as in the case of **Father Gapon**) and executioners.

The Provisional Government's abandonment of the secret police was not simply a reaction to demands from the people to get rid of it. From February until October 1917, those governing were more focused on wartime security, and therefore established the Counter Espionage Bureau of the Petrograd Military District. This was designed to weed out those who attempted to undermine the war effort, which inevitably included Bolsheviks. Some historians have argued that the wider use of a secret police force would have prevented the Provisional Government from failing. This **counterfactual argument** is not especially convincing, given the overall weaknesses of the regime.

The All-Russian Extraordinary Commission for Fighting Counter-Revolution and Sabotage (the *Cheka*)

The *Cheka* was established in December 1917 under the Bolsheviks and was headed by a Polish communist, **Dzerzhinsky**. As the official title suggests, this type of secret police was intended to have the specific role of dealing with those who opposed the revolution. Initially, it was similar to previous forms of the secret police in that individual trouble makers were targeted. But by the summer of 1917 there was a shift towards clamping down on groups considered to be displaying 'bourgeois' elements and counter-revolutionary behaviour. A particular target was those associated with left-wing Socialist Revolutionaries, especially after members of this group were linked with an attempt to assassinate Lenin in August 1918. In fact, what made the *Cheka* very different from previous variants of the secret police was the way in which they used terror to victimise people not just because of their actions but more generally, as a result of *who* they were. Thus, one of Dzerzhinsky's instructions to *Cheka* members was not to

> ... demand incriminating evidence to prove that the prisoner has opposed the Soviet government by force or words. Your first duty is to ask him to which class he belongs, what are his origins, his education, and his occupation. These questions should decide the fate of the prisoner.

The *Cheka* were a very nasty and ruthless set of individuals. Probably the best-known example of their work was the execution, without trial, of the Romanov family at Ekaterinburg in July 1918. Throughout the period of the Civil War, there were many more examples of *Cheka* brutality. Under the guidance of Trotsky and Dzerzhinsky, the *Cheka* formally implemented the **Red Terror**. Part of this involved enforcing War Communism (especially grain requisitioning), the '**Labour Code**', the elimination of *kulaks*, the administration of **labour camps**, and the **militarisation of labour**.

Once the Civil War was over, the Bolsheviks saw the need to improve their somewhat tarnished image, which meant getting rid of the *Cheka*. It was disbanded by Kamenev in 1922 and replaced by the State Police Administration (GPU). The latter was expanded in 1924 and renamed the United State Police Administration (OGPU). Although OGPU was not as brutal as the *Cheka*, it was still the secret police and therefore maintained a presence that instilled fear in the general populace. It was also entirely under the control of the Communist Party of the Soviet Union (CPSU).

Counterfactual argument
An argument based on what might have happened rather than on what actually did occur.

Red Terror
Fear engendered by the Bolsheviks through the threat of arrest, imprisonment, exile and/or execution.

Labour Code
Rules for the deployment and control of labour.

Labour camps
Punishment camps where political opponents were set to hard labour. They were placed in the more inhospitable parts of Russia such as Siberia.

Militarisation of labour
Workers were forced to work either as labourers or soldiers.

Felix Dzerzhinsky 1877–1926
A Polish communist who came out of exile as a result of the February revolution. He was appointed as head of the *Cheka* (1917–26) because of his ruthlessness, reliability and total dedication to the cause.

**Genrikh Yagoda
1891–1938**
Held the position as
Commissar of the
Interior (NKVD)
(1934–6). He and
his associates were
dismissed seemingly
for being too
honest.

**Nikolai Yezhov
1895–1939**
Replaced Yagoda as
Commissar of the
Interior (1936–8)
which from 1936
onwards
incorporated the
work of OGPU.

**Lavrentiy Beria
1899–1953**
Initially paved a
political career
through the post of
Transcaucasia Party
Secretary (1932–8).
He replaced Yezhov
as head of the
NKVD (1938–53)
and became feared
for his lack of
scruples and cold-
heartedness.

The People's Commissariat for Internal Affairs (NKVD)

By 1930, Stalin had started to introduce a very personalised form
of rule (that is, his personal dictatorship). Coupled with his
collectivisation programme, Five-Year Plans and attacks on
national minorities, signs of opposition became more apparent.
Thus, the role of the secret police changed once more. The
NKVD, formed in 1934 and headed by **Yagoda** (later **Yezhov**),
was a reversion to a *Cheka* tool of repression. Some historians
though, have pointed out that NKVD broke the pattern of secret
policing by creating a more permanent form of terror. The
NKVD was unique in that it became crucial to the imposition of
the purges and show trials that continued until the early 1940s.

What also stood out with respect to NKVD activity was the
rigour and intensity used to gather evidence against conspirators.
Of particular note was the way in which damning evidence was
gathered to be used against communists who had previously been
held in high esteem, that is, Bukharin, Kamenev, Zinoviev and
Trotsky. In fact, Trotsky was eventually assassinated, in 1940 in
Mexico, by an NKVD agent using an ice pick. The NKVD was
also revered for the way they helped administer the prison camps
or *Gulags*. Given that over 40 million people were eventually sent
to *Gulags* during the Stalinist regime, it was essential for Stalin to
use a body of people who were totally committed to repression
tactics.

Given the paranoia and insecurity displayed by Stalin, it is not
surprising that even the NKVD came under suspicion as being
conspiratorial. In 1938, Yezhov was blamed for the emergence of
an anti-purge campaign. He was quickly replaced by **Beria** who
proceeded to arrange the execution of Yezhov and his close
allies. In fact, by the start of the Second World War, the NKVD
had itself been purged of around 20,000 members who had
committed a variety of misdemeanours.

The disbandment of the NKVD

The tarred reputation of the NKVD led to it being disbanded in
1943. It was initially replaced by the People's Commissariat for
State Security (NKGB) with Beria at the helm. In 1946 Beria and
the NKGB claimed to have fulfilled their mission which was to
quell the unrest from ethnic minority groups.

The coming of the Ministry for State Security (MGB) and Ministry of Internal Affairs (MVD)

The NKGB was subsequently replaced by two bodies, the Ministry
for State Security (MGB) and the Ministry of Internal Affairs
(MVD). The MGB, as its title suggests, was responsible for
ensuring that the general population was kept in line. The MVD
was really another version of the NKVD. In 1953 these
organisations were merged to form a large version of the MVD.
Control of this body was placed in the hands of Beria. Most
senior party members feared Beria. Khrushchev in particular was
worried that he was planning some kind of coup against senior

politicians in control of government. Fairly soon after gaining control of the Party Central Committee, Khrushchev ordered Beria to be arrested and tried. In December he was executed.

The reorganisation of the MVD

The demise of Beria provided Khrushchev and other party members with the opportunity to break away from the past. Part of the destalinisation process involved reshaping the security services so that it seemed that they were less threatening. Thus, in March 1954, the MVD was reorganised into two departments. One was a much refined and rationalised version of the original MVD which retained the same title. This was to be solely responsible for dealing with 'ordinary' criminal acts and civil disorder. The other was called the Committee for State Security (KGB) which was to focus on the internal and external security of the USSR. Included in the remit of the KGB was the need to spy on enemies and gather intelligence, both important during the **Cold War** period.

The MVD and the KGB were placed under the direct administration of the party and it therefore became much easier to monitor security measures and law enforcement in general. The new structure, coupled with the genuine desire to move away from the severe repression of the Stalinist era, had a noticeable impact on Russian society. Until 1964 the number of political arrests plummeted. The use of *Gulags* largely disappeared and torture of dissidents appeared to be a thing of the past. By 1960, it is estimated that there were only about 11,000 counter-revolutionaries in captivity, a far cry from the 1930s and 1940s.

The army

At the start of the period the army numbered around 1,400,000 men. Most were forced conscripts from the serf class and could be expected to commit themselves to at least 25 years' service. The officers were drawn purely from the nobility. At any point in time, the army could be used to deal with internal law and order issues as well as to engage in wars.

The Crimean War (1853–6) revealed a number of deficiencies in military provision. Out of the 800,000 men that served, a significant number withdrew from combat due to poor health. The Russians also suffered a huge number of casualties. The dismal military performance, coupled with the Emancipation Edict in 1861, led to some important military reforms (see pages 153–4).

Russification under Alexander III led to the army having an enhanced role as a peace-keeping force and regulator of regional frontiers. On occasion, this function was compromised as soldiers contributed to disturbances. A good example of this was at Kishinev in 1903 when Cossacks joined in on attacks against Jews.

There were also times when armed forces seemed to use excessive force. On Bloody Sunday, 1905, troops opened fire on peaceful protesters, including women and children. About 200

Key term

Cold War
A state of tension and hostility between the Soviet bloc and Western powers after the Second World War. However, the hostility did not spill over into actual fighting between the two power blocs.

Key question
How far was there more continuity than change in the way the army was used to control opposition in the period from 1855 to 1964?

people died on the spot and around 800 were wounded (although there were a variety of reports of the event which gave wildly different figures).

The army and strikes

From 1905 to 1917 the army was used fairly frequently to dismantle strikes, protests and riots. The social unrest of February 1917 (see pages 33–4) was dealt with forcefully by the army under the guidance of General Khabalov. Furthermore, the strikes and protests of July 1917 were put down using the military (see pages 34–5). However, the summer of 1917 was pivotal in that the Kerensky offensive against Germany failed and many troops deserted. This seemed to affect the morale of soldiers who had been given the task of restoring domestic law and order.

The formation of the MRC

In February 1917, troops had already displayed a propensity to desert and join protesters. It is estimated, for example, that about 150,000 members of the Petrograd Garrison supported revolution at that time. In March, soldiers and sailors formed committees to protest against the government's Declaration of War Aims. July saw sailors from Kronstadt take to the streets to complain about Russia's involvement in the war. By October, Lenin and Trotsky had realised that the bulk of the military were unlikely to support the Provisional Government if a Bolshevik takeover was attempted. With this in mind, they encouraged soldiers, especially from Petrograd, to form the Military Revolutionary Committee (MRC), which was to become the vanguard of the revolution.

During the October Revolution, the MRC and the **Red Guard** seized power, with little bloodshed, from Kerensky. They quickly commandeered transport, public buildings, utilities and the **Winter Palace**. Interestingly, this appeared to involve minimal strategic planning; Trotsky made the observation that even if a few hundred soldiers had remained loyal to the Provisional Government the revolution could have been averted.

Once the Bolsheviks took over they continued to deploy the military to maintain stability and to consolidate power. Troops were used to deal with flash strikes by civil servants and financial workers. The war issue (how to end Russia's involvement in the First World War) was tackled by a change in military personnel at the top with General Dukhonin being replaced by General Krylenko. The Constituent Assembly was stopped from meeting on its second day by Bolshevik sailors.

The importance of the Red Army

But the most dramatic utilisation of the military occurred via the construction of the Red Army. Under the guidance of Trotsky, the Red Army was instrumental in enabling the Bolsheviks to win the Civil War. At the start of the war, the Red Army hardly existed but by the end it consisted of over five million conscripts.

Key terms

Red Guard
A general term to denote armed supporters of the Bolsheviks especially in the second half of 1917.

Winter Palace
Official residence of the tsars in St Petersburg.

Such a large force proved more than a match for the White opposition who could only muster about 500,000 troops in total. It should be remembered that the army was also used to impose, along with the *Cheka*, War Communism (see page 14). Despite instilling a more disciplined approach to the running of the army, Trotsky still faced the problems of desertion and military personnel joining rebellions. The most notable example was in February 1921 when sailors at Kronstadt mutinied. Trotsky ordered 50,000 troops to recapture the island but this was achieved only at the cost of 10,000 Red Army deaths. Those rebels who were captured were executed or exiled to the Arctic.

Stalin's use of the army

The use of the military to help implement economic policy was furthered by Stalin. The Red Army was once again required to requisition grain, this time as part of collectivisation. It also had a role in administering the purges and creating the **Great Terror**. Ironically, the military leadership was consistently perceived as a threat, by Stalin, to his position. He therefore included a number of key military figures in the **Great Purge** of 1936–8. During the spring of 1936 generals and marshals were arrested, tried and executed including the great Civil War hero Marshal Tukhachevski. By the end of the purge, over 40 per cent of the top echelon of the military had disappeared and were not replaced. This was all very illogical given rising international tensions. Such tensions arose as a result of the Nazi seizure of power (1933) and the imposition of Hitler's expansionist foreign policy.

The army in the Second World War

Russia's involvement in the Second World War resulted in enormous military casualties. There were some examples of desertion but this was considered treachery of the highest order. Stalin ordered all Russian troops to fight to the death ('to the last drop of blood'), a policy that is usually offered as part explanation for the successful defence of Stalingrad and Moscow. Civil unrest at this time and immediately after the war was virtually non-existent; any that did exist was not supported by soldiers and was dealt with mainly by the NKVD.

The army after the Second World War

From 1945 to 1953, military leaders were still treated with suspicion despite their heroics during the war. Marshal Zhukov (Chief of Staff of the Russian armed forces during the Second World War), for example, was removed from the Party Central Committee and exiled from Moscow. Alongside alterations to the military leadership was a change in emphasis concerning the role of the armed forces in general. Internal security was still of concern as exemplified by the role of the army in helping unravel the Doctors' Plot (see page 77) and in the arrest, trial and execution of Beria (see page 81–2). But, by the time Khrushchev

Key terms

Great Terror
The period from 1936 to 1938 when the terrorisation of the Russian people reached a peak.

Great Purge
The period from 1936 to 1938 when thousands of people were arrested, convicted and executed for committing 'counter-revolutionary' crimes.

came to power, the armed forces were far more focused on resolving international conflicts. With *détente*, an easing of tensions occurred, which in turn led to a reduction in the size of the army from 3.6 million to about 2.4 million. Nevertheless, there were still flashpoints that required a distinct military presence. The shooting down of a US spy plane over Russian airspace in 1960 and the Cuban Missile Crisis of 1962 illustrated that Russian leaders could not afford to be too complacent about how they deployed their military resources.

Key term

Détente
A relaxation in tensions between states during the period of the Cold War, although it is usually applied to the period from 1963 to the late 1970s.

Essay focus

The role of the military in suppressing opposition is often overlooked. Essay 1's focus has a very synoptic paragraph (5) on the importance of this factor (see pages 96–7). Note that only a brief comment is made about the army in Essay 2 (pages 99–101).

Key question
How effectively did the tsars use censorship compared with the communists to control opposition in the period from 1855 to 1964?

Censorship
Censorship under Alexander II and Alexander III
Under Alexander II, Russia experienced *glasnost* (the policy of openness) for the first time. In 1865 there was a relaxation of censorship; daily newspapers and foreign books from this time onwards were not censored before going to print. However, the government retained the right to withdraw publications thought to include 'dangerous orientation' (that is, criticism of the ruling élite). Government departments also published newspapers (*Ruskii*) that provided information on official items. The result was an increase in the circulation of newspapers, periodicals and books as illustrated by the statistics below:

- 1855: 140 periodicals (60 official)
- 1855: 1020 books published
- 1864: 1836 books published
- 1872: the first Russian translation of volume 1 of Marx's *Das Kapital* was published
- 1894: 89 newspapers
- 1894: 10,691 books published (roughly the sum total published in the USA and Britain).

In general, publishers found it relatively easy to print material that questioned the role of government especially when it came to its handling of economic and social problems.

The reactionary rule of Alexander III (1881–94) resulted in a clampdown on publications. The relatively high number of books published in 1894 was a result of an easing in censorship rules by Nicholas II. Officials censored written material before it was published and closed down certain newspapers, journals and educational institutions. Despite this some artistic and creative works were actually promoted especially if they were deemed to be patriotic (for example, the works of the composer Tchaikovsky).

Censorship under Nicholas II

When Nicholas II came to the throne a reversion to the *glasnost* of Alexander II occurred. A considerable expansion of the press in 1894 took place; for example, the number of different periodicals in circulation increased threefold from 1900 to 1914. Pre-publication censorship once more disappeared although publishers could still be fired or closed down for circulating subversive material. An interesting development during this time was the emergence of newspapers aimed at the proletariat. This included the '*Kopek* newspaper' (the penny paper) which, within two years of its appearance reached a circulation of 25,000. Also significant was the reporting of political matters discussed in the *Duma* although the finer details of what was debated were occasionally omitted or changed. Thus, for example, in 1912, when correspondence from Rasputin was being analysed, the press were told to report the matter by making reference to the 'dark forces near the throne' (instead of using Rasputin's name). All in all, by the time of the outbreak of the First World War, Russia had joined the other major Western nations in contributing to a worldwide media network.

Censorship during the First World War

Russian people, especially troops, were subject to censorship during the First World War in a similar way to the peoples of the other combatant countries. Troops at the front gained most of their 'news' from foreign broadcasts (including the fall of the Romanovs). When the Bolsheviks seized power, one of the first measures was to abolish press freedom altogether so as to suppress 'counter-revolutionaries'. Some workers' groups, such as the printers, opposed this only to experience the wrath of the Military War Committee (MRC). By the 1920s, reporting was totally under the control of the Bolsheviks. In 1921, the Agitation and Propaganda Department (Agitprop) was founded with the main aim of creating an idealised picture of Russian life. Schools, cinemas, the radio and libraries were all under the constant surveillance to ensure that the populace was denied access to counter-revolutionary material. However, writers who supported the new regime flourished. They were known as 'Fellow Travellers'. The Association of Proletarian Writers (APW) was formed to support those, such as Shokolov, who wanted to pursue 'new ideas'. On the other hand, writers, such as Zemyatin, who predicted the coming of a totalitarian state were labelled subversive and were victimised.

Censorship under Stalin

Under Stalin, censorship was taken to a new level. By 1932, all literary groups were closed down (including APW); anyone wanting to write and publish had to join the Union of Soviet Writers (USW). During the first congress of the group in 1934, it was announced that all members had to produce material under the banner of '**socialist realism**'. This involved writing to depict

Socialist realism The 'official' way of writing to reflect the heroic efforts of workers and peasants to ensure the success of communism.

Key term

'revolutionary reality' that is, the struggle of ordinary people to overcome oppression. All work was to be written in a language that the bulk of the population would understand and was to be approved by the party. For those with a burning desire to write creatively, the USW caused much consternation. Some writers, such as Pasternak, changed their beliefs to fit in with the wishes of the USW. Others who rebelled were arrested, sent into exile (and/or labour camps) or executed. Some committed suicide while others, such as Bulgakov, were simply forgotten.

The Second World War and the New Soviet Man

A high degree of censorship continued throughout and after the Second World War. Stalin was especially concerned to doctor information about the rest of the world. Radio airways were distorted, news was fictionalised and restrictions were put on all of the arts to prevent bourgeois behaviour. Writers were still valued highly as the 'engineer of men's souls' (Stalin) but only if they focused on glorifying Russia's achievements and promoted the concept of the **New Soviet Man**.

Censorship under Khrushchev

Under Khrushchev, censorship was eased in a similar way as under Alexander II and Nicholas II. Books and libraries proliferated so that by the late 1950s nearly 65,000 books were being published per year, twice the number that came out in the mid-1920s. By 1959, there were 135,000 libraries containing around 8000 million books, a 10-fold increase on the numbers for 1913. The Lenin library alone, based in Moscow, held 19 million texts. Newspapers also flourished with a total readership of nearly 60 million by the early 1960s. But, despite the variety, the most popular papers were *Pravda* (paper of the Communist Party), *Izvestiya* (paper of the government) and *Trud* (paper of the Trades Unions Council). However, even with greater accessibility, news was still distorted.

Propaganda

The use of propaganda by all leaders was closely linked to censorship. However, propaganda as a tool of repression was not really used by the tsars until after 1905. The advisers to Nicholas II then attempted to promote his image through pamphleteering, portraits, photographs and staged events. In 1913, the tercentenary celebrations of the Romanov dynasty were designed to raise the popularity of tsarist rule. Given the reception to the events from the public this form of propaganda was very successful. During the First World War there was a significant increase in the number of pictures in circulation that showed how the Tsar was in control. It was considered crucial to do this given how disastrously the war seemed to be progressing. But the real masters of the use of propaganda were the communists.

Key term

New Soviet Man
The ideal Soviet citizen – one who was hard working, law abiding, moral and totally supportive of the Communist Party.

The use of slogans

The Bolsheviks were adept at using slogans to get their message across to the population such as 'Peace, Bread and Land' and 'All Power to the Soviets'. As with Nicholas II, pamphlets, tracts (for example, *What is to be Done?*), newspapers, photographs, portraits, posters and statues were used by the Bolsheviks to promote the regime and inculcate the people with an ideology that was deemed to be in their best interests.

The cult of personality

The main difference was that with Lenin and Stalin a cult of personality was purposely engendered. The intention was to present the leaders as heroes to be worshipped with

Figure 2.2: A propaganda poster photographed in 1967 of Lenin showing the words 'Lenin lived, Lenin is living, Lenin will live'.

Figure 2.3: 'Moscow by Stalin'. The text at the bottom reads: 'Under the leadership of the Bolshevik Party, under the guidance of the Leninist Central Committee and the sacred leader of the proletariat Comrade Stalin – onward to the heights of joy and happiness of mankind.'

unquestioning loyalty. With this in place, it was then much easier to rule in a dictatorial fashion. Examples of the cult being implemented included the following:

- the imagery of Lenin continued to be displayed after his death
- the embalming and display of Lenin's body in the mausoleum in Red Square
- the renaming of Petrograd as Leningrad (1924)
- the renaming of Tsaritsyn as Stalingrad (1923)
- the slogan 'Stalin is the Lenin of Today' (1924)
- various posters, photographs and statues depicting Stalin as a man of the people (usually dressed as a peasant).

Newspapers

Under the communists, propaganda characterised the make-up of most government institutions. Unsurprisingly, the main newspapers, *Pravda* and *Izvestiya*, were purely propaganda tools. Under Stalin, they were used to good effect to promote the achievements of the Five-Year Plans.

Groups

Special youth organisations were established (the Pioneers and *Komsomol*) to protect the young against the 'degeneracy of bourgeois culture'. *Komsomol* members were encouraged to tell tales on those who criticised their glorious leaders. They were also asked to prove their loyalty by working on construction projects such as at Magnitogorsk and by implementing collectivisation. Total membership increased fivefold from 1929 to 1941.

The arts

The arts were manipulated to present a popular culture that emphasised the role of the 'little man' and traditional values. Any trends that veered from the norm, such as jazz music, recreational drug use or engagement in homosexual acts, were 'banned'.

The Stakhanovite movement

The workplace was targeted with propaganda with the intention of raising productivity. The best example of this was the creation of the **Stakhanovite movement**. Even leisure pursuits were targeted as providing opportunities to promote communist ideals. For example, much time, effort and money was invested in the Dynamo and Spartak Moscow football teams to show to the rest of Europe how successful Russian people could perform under Communist rule. Thus, the propaganda was all pervasive and integral to the establishment of totalitarian rule.

The use of film and the cinema to promote communism

Film and the cinema were also used to promote communism. The film industry started to get underway in 1907. The cinema quickly grew in popularity so that by the time of the October

Key term

Stakhanovite movement
Based on the extraordinary efforts of the Donbas miner, Alexei Stakhanov, who produced way above the normal quantity of coal per man-shift. He was turned, using propaganda, into a 'model' worker for others to copy. Those who did, creating a Stakhanovite movement, were given special rewards such as red carpets and holidays in Moscow.

Revolution of 1917, there were over 1000 cinemas. Production and direction of films were loosely based on the format used in the West but by the late 1920s Stalin was using the cinema to promote collectivisation and his Five-Year Plans. Under the guidance of the Council of People's Commissars, Soviet cinema was immersed in 'socialist realism' although, as with the printed word, more freedom to be creative was allowed after Khrushchev's destalinisation speech. In 1959, 145 films were made and the number of cinemas had increased to nearly 59,000. Nevertheless, much of what the Soviet public got to see still revolved around the transmission of political ideology rather than pure entertainment.

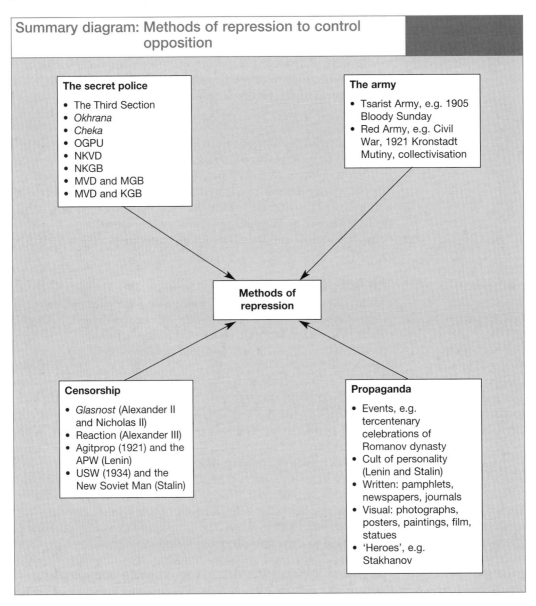

Summary diagram: Methods of repression to control opposition

The secret police
- The Third Section
- *Okhrana*
- *Cheka*
- OGPU
- NKVD
- NKGB
- MVD and MGB
- MVD and KGB

The army
- Tsarist Army, e.g. 1905 Bloody Sunday
- Red Army, e.g. Civil War, 1921 Kronstadt Mutiny, collectivisation

Methods of repression

Censorship
- *Glasnost* (Alexander II and Nicholas II)
- Reaction (Alexander III)
- Agitprop (1921) and the APW (Lenin)
- USW (1934) and the New Soviet Man (Stalin)

Propaganda
- Events, e.g. tercentenary celebrations of Romanov dynasty
- Cult of personality (Lenin and Stalin)
- Written: pamphlets, newspapers, journals
- Visual: photographs, posters, paintings, film, statues
- 'Heroes', e.g. Stakhanov

Key question
How useful and appropriate were the reforms used by the tsars and communists as a tool to control opposition?

3 | Reform as a method to deal with opposition

The tsars and reform

All Russian rulers throughout the period used reforms as a means of controlling the behaviour of the population. The tsars tended to implement political, economic and social policies to appease opposition. Alexander II hoped that by freeing the serfs they would simply be happier with their lot and be more reluctant to riot (hence his view that it would be better to reform from above than from below). Nicholas II introduced the *Duma* to quieten those who clamoured for constitutional reforms. The Provisional Government also passed liberal reforms such as the dismantling of the *Okhrana* which they hoped would create more stability. This approach did not seem to work as the more freedoms that the Russian people had, the more obstreperous they became. However, their behaviour was likely to have been dictated by the view that reforms did not go far enough and that what they were left with was still a highly authoritarian form of rule.

The communists and reform

In contrast, the communists used reforms to deal with opponents in a more direct fashion. War Communism (see page 10), collectivisation (see pages 117–20) and the Five-Year Plans (see pages 110–13) were all combined with repressive measures to ensure that they were successfully implemented. There was little scope to question the efficacy of these reforms. It was made clear that collectivisation, for example, involved making tremendous sacrifices that were for the good of the motherland. Anyone who disagreed was exiled or executed. Thus, reforms had the double benefit for rulers of stimulating economic growth while enabling opposition to be kept in check.

Summary diagram: Reform as a method to deal with opposition

The tsars and reform	The communists and reform
• Reforms used indirectly to appease the population and control opposition • Reforms often led to an increase in opposition	• Reforms used directly to control opposition • Reforms tended to crush opposition

4 | Conclusion

The nature of opposition

The 'nature of opposition' is quite a vague term. 'Nature' refers to what characterised opposition. This, in turn, depends on how 'opposition' was and is defined. The word refers to those who disagreed with the ideas, policies and actions of individuals and groups that governed Russia. However, there was often a difference between 'real' opposition and 'perceived' opposition. Real opposition was characterised by certain people speaking out against rulers or taking direct action to influence their behaviour. Some historians, though, have pointed out that opposition was not always easy to detect as it could have taken the form of a pattern of behaviour that did not obviously seem to represent disobedience or dissidence against rulers, for example, deciding not to attend the tercentenary celebrations of the Romanov dynasty. This could partly explain why some Russian leaders believed opposition to exist even though the evidence was flimsy. Stalin, for example, undoubtedly displayed a great deal of paranoia when dealing with those he perceived to be enemies within the Communist Party.

Opposition from outside and inside the ruling élites

Opposition, quite obviously, occurred not only outside but also inside ruling élites. With the tsars, outside mainly meant from emerging political parties or loosely organised groups of workers and peasants. Inside refers to members of the aristocracy, especially those high up in the military who 'advised' the Tsar on the most appropriate policies to adopt. With the Bolsheviks and communists outside opposition was similar to that faced by the tsars. Inside opposition was different; this came from fellow party members, who, depending on who was the leader, would be viewed as opponents if they were considered to be factionalists. Both the tsars and the communists also experienced two other forms of outside or external opposition. One was that provided by nationalist minorities and the other was from other countries. The latter was most obvious during times of total and limited war (see Chapter 4) but also during peacetime, especially from 1921 onwards. Britain, for example, was very wary of communism and British politicians were reluctant to form any kind of political, military and economic alliances with Soviet leaders. One of the consequences of this was that Stalin felt he had no option but to form a pact, in 1939, with Nazi Germany (see pages 172–3).

The extent of opposition

The extent of opposition can partly be measured by reference to numbers affiliating to opposition groups, although statistics for this are difficult to obtain and interpret. Also, even where figures are available, it is important to remember that large numbers did not necessarily constitute more significant and effective opposition.

The effectiveness of opposition can be viewed with respect to whether those who opposed rulers achieved their specific aims. It also needs to be considered from the perspective of rulers; the effectiveness of the tools used to control opposition is an equally important measurement of the overall impact of opposition.

The methods used to deal with opposition

The tsars and communists used a variety of methods to deal with opposition. These can be grouped under forms of repression (physical force, propaganda and censorship) and reform (economic, social and political). All rulers used a mixture of repression and reform. However, historians often point out that under Stalin repression was taken to a higher level particularly through the extermination of the *kulaks*, the purges and the show trials.

Finally, the reader should bear in mind that a degree and certain type of opposition is considered to be a healthy, positive feature of a society that is 'free' and truly democratic. There were times when this was partly acknowledged by Russian rulers but one theme that appears to be constant throughout the period is that all rulers, even those of a more reforming inclination, justified resorting to repression as a way of preserving the state.

Further questions for debate

1 'Political parties only posed a serious threat to the stability of Russian government during the period of the First World War (1914–18).' How far do you agree with this statement?

2 How far did the motives of opponents to Russian rulers change from 1855 to 1964?

3 Assess the reasons for the differences in the scale of peasant opposition to rulers from 1855 to 1964.

4 How effectively did different regimes deal with opposition from national minorities from 1855 to 1964?

5 How far did the methods used to deal with opposition change from 1855 to 1964?

Advice on answering essay questions on explanation

The following essays are responses to a question that demands explanation of the different policies towards dealing with opponents that occurred over time. This means that answers should focus on the analysis and evaluation of a range of reasons that help explain the actions of the tsars and communists. A number of key steps should be taken to ensure that such a question is answered successfully:

- First, the response should be planned carefully using a spider-web diagram. This will enable reasons to be written out laterally so that they can be reflected on before a judgement is made about which is most important.
- Second, factors should be grouped thematically (for example, different strategies and tactics used by the opposition, different ideologies of the regimes) rather than chronologically.
- Third, the reasons should be written about in order of relative importance starting with the most important.
- Fourth, reasons should be linked, where appropriate, to strengthen the argument being presented and to ensure that the answer retains fluency.

- Finally, the response should end with a conclusion that contains a judgement about the relative importance of the reasons discussed. This should be in line with what is presented in the main body of the answer.

Read each of the following essays carefully. Each essay was written in one hour and without the use of notes. Note any strengths and weaknesses and compare your views with those of the assessor. Marks should be awarded for each of the two assessment objectives described in the tables at the end of the book (see pages 192–3).

Two important points need to be noted about the content required to answer this question:

- First, information on the extent of success of opponents can be found in other chapters especially Chapters 1 and 3. You will probably need to read these chapters before using the essays at the end of this chapter. Remember that one of the key objectives of the OCR Themes paper is to get students to think and write synoptically. In other words, you should be able to draw on your knowledge and understanding of *all* of the different sections in the OCR Themes specification for Russia and its Rulers 1855–1964 to answer any *one* particular question.
- Second, some of the examples used in the essays to support key points will not necessarily be found in this book. This has been purposefully done to remind students of the need to read widely so that they can accumulate a range of different material that they can use as 'evidence'. To this end students would do well to consult a number of the texts mentioned on the reading list at the end of this book.

Also, remember that the Themes paper is about writing synoptically to cover a 100-year period and applying historical concepts to historical problems (change/continuity, similarity/difference and cause/consequence). The learning and use of facts is only important insofar as it will prevent the student from providing over-generalisation and assertion in essays.

Essay 1: Explain why the opponents of the tsars from 1855 to 1917 were more successful than those who opposed the communist regime from 1917 to 1964

1 The opponents to the tsars were primarily more successful as the circumstances they found themselves in were more conducive to concessions being made by rulers which in turn allowed opposition groups to flourish. The Bolsheviks, in particular, exploited adverse conditions created by war and industrialisation to promise a brighter future for all Russians. Once the population supported the notion of revolution the communists then proved to be very skilful and ruthless in ensuring that anyone who veered from the revolutionary path was severely dealt with. The Stalinist era saw the emergence of totalitarian rule and zero tolerance of any kind of dissent. During the rule of Khrushchev there was more tolerance of dissidents in an attempt to win back support from the West but there was still little

1 This is a very clear and solid start. The line of argument to be taken is stated in a well-structured and forceful manner.

threat to the communist regime. Thus, the success of opposition was dependent not just on political, economic and social change but on how those in authority chose to deal with such change.

2 The context within which opposition to regimes operated goes a long way to explaining different levels of success. The tsars were involved in four major wars from 1855 to 1917, three of which were disastrous and prompted major changes to the way Russia was governed. These changes all involved the creation of a more liberal climate in Russia and one in which opposition thrived. Alexander II issued the Emancipation Edict in 1861 partly as a result of the Crimean War. This in turn was linked to reforms of local government and in particular the creation of the *Zemstva* which proved to be a useful vehicle for those wishing to challenge the ruling élite. Nicholas II introduced his October Manifesto and the *Duma* after the failings of the end of Russo-Japanese war in 1905. Again, this allowed opposition groups to freely express their views even though the Fundamental Laws attempted to restrict freedoms. The Provisional Government also introduced liberal measures such as the disbandment of the *Okhrana* and the toleration of the soviets. Under the communists, wars never had the same impact. The Civil War was promoted as the chance to eradicate all of those who were against a just cause, that is, the workers' revolution. The Second World War was used to bring Russian people closer together to fight a common enemy and it was notable that there was virtually no domestic social unrest at that time.

3 Another contextual factor of equal importance was the changing state of the world economy. The tsars carried out economic reforms in attempt to keep up with the rapidly industrialising West. Unfortunately, these reforms stimulated discontent among the population that was easily exploited by opposition groups. The emancipation of the serfs created land ownership issues that were never resolved by the tsars and this was bitterly resented by peasants. Industrialisation led to rapid urbanisation and associated public health problems. The growing urban proletariat became more conscious of their existence as a separate class and began to organise themselves, with the help of groups such as the Social Democrats and Socialist Revolutionaries, to campaign for better conditions. The Bolsheviks, mainly by dominating the Soviets, proved particularly adept at exploiting deteriorating living and working conditions to gain support for their eventual takeover of the Provisional Government. The communists were fortunate in that a platform for further industrialisation had already been laid. This, combined with the highly repressive tools of government employed, ensured that they were able to deal with any opposition to their own economic policies with relative ease. War Communism, the New Economic Policy, collectivisation and the Five-Year Plans were all 'sold' to the population as necessary if Russians were to live in a more just and equitable society.

---

2 An interesting and relevant point is made here about how war influenced the growth of opposition under the different regimes. Good synoptic skill is displayed in explaining this factor.

3 An attempt is made here to evaluate another contextual factor (economic performance) although it is not fully explained as to why this is 'of equal importance' to the issue discussed in the previous paragraph.

4 Linked to changing contexts was the way in which different regimes went about dealing with opposition. Challenges to authority were more successful under the tsars as opposition faced a less systematic, consistent and focused use of the secret police than under the communists. Generally, the tsars went for a mixture of reform and limited repression dependent on circumstance. All of the tsars used the secret police to deal with riots, strikes and agitation caused by individuals. However, the *Okhrana*, as introduced by Alexander II in 1880, targeted the actions of ringleaders and small dissident groups in the hope that this would deal with the root cause of unrest.

The communists used the secret police in a very different way. Both the *Cheka* and later the NKVD were used to launch a class war against social groups that were considered to be bourgeois and anti-revolutionary. The targeting, in particular, of so-called *kulaks*, wreckers and 'rightists' invoked terror and fear which meant that those who might have posed a serious threat to communist regime were generally reluctant to do so.

The difference in treatment is born out in the statistics related to arrests, deportations and executions. Under the tsars, thousands were executed and exiled. Under Lenin and, more significantly, Stalin millions were purged through the use of show trials, transportation to Gulags or shootings. It is estimated that by the mid-1930s the NKVD was responsible for sending over 40 million people to the Gulags. Even the NKVD was not exempt; in 1938 20,000 of its members were purged under the guidance of Beria. Thus, the scale of repression by the secret police under the communists was such that it was virtually impossible for any opposition to gather momentum.

5 The armed forces were also used to monitor and control opposition by both regimes. Again, there were differences in how and the extent to which this tool of repression was used. Alexander II's main intention was to reform the army after its disastrous performance during the Crimean War. There were few instances during his reign of the military being used to quell unrest although generally there were not many examples of wide-scale disturbance. Alexander III used the modernised and better equipped army in the Russification process but this tended to increase resentment and opposition rather than lessen it. The most dramatic example of military use against opponents to the tsars happened in 1905 when the army shot dead over 200 protesters who marched on the Winter Palace. Bloody Sunday, as the incident was called, again led to even more discontent and seemed to result in some opposition groups gaining greater resolve to topple the tsar. By 1917, many soldiers had become disillusioned with the war and were reluctant to support the tsarist regime. Those left at home to deal with civil disobedience became increasingly reluctant to deal with peasant and worker protesters. This was partly due to the propaganda efforts of the Bolsheviks but also because soldiers were hesitant to repress those who were campaigning against something that they sympathised with. The effect was that many deserted to

4 The material used here has been well synthesised. The links mentioned in the opening sentence could have been made more explicit.

5 Again, the factor under discussion has been well presented and it is important to note how the candidate has taken the opportunity to make comment about the later part of the period.

join the ranks of strikers and protesters. Under the communists such desertion never really happened. When it did, as in 1921 at Kronstadt, it was ruthlessly dealt with. Both Lenin and Stalin realised the importance of keeping the military on board if they were to remain in power. This is why they spent so much time, effort and resources on expanding and maintaining the armed forces. Hence, Lenin ordered Trotsky to build the Red Army as he knew this was vital to winning the Civil War and to help bring stability to Russia after the conflict. Stalin continued to expand the military; the Five-Year Plans were mostly designed to equip the armed forces with the hardware they needed to deal with both internal, but more importantly, external threats. The Great Patriotic War proved that Stalin's policy was correct. It also showed that, unlike during the First World War, desertion was not an option. Stalin ordered that during the Battle for Stalingrad soldiers would fight to the death and that if they attempted to surrender they would be shot. Despite destalinisation, Khrushchev showed that he was not afraid to use the army to deal with opponents when he sent troops and tanks to put down the 1956 Hungarian rising. Therefore, under the communists, the military was considered a more important tool in keeping opposition in check than under the tsars.

> 6 Sustained, well-focused material is used here. The compare and contrast approach adopted from the start is continued.

6 When it came to the use of censorship and propaganda to deal with opposition, the tsars were again less methodical and rigorous than the communists. In 1865, Alexander II actually relaxed censorship laws which led to an increase in the publication of books and periodicals. After a return to censorship during the reign of Alexander III, Nicholas II reverted to a more liberal approach. Publications increased threefold from 1900 to 1914 and included the circulation of the penny paper aimed primarily at the proletariat. The freedoms given to the press were aimed to appease opposition but actually allowed it to proliferate. The communists resorted to a much harder line. The Bolsheviks abolished all press freedoms to counter anti-revolutionary activity. The news was manipulated through Agitprop, established in 1921. Individual writers were forced to join the Association of Proletarian Writers so that their work could be monitored. This was further tightened by Stalin when he established the Union of Soviet Writers in 1932. No dissent from the party line was allowed to be expressed in print. Any writer that attempted to do this was either exiled or executed. Only after Khrushchev's destalinisation programme was there any relaxation of censorship. The implementation of censorship was closely tied to the use of propaganda although this was far more obvious under communist rule. The only tsar to use propaganda was Nicholas II although he did so reluctantly. After the events of 1905, attempts were made through the printed word to promote a positive image of Nicholas. The focus on the use of propaganda reached a peak in 1913 with the tercentenary celebrations of Romanov rule. They were designed to whip up national fervour and adoration for the Tsar and, if photographs of the events are anything to go by, the Tsar achieved his aim. However, within four years the Romanov dynasty had been

overthrown and it was the communists who showed how effective propaganda could really be in helping to control opposition. Both Lenin and Stalin focused on creating a cult of personality. Posters, photographs, statues, written articles and broadcasts were all used to promote Russian leaders as heroes to be worshipped. Ordinary citizens who carried out worthy deeds were held up as examples for others to follow. Of particular note was the case of Pavlik Maraozov who was hailed as a loyal communist youth for denouncing his father as a kulak. All aspects of Russian life were influenced by the communist propaganda machine including the media, education, the arts, work and leisure. It was virtually impossible to escape promotion of communism as the only way worth living. In this sense, the population was indoctrinated which greatly lessened the chance of any kind of opposition proliferating.

7 The nature and extent of opposition under the two different regimes had less of an impact on its success. Throughout the period, there was never a united opposition against rulers. The People's Will, a minority group that broke away from the Land and Liberty movement, was successful in assassinating Alexander II in 1881 but this did not lead to the end of Romanov rule; in fact it resulted in the period of the Reaction. The Social Democrats, formed in 1898, were in disarray by 1905, having split into the two factions of the Mensheviks and Bolsheviks. The Bolsheviks remained a minority opposition group and it was extraordinary that they were eventually responsible for overthrowing the Provisional Government. The Socialist Revolutionaries that came into being in 1901 had divided into the 'left' and 'right' in 1905 and the liberals consisted of the Kadets and Octobrists. Divisions in opposition continued under the communists with the uncoordinated activity of the Whites and Greens during the Civil War, the continuation of the left and right split during the time of Lenin and the fragmented dissent from some peasants, workers, Politburo members, military leaders and national minority groups during the time of Stalin. Thus, at no time was the unity and strength of opposition a decisive factor in determining its success.

> 7 This paragraph contains a well-expressed and strong argument that adds balance to the response.

8 Opposition under the tsars was more successful than under the communists mainly because the tsars were never consistent and systematic enough in destroying it. In attempting to appease dissenters, reforms were allowed which only resulted in a strengthening of opposition. The communists on the other hand, were adept at blending different tools of repression together to ensure that anti-revolutionaries were never allowed to flourish. They were especially good at exploiting circumstance and ensuring that tough measures were always promoted as being in the best interests of the people. Even when reforms seemed 'genuine' they were often disguised so that the Russian people were never free from being under the total control of a communist dictatorship.

> 8 The conclusion makes a judgement which follows on from the main part of the essay.

> **Assessment for Essay 1**
>
> Uses a wide range of accurate, detailed and relevant evidence. Accurate and confident use of appropriate historical terminology. Answer is clearly structured and mostly coherent. **[Level IA: 18 marks out of 20]**
>
> Shows a good understanding of key concepts relevant to the question set. Good synthesis and synoptic assessment of the whole period. Answer is consistently analytical with developed and substantiated explanations. **[Level IA: 38 marks out of 40]**
>
> The overall mark of 56 would take this into the A* bracket. If the answer has a weakness it lies in an assessment of the relative importance of factors. This, on balance, has been done implicitly.

Essay 2: Explain why the opponents of the tsars from 1855 to 1917 were more successful than those who opposed the communist regime from 1917 to 1964

1 The introduction discusses the nature of opposition under the different regimes but gives no indication of why levels of success varied.

1 There was always opposition to tsarist rule but this was not always the case with the communist regime. The tsars faced opposition from a number of individuals and groups including the Populists, the Socialist Revolutionaries (SRs), the Social Democrats (SDs) and Liberals. Under the communists, opposition groups were banned but there was still resistance. One key similarity between the tsars and the communists is that they both faced opposition from national minorities seeking to gain independence.

2 This section is quite full but very descriptive. A chronological approach has been adopted whereas a thematic structure would have been better.

2 Alexander II faced opposition from Populists such as Land and Liberty who believed that by preaching to peasants about inequality and injustice they would rise up and overthrow the autocratic tsarist regime. However, 'Going to the People' as it was called failed as the peasants didn't like being told what to do and Land and Liberty was divided over what was the best strategy to adopt. A splinter group called the People's Will (formed in 1879) believed that the only way to create effective change was through the use of violence. One of their aims was to assassinate the Tsar in the hope that autocracy would then be replaced by democracy. When they finally achieved their aim, in 1881, this only led to a backlash from the new Tsar, Alexander III. Thus, violent methods did not lead to a long-term solution to issues relating to authoritarian rule.

3 The chronological approach is continued although there is far more of an attempt in this section to offer explanation.

3 Alexander III thought his father had been too soft on opposition which helps explain why groups such as the People's Will achieved some success. The response was to introduce more repression and overturn some of the reforms made by Alexander II. Despite this, better organised opposition groups emerged and developed after 1881. The Socialist Revolutionaries carried on the tradition of the People's Will by using violent methods to achieve their aims. From 1901 to 1905 they assassinated thousands of politicians including Grand Duke Sergei. They were also successful in getting much widespread support from peasants. The main reason for this was they promised to deal with peasant land issues if they gained power. This was something that the tsars had failed to do after the issuing of the 1861 Emancipation Edict.

4 Another important group was the Social Democrats who formed in 1898. They were Marxists who believed in revolution but were less violent in outlook than the SRs. However, like the SRs, they were divided in opinion over the best strategies to adopt to achieve their aims. Eventually it was the Bolshevik splinter group that, in October 1917, finally overthrew the Provisional Government. This was an astonishing achievement given that the Bolsheviks did not have the level of support that other groups had. What this illustrates is that the reason for the success of the opposition in 1917 was more to do with the weaknesses of the Provisional Government rather than the strengths of the Bolsheviks.

4 Again, there is quite a good attempt here to offer explanation. The paragraph also illustrates how a theme, the strategies and tactics of the opposition, could be used to provide a reason for the success of opposition under the tsars. The structure of the essay could have been improved if mini-themes such as this had been developed synoptically (i.e. one theme covering the whole period per paragraph).

5 There was also opposition to the tsars from liberals who wanted to change the system from within. As they were more moderate in their views, the tsars seemed more willing to listen to their demands. Their main objective was to achieve the setting up of a democratically elected Constituent Assembly. The October Manifesto of 1905 and the subsequent setting up of the *Duma* indicated that, to some extent, the Liberals were successful. The 'new' liberals that emerged after 1905, especially the Kadets and Octobrists, went on to play an important role in influencing the business of the *Duma*. But, it should be remembered that the reforms made by Nicholas II were not simply due to pressure from liberals; demonstrations and strikes from peasants and workers that occurred in 1905 also influenced the Tsar's thinking. It is also worth noting that through the Fundamental Laws, Nicholas II was able to manipulate the make up of the *Duma* and control the influence that opposition groups had.

5 This paragraph contains some useful material but drifts from explaining why the liberals were partly successful in achieving their aims. However, there is a sound piece of analysis at the end concerning why liberal success was limited.

6 To sum up the situation with the tsars, opposition was successful at times because it gradually became better organised and leading opposition groups learned how to appeal to the masses more effectively. Equally important was the fact that the tsars were not consistent in the way they dealt with opposition. Reforms were made which seemed to appease the people but they also led to more liberal thinking and behaviour and, therefore allowed opposition to flourish. When repression was used it seemed to cause backlash and resentment which boiled over into a full-scale revolution in 1917. If the tsars had stuck more rigidly to autocracy then maybe the revolution would not have occurred.

6 This is a well-considered synthesis of the reasons for the varying degree of success of opposition under the tsars. But, it is bolted on to the previous paragraphs. More effective planning would have ensured that this material was blended in more appropriately.

7 By contrast, the communists did stick to repression as a way of dealing with those who opposed them. Lenin effectively used the *Cheka* and the Red Army to defeat the Whites and Greens during the Civil War. He used the same bodies to enforce War Communism. Stalin took repression to another level by employing the NKVD (that replaced the *Cheka*) to 'police' collectivisation and his Five-Year Plans. The secret police were involved in the arrest of bourgeois elements, 'wreckers' and saboteurs who were put on trial and either then sent to labour camps (*Gulags*) or executed. Show trials and purges (especially during the early 1930s) were employed to spread Terror.

7 This is a well-synthesised paragraph that focuses on repression under the communists and which shows a fair understanding of change and continuity over time. It could have been improved by emphasising that Lenin and Stalin used reforms to repress and that this approach was reinforced through the deployment of more direct methods (secret police, purges, etc.).

All of this was reinforced by the use of propaganda and censorship. It was the systematic and integrated way in which Stalin used repression which led to the elimination of opposition throughout his period of rule.

8 It could be argued that there was more opposition during the period of communist rule than is often supposed. But, the difference, compared with the tsarist period, was that opposition was less well organised and widespread. The communists banned political parties and the use of Terror meant that people were afraid to form organisations that might have the collective power to topple the ruling élite. During Khrushchev's period in power, destalinisation led to a slackening of control over the population and, once again, a rise in protests. However, Khrushchev still consistently used the Red Army and the secret police to keep opposition in its place. This was especially true of states such as Hungary who wanted to break away from the USSR. In 1956, Khrushchev sent Russian tanks to suppress the dissident regime of Nagy.

9 To conclude, opposition under the tsars was more successful during the communist period of rule due to effective organisation, strategies, tactics and leadership. An inconsistent approach to dealing with opposition by the tsars and the Provisional Government also contributed to success. Under the communists, opposition had very little success simply because the ideology and methods employed by the leadership did not allow this to happen. Nevertheless, the only time during the whole period when opposition could be said to be genuinely successful was in October 1917. Even then, this had as much to do with the effects of the First World War as it did with the relative strengths and weaknesses of regimes and their opponents.

8 There is some good analysis and evaluation here but some of the observations needed supporting with 'evidence'. The point about Khrushchev is well made and indicates an awareness of the need to cover the whole period.

9 A solid conclusion that focuses on making judgements.

Assessment for Essay 2

Uses mostly accurate, detailed and relevant evidence, which demonstrates a competent command of the topic. Generally accurate use of historical terminology. Answer is structured and mostly coherent. **[Level II: 14 marks out of 20]**

Sound understanding of key concepts relevant to analysis and mostly focused on the question set. The answer is something of a mixture of analysis and explanation but also description of events. Some of the analysis is uneven and there is a drift, in places, away from synthesising material. **[Level III: 25 marks out of 40]**

The overall mark of 39 would result in the award of a high grade C. The candidate has covered a good range of relevant material but needed to focus more on explaining *why* rather than *how* some opposition was more successful than others. The chronological approach adopted hinders attempts to analyse and evaluate the key issues effectively.

3 Impact of Dictatorial Regimes on Economy and Society

OVERVIEW

This chapter analyses the effects of the tsarist and communist regimes on the Russian economy and society. The main focus is on the pace and extent of change. It is also important to consider the relationship between policies and economic and social change. Were reforms put into place to improve working and living conditions or did government policies lead to a deterioration in the quality of life for the Russian people? These issues will be tackled under the following headings:

- The extent of economic change
- The extent of social change
- Living and working conditions of rural and urban people
- Civil rights
- Conclusion: the pace and extent of economic and social change

Note making

Arrange your notes under the sub-headings in each section. Keep them concise but include a decent range of examples, including statistics, to illustrate key points. You may wish to experiment with different types of note taking for each key section, for example, spider diagrams, mind maps, charts, tables. Also, be aware of the need to be clear about some of the technical language used in this chapter, for example, industrialisation, economy, economic growth. Sometimes students use words inappropriately and out of context which can detract from the quality of response to examination questions.

1 | The extent of economic change

Industrialisation

Key question
How far was industrialisation throughout the period motivated mainly by a desire to catch up with the West?

Industrialisation is the term given to the manufacture of goods in workshops and factories. Throughout the period from 1855 to 1964 Russian leaders were keen to accelerate the industrialising process although there was a consistent emphasis on heavy (iron, steel, coal and engineering) as opposed to light industry. This was connected to the main motive for industrialising which was to 'catch up with the West'; the great Western powers, especially Britain, France and Germany (after 1871) had seemingly based their economic progress on the development of the iron and coal industries. Russian leaders sought to emulate the industrial revolutions that had occurred in these countries as they believed this was the obvious way to increase and maintain world power status. However, the methods used to achieve this varied from leader to leader according to the circumstances they found themselves in.

Russian industrialisation proceeded through different phases due to differences in political leadership but also because of a changing world context. However, a common thread that affected development was the relationship with agricultural activity and the peculiar nature of Russian society. This needs to be borne in mind when analysing and evaluating the following stages of growth.

Alexander II and the proto-management of the economy

Before Alexander II (1855–81) there had been a reluctance to engage in industrialisation as this was associated with the rise of an urban proletariat, which, in other countries, had displayed a propensity to revolt. However, Alexander II recognised that the threat of peasant unrest was just as great and that this could be dealt with to an extent by moving rural workers off the land and into industry. Factories warranted a '**new work discipline**' from which evolved a way of controlling the activities of the bulk of the population.

Therefore, the rule of Alexander II marked a more committed move towards state involvement in industry with the appointment of Mikhail Reutern (1862–78) as Minister of Finance. He adopted a sensible approach that revolved around continued railway construction, the attraction of foreign technical expertise and the employment of foreign investment capital. As a result modernisation and expansion occurred within the 'staples' (iron, coal, textiles) as well as the newer industries (for example, oil). For example, Ludwig Loop from Manchester helped develop the Russian textile industry and the Nobel brothers were responsible for the growth of the modern oil industry around Baku in the Caucasus.

Equally impressive was the work of the Welshman, J.J. Hughes, who transformed iron and steel production at Ekaterinoslav. He was employed in 1871 by the Russian government as an expert in

Key term

New work discipline
Factory owners introduced strict rules and regulations that were required for employees to work safely and efficiently with machines. This was especially important for recruits from the countryside who were used to working according to 'nature's clock'.

the manufacture of armour plate. By 1884 his New Russian Coal, Iron and Railmaking Company was the largest producer of pig iron in the whole of the empire. By the start of the twentieth century Hughes and his associates were also responsible for about half of the steel production of Russia. This was accompanied by social investment; Hughes constructed a new town, Yuzovo, replete with English schools, public houses and, by 1904, 32,000 Welsh Russians! This was a clear demonstration of the value of employing foreign technical expertise to move Russia forwards and was a trend that continued throughout the period.

Railway construction

The use of foreign expertise was not entirely new and this was well illustrated in the field of railway construction. The first railway in Russia was completed in 1837 during the reign of Nicholas I and was the work of Gerstner, an Austrian. This was followed by the more ambitious St Petersburg to Moscow line which opened in 1851. The project was stimulated by the success of the Manchester to Liverpool railway although the final design and construction were mainly influenced by the American engineer George Washington Whistler. It was built to a very high technical standard and illustrated that where there was a will there was also a way for Russia to keep up with Western counterparts.

Reutern built on this foundation so that there was a sevenfold increase in the amount of railway track opened from 3532 km in 1862 to 22,498 km in 1878. Through the capacity of railways to 'break bulk' (carry large quantities of heavy, bulky goods) at speed, this expansion gave a significant boost to the industrial sector. It was undoubtedly a major reason for the doubling of industrial output and an average annual growth rate of six per cent during Reutern's term of office. In fact, Clive Trebilcock has claimed that this was 'the country's first respectable performance in manufacturing' and so impressive that it allowed Russia to cushion itself against the European economic depression from 1873 to 1882.

Railway construction further illustrated the importance of attracting foreign investment capital. Reutern secured foreign monies and investment through a variety of novel approaches including the issuing of **government bonds**, **taxation exemptions** and **monopoly concessions**. Some of the money that went straight to the Russian government was used to protect railway projects against failure. Wherever possible, construction was placed in the hands of private contractors (as was the norm in the West) and, to secure their services, the government made guarantees to bail out projects if they encountered financial difficulties. This inevitably resulted in a certain amount of corruption (for example, financial help was given to certain companies when it was not really needed) as well as an expensive transport system. Due to the very high costs of construction and operation, about 94 per cent of railway lines were in private hands by 1880.

Key terms

Break bulk
The carriage of low-value, high-density goods in large quantities. That is, heavy, bulky goods such as coal and iron ore.

Government bonds
A way of investing in the government by buying bonds (loan certificates) and cashing them in at later date with interest.

Taxation exemptions
Being allowed to pay lower tax in return for lending money to the government.

Monopoly concessions
Being given the right to be the only seller of a particular good.

According to Clive Trebilcock, Reutern created the 'first (proto) state managed exercise in industrial advance' but, as with other economic ministers, his efforts were cut short by the coming of war (Russo-Turkish War, 1877–8). Nevertheless, he paved the way for others to follow, especially Sergei Witte.

Reforms after the death of Alexander II

After Reutern's demise and the assassination of Alexander II in 1881, further economic reforms were enacted by the new Finance Minister, Nikolay Bunge (1882–6). These included fiscal amendments (the abolition of Salt Tax in 1881, a tax on salt, and in 1886 the Poll Tax, a tax based on the number of people in a household), the creation in 1883 of a **Peasant Land Bank** and a move towards greater state ownership of the railways. The latter started a process that eventually led to 69 per cent of the system being under public control by 1911.

This more liberal approach did not last long as Alexander III blamed Bunge for a dramatic fall in the value of the rouble in the mid-1880s and replaced him with Ivan Vyshnegradskii (1887–92). This man was more of a hardliner but managed to balance the government budget while also making a surplus of income. He achieved this through more efficient utilisation of income from taxes, railways, crown properties, the state bank and treasury. More significant was the revenue raised through the **Medele'ev tariff of 1891** and income gained by exporting large amounts of grain even when there was the prospect of a domestic shortage and starvation. The 1891 famine was seen partly as a result of Vyshnegradskii's policies, and despite his other achievements, he was forced to give way to Count Witte (1893–1903).

The 'Great Spurt'

The appointment of Witte marked a distinct break from the past. Previous ministers had attempted to stimulate Russian industrialisation but in relative terms their achievements were modest. By 1893, Russian economic activity still revolved predominantly around agricultural production. Witte was the first one to show total commitment to industrialisation in an attempt both to compete with other industrialised nations and to improve Russian military capability. This was to be achieved mainly at the expense of agriculture (part of the so-called 'substitution' effect, with more investment being made in industry than agriculture), which caused suspicion and consternation among sections of the Russian élite. Witte claimed that 'all thinking Russia was against me' which emphasises how radical he thought his approach was. The main strands of his plan were as follows:

- Witte resurrected Reutern's idea of encouraging foreign experts to come to Russia.
- Witte also went back to the idea of taking out foreign loans, raising taxes and interest rates to boost available capital for investment in industry.

Key terms

Peasant Land Bank A bank especially set up by the government to allow peasants to borrow money at relatively cheap rates to allow the purchase of land.

Medele'ev tariff of 1891 Named after Dimitry Medele'ev who put together a 700-page book of tariffs (taxes) that should be applied to all imports of goods.

- A major development was the placement, in 1897, of the rouble on the **gold standard**. The idea behind this was to give potential investors confidence in the value of the Russian currency.
- Witte insisted that most investment went on heavy industry and the railways as this was what had made Britain, France and Germany great economic powers and had already reaped some dividends for Russia.
- Further industrialisation was to be planned and managed mainly by the state with a move away from private enterprise.

The effect of this was a so-called 'Great Spurt' in economic and industrial activity which resulted in the following:

- Coal production doubled and that of iron and steel increased sevenfold.
- A stimulus was provided to the development of more specialist and 'new' technologies in the oil and chemical industries.
- The total amount of railway track opened rose from 29,183 km in 1891 to 52,612 km in 1901. Much of this was facilitated by the stupendous growth in capital from abroad which increased on average 120 per cent every year from 1893 to 1898.
- Income earned from industry shot up from 42 million roubles in 1893 to 161 million roubles by 1897.

There was also indication that Russia had at last started to catch up with other industrialised nations; by 1900, for example, France had been ousted into fourth place in world iron production. All of this, according to Trebilcock, led to an annual average rate of increase in industrial production of 7.5 per cent, 'far exceeding Russian achievement for any comparable period before 1914 and establishing one of the most impressive performances in late nineteenth-century Europe'.

Criticisms of Witte's policies

However, some historians have argued that Witte's achievements have been exaggerated. First, Witte focused on the development of heavy industry and neglected other parts of the industrial sector such as engineering and textiles. This was short-sighted, as to an extent the demand for metals (and hence coal) came from other industries such as cotton textiles. Second, the reliance on foreign capital has been criticised as being dangerous as loans could be recalled at short notice and reliance on foreign technological expertise stunted the emergence of home-grown talent. Third, although the railway system expanded considerably it was still very costly and not as impressive as what existed in other parts of Europe. By 1914, for instance, Russia had 11 times fewer kilometres of track per unit of land than Germany. Most railway investment was made in the Trans-Siberian line started in 1892 (but never fully completed). Although this greatly aided the industrial and agricultural expansion of Siberia it was rushed and poorly constructed. Finally, Witte paid scant attention to agriculture which caused rural discontent and distrust from other members of the government. This was one of the key reasons for his downfall in 1903.

Some believe that Witte's industrial programme was a dress rehearsal for Stalin's industrialisation of the 1930s. There are similarities but there was no 'natural' progression from one to the other. The First World War and the Russian revolutions ensured further twists in the move to greater industrialisation.

The First World War and industrialisation

In August 1903 Witte was dismissed from his post. Nicholas II had developed an **expansionist foreign policy** which Witte opposed mainly on the grounds of cost. This also coincided with a dip in the economy. However, Witte's fall in favour was short lived. After a disastrous war against Japan (1904–5) and the social unrest of 1905 Witte was appointed Prime Minister. Pyotr Stolypin was put in place as Minister for Finance and their joint efforts resulted in a revival of the economy. From 1909 to 1913 industrial output increased on average by seven per cent a year and gross national product (GNP) by 3.5 per cent a year.

Some historians have reflected on this economic performance after 1905 and argued, counterfactually, that without the First World War Russia would have caught up rapidly with the West. Other evidence suggests this would not have been the case. By 1913 the overall production levels in particular industries still lagged considerably behind those of competitors. For example, Russian coal production at the start of the war was 10 per cent of that produced by Britain and **GNP per capita** was only 20 per cent of that found in Britain. Although production had increased in many industries productivity had not. The factories that were in operation employed vast amounts of labour to compensate for a lack of investment in modern technology and equipment. Despite this the vast number of industrial workers were employed in small-scale, handicraft-based enterprise; this was not the sign of a developing economy. Many of the gains that appeared to be made on behalf of the Russian people were masked by a substantial increase in the size of the population. Given the lack of attention paid to agriculture the chances of further periods of starvation were high.

The fact that the Russian economy fell apart during the First World War adds further weight to the argument that Witte's reforms had only a short-term positive effect. Despite having the largest stock of gold reserves in Europe in 1914, this was still not enough to pay for the armaments required to fight a successful war. Industry struggled to meet the demands of the armed forces and the railway system was found to be wanting with respect to efficiency. More money was borrowed from abroad, taxes increased even higher and the gold standard was abandoned. This led to rampant inflation. The price of fuel and food quadrupled in the first two years of the conflict and wages failed to keep up. The First World War was yet another disastrous war for Russia but this time with far more dramatic consequences. By the end of 1917 the Romanov dynasty had ended and was

---

Key terms

Expansionist foreign policy
Foreign policy that involved the acquisition of territory from other countries (or sometimes expanding influence over such territory).

GNP per capita
Gross national product per head of the population. This is often used as a measure of living standards.

replaced by Bolshevik rule; this marked a major turning point in the way the Russian economy was to be managed.

War Communism and the New Economic Policy (NEP)

By November 1917 Lenin had started to deal with the exigencies of war by introducing State Capitalism. This involved the state taking complete control of the economy until it could be 'safely' handed over to the proletariat. This was not part of some grand plan; it was simply a reaction to the crisis situation that the Bolsheviks found themselves in. Nevertheless, it still fitted with (or was made to fit) Bolshevik ideology. State Capitalism was introduced by way of the following:

- November 1917 Decree on Land. This involved the division of private landholdings that were then handed over to peasants.
- November 1918 Decree on Workers Control. Workers' Committees were given 'extra' powers to run factories.
- December 1917 Formation of the Supreme Economic Council (SEC). The SEC was formed to manage key industries that were **nationalised** by the Bolsheviks. This did not prevent 'local' nationalisation occurring via soviets (workers' councils). The nationalisation process was therefore tightened by two further decrees: one in the summer of 1918 and the other in the spring of 1919. These resulted in the nationalisation of all enterprises employing more than 10 workers and without compensation. The effect was to create over 30,000 nationalised economic entities by 1920 ranging from windmills to huge steel plants. The SEC soon struggled to cope with the management of this (and was soon made subservient to the more powerful Council of Labour and Defence, personally chaired by Lenin).

Lenin obviously believed centralised control of this nature was essential if Russia was to survive the effects of war. However, there was much opposition to it both within and outside the party. This was further fuelled by the signing of the Treaty of Brest-Litovsk in March 1918. Russia struck a peace deal with Germany but only after agreeing to hand over valuable territory. For Lenin, this was an essential move as it shortened a conflict that was likely to end in total ruination of the economy. He also knew that it was likely to hasten the move towards civil war and the creation of further economic problems.

The Civil War (1917–21) pretty much nullified any positive impact that State Capitalism may have had. Industrial output in a number of sectors fell dramatically. Inflation had got so out of hand that the rouble by October 1920 was worth only one per cent of its value in 1917. This resulted in the virtual abandonment of the currency so that, for example, 90 per cent of all wages paid to workers by the start of 1921 were '**in kind**'. Some services such as tram rides were free as it was impossible to pay for them. Such a drastic situation clearly required a change of approach.

Key terms

Nationalised
The state control of industry and commerce by taking ownership of the means of production, distribution and exchange of goods and services.

In kind
Payment other than by using money, such as the exchange of goods and services.

War Communism

During the Civil War, Lenin used State Capitalism alongside grain requisitioning to create what was labelled War Communism. The key features of War Communism were as follows:

- Nationalisation (state control) of larger enterprises and a state monopoly of markets for goods and services. The nationalisation of industry and state monopoly of markets caused unrest as it meant that individuals lost the freedom to produce and sell goods at a time, price and place that suited them. They lost all ownership and hence control over the means of production, distribution and exchange.
- Partial militarisation of labour. The militarisation of labour was also disliked as people were forced to work solely to meet the needs of the war.
- Forced requisitioning (taking) of agricultural produce. Grain requisitioning was the most hated policy as it involved taking away surpluses of food and grain which meant a disincentive to grow more than was actually needed by an individual household. Often, the majority of food would be taken from a household to feed the army and urban workers. The overall result was starvation in rural areas.

By 1921 workers, peasants and party members were clamouring for something 'new' to resolve the hardships caused by both the First World War and the Civil War. It is debatable as to how far Lenin viewed War Communism as a short-term emergency measure but he was quick to change tack and replaced it with his New Economic Policy (NEP).

New Economic Policy (NEP)

The key features of the NEP were as follows:

- Denationalisation of small-scale enterprise and a return to private ownership. This was to allow small workshops to flourish to produce consumer items such as clothes and shoes.
- The continuation of state control of heavy industry but with the use of trusts. These organisations were to pay strict attention to accounting procedures and were responsible for the purchase of raw materials and equipment and the payment of wages.
- Rejuvenation of trade through the removal of restrictions on the private sales of goods and services. Shops flourished, rationing was ended and a new, revalued rouble was introduced.
- A return to the encouragement of foreign trade, investment and the import of foreign expertise.
- An end to grain requisitioning and a return to peasants being allowed to sell surpluses in local markets.

The short-term impact was impressive. Industrial output increased rapidly and this was reflected in the greater amount of food and consumer goods found in shops and markets (see Table 3.1). This was linked to the emergence of a new breed of

Table 3.1: Russian agricultural and industrial production 1921–6

	1921	1922	1923	1924	1925	1926
Grain harvest (millions of tonnes)	37.6	50.3	56.6	51.4	72.5	76.8
Sown area (millions of hectares)	90.3	77.7	91.7	98.1	104.3	110.3
Industrial (factory) production (millions of roubles at 1926–7 value)	2,004	2,619	4,005	4,660	7,739	11,083
Coal (millions of tonnes)	8.9	9.5	13.7	16.1	18.1	27.6
Electricity (million of kilowatt-hours)	1,945	775	1,146	1,562	2,925	3,508
Pig iron (thousands of tonnes)	116	188	309	755	1,535	2,441
Steel (thousands of tonnes)	183	392	709	1,140	2,135	3,141
Cotton fabrics (millions of metres)	105	349	691	963	1,688	2,286
Rail freight carried (millions of tonnes)	39.4	39.9	58.0	67.5	83.4	–*

*Data not available.
Source: A. Nove, *An Economic History of the U.S.S.R.*, Allen Lane (1969).

entrepreneur, the **Nepman**. By 1923 Nepmen were responsible for over 60 per cent of retail trade but they had already started to annoy people with their underhand wheeling and dealing. Another cause for concern by that time was the emergence of what Trotsky called the 'scissors crisis'. The supply of food increased at a rate that far exceeded domestic demand, resulting in a swift fall in prices. In comparison, the supply of manufactured goods increased at a much slower pace which left prices relatively high. Peasants were therefore reluctant to sell surpluses at low prices but the frustration was that industrialists needed them to do this so that they could afford to buy their products. As the historian J.N. Westwood has pointed out this was 'less serious than it seemed at the time' and the Bolshevik government quickly found a way of resolving the problem.

As with War Communism, the NEP was promoted by the Politburo as 'a temporary deviation, a tactical retreat'. Despite this, debate raged over the extent to which the NEP was a betrayal of the October Revolution. This was partially resolved with a demand for political unity after the fright of the 1921 Kronstadt rising (see page 84). With the death of Lenin, though, in 1924, and the ensuing power struggle, the divisions within government widened and centred around the efficacy of the NEP. Those in favour of continuation were known as the Rightists (right opposition) and those that opposed were called the Leftists (left opposition). During this time Stalin remained fairly ambivalent about the NEP but as the longer term effects of it were felt he became a major critic. This coincided with him taking leadership in 1929 and it was not long before he abandoned the NEP and created the Great Turn.

Nepman
The 'new' type of businessman that emerged as a result of the NEP.

Key term

Stalin, Khrushchev and the Five-Year Plans

There were two general aims that underpinned Stalinist economic policy. One was to launch a war against Russia's tsarist past. Stalin believed that Russia had failed to keep up with the West due to the incompetence of the tsarist regimes but more generally because the tsars were enemies of the workers. Only with a system that allowed more worker autonomy and that encouraged workers to believe that they were the key to economic success, would Russia become a major industrial force. The second aim was to prepare for potential conflict with Russia's capitalist enemies. The development of heavy industry was the key to expansion and modernisation of the armed forces which was essential to the defence of Russia. These aims were also linked to the wish for **economic autarky**.

Stalin believed that the only way his aims could be achieved was by abandoning the NEP completely and replacing it with a policy that revolved around strict state control and centralised planning. Industrialisation was to be stimulated through the setting of production targets. These targets were to be achieved over a five-year period. From 1929 to 1964 there were seven Five-Year Plans. Ironically, this policy involved very little strategic planning in the modern sense. Targets were set by the ruling élite and were often based on very flimsy research. Managers at local level were ordered to achieve them and were in constant fear of failing.

In theory, there was a structure to the target setting and planning process. It resembled the following:

- Initial targets were stipulated by key officials in the party. **Gosplan** (the State Planning Commission) was given the task of researching and calculating figures needed for target setting for individual industries.
- Targets and other appropriate information were then passed on to industrial commissariats to frame a plan of some sort for clearly defined areas of economic activity. Initially there were four commissariats (heavy industry, which was the most important, light industry, timber and food). By the beginning of the third Five-Year Plan there were 20 of these bodies.
- The 'plans' were then passed on to regional managers/directors to implement. In reality, the plans were little more than very detailed instructions about what had to be achieved. There was very little guidance on how targets were to be arrived at and on the availability of resources needed to support the planning process.

The first plan was officially introduced in spring 1929 at the 16th Party Congress. As it was outlined then, it rather bizarrely covered the period from October 1928 to September 1933. In practice, the first plan, as with the second, did not run its full course. This was due to the government exaggerating achievement, claiming that the plans were so successful, in hindsight, that targets had been met well ahead of schedule. The reality was that workers had struggled to meet what were totally unrealistic targets especially after Stalin audaciously decided to revise them upwards towards the end of each plan. Nevertheless centralised planning was the main characteristic of industrialisation until the end of the period. A summary of what was achieved can be seen in Table 3.2 on page 112.

Key terms

Economic autarky
When a country can provide all of the resources it needs without having to trade.

Gosplan
A group originally set up in 1921 to plan for industrialisation and economic growth.

Table 3.2: Achievements of the Five-Year Plans 1928–60

Product	1928	1940	1945	1960
Electricity (millions of kilowatt-hours)	5.0	48.3	43.3	292
Oil (millions of tonnes)	11.6	31.1	19.4	148
Coal (millions of tonnes)	35.5	166	150	510
Gas (millions of cubic metres)	0.3	3.4	3.4	47.2
Steel (millions of tonnes)	4.3	18.3	12.3	65.3
Tractors (thousands)	1.3	31.6	7.7	238
Plastics and synthetics (thousands of tonnes)	–	10.9	21.3	312
Clocks and watches (millions)	0.9	2.8	0.3	26
Cement (millions of tonnes)	1.8	5.7	1.8	46

Source: J.N. Westwood, *Endurance and Endeavour: Russian History 1812–2001*, Oxford University Press (2002).

The statistics in Table 3.2 need to be treated with some caution. They are based partly on 'official records' but also on adjustments made by historians to compensate for inaccuracy. Under the first two plans, managers quite obviously submitted false claims about production levels as they feared the possible consequences of not achieving the targets that they were set. Fabrication of production levels backfired on the managers when Stalin became so impressed with achievement that he revised the targets. However, it is understandable why they did this given the climate of fear that had been manufactured. Nevertheless, the statistical 'evidence' suggests that each plan had a fair amount of success. Interestingly, the greatest achievement would appear to be during the post-war period. Much of this was down to ordinary Russian people working extraordinarily hard to rebuild their country rather than effective planning. Khrushchev's continuation of centralised planning resulted in further economic growth and more diversification in what was produced. But, his first plan was abandoned and his second correlated with a slowdown in the rate of growth which makes Khrushchev's achievements less impressive than Stalin's.

All of the plans had strengths as well as limitations as outlined in Table 3.3.

Key term

Consumer industries
These included any industries producing goods and services for direct consumption by the population (for example, those producing clothing, ovens, cooking utensils, toys for children).

Table 3.3: Successes and limitations of the Five-Year Plans 1928–65

Plan	Successes	Limitations
1: Oct. 1928–Dec. 1932	There were significant increases in the output of heavy industry The engineering industry developed considerably especially with respect to the production of machine tools and turbines New specialised industrial centres emerged, for example, Magnitogorsk in the Urals Agriculture was stimulated as tractor works expanded	**Consumer industries** were neglected causing discontent among certain sectors of society Small specialist workshops disappeared A shortage of skilled workers was apparent. This was partly due to show trials and purges Although production levels rose, targets were not met. There was quite a dramatic shortfall in some industries such as chemicals

Table 3.3: Successes and limitations of the Five-Year Plans 1928–65 (*cont'd*)

Plan	Successes	Limitations
2: Jan. 1933–Dec. 1937	The electricity industry took off and heavy industry built on the base laid by the first plan. Over 4500 new enterprises were started	Consumer industries continued to decline although some flourished, for example, footwear, meat packaging, ice-cream
	Engineering became self-sufficient and no longer relied on imports of specialist equipment	The oil industry was very slow to expand compared with Western counterparts
	Something resembling a genuine transport and communications network was put in place	
	The chemical industry made up for the lack of progress during the first plan	
	Certain metals were mined for the first time – tin, zinc and copper	
	Specialised training schemes for workers were implemented	
	Targets were scaled down and a more rational approach to planning was adopted	
	The commissariats were better organised and more effective	
3: Jan. 1938–June 1941	Production and productivity in heavy industry continued to be impressive although regional variations became more apparent	Russia's entry into the war (1941) led to a diversion of resources to fuel the war effort
	There was a notable improvement in the quantity and quality of armaments produced	There was a shortage of raw materials
		There was generally a slowdown in the pace of progress. Some historians have attributed this to the purges as well as the war
		By the end of the third Five-Year Plan there were many features of a lack of planning: shortages, bottlenecks and a lack of 'expert' workers
4: 1946–50	Seemed to be linked to a rapid recovery of the economy. Pre-war production levels were reached within three years	Russian people were placed under extreme pressure to help Russia get back on its feet
5: 1951–5 (presented in Oct. 1952)	This was a period of fairly rapid growth especially with respect to agricultural equipment	Too many resources were devoted to 'projects' that had little positive economic benefit, for example, hydroelectric schemes
6: 1956–60	There was a shift from the old staple (for example, textiles) to modern industries, for example, plastics and synthetics	Over-optimistic targets were set, resulting in the plan being abandoned after two years
	Consumer goods became more prevalent	
7: 1959 (revised to 1961)–65	Substantial increase overall in production of a range of goods	Signs that the rate of growth in production slowed down especially when compared with rivals such as the USA
	Setting of more realistic targets	

Summary diagram: The industrialisation of Russia

Under the Tsars
- The growth of proto-industry/early factory system, production plants and the railway
- The 'Great Spurt'
- The impact of the First World War

Result: rapid economic growth at times comparable with Western counterparts

↓

Industrialisation
- All rulers, except Khrushchev, focused on the development of heavy industry to the detriment of consumer industry

↑

Under the Communists
- State Capitalism
- War Communism
- Centralised planning: the seven Five-Year Plans

Result: rapid, but variable economic growth, greater than under the tsars and comparable with Western counterparts

---

Agriculture

Agriculture remained an important industry in its own right throughout the period. The majority of the population continued to be employed in agricultural work despite moves to industrialise Russia. The tsars and the communists had two things in common when it came to agricultural policy making. First, agriculture was always seen as subservient to the needs of industry. Thus, government policies focused on reforms that increased food production and productivity to provide sustenance for the expanding urban proletariat. Second, those who worked on the land were treated as second-class citizens. The poor treatment of peasants reflected the view that industry had to come first so that Russia could catch up and compete with the West.

Key question
To what extent did government policies have a positive impact on the development of agriculture during the period from 1855 to 1964?

Land ownership

The issue of peasant land ownership was one that all Russian rulers failed to deal with effectively. Under the tsars, land redistribution policies never met the rising expectations of the peasants. Under the communists, all land was appropriated and it was managed by the state. However, this simply fuelled resentment especially as it was evident that the ruling élite and hangers-on kept aside a fair amount of land for personal use.

The emancipation of the serfs 1861

The issue of land ownership started with the Emancipation Edict of February 1861. Before the edict peasants were the property of landowners or the state and lived and worked under a system known as serfdom. Being a serf meant that you were under the total control of a noble or the state and had no access to land. Yet peasants claimed they had a kind of 'natural' right to the land as they were the class in society that were constantly working the soil to feed the Russian population. Labour and military services were provided in return for food and shelter. Serfdom was really a form of slavery.

The conditions laid down by the edict were as follows:

- All privately owned serfs were freed. Those kept by the state were to be emancipated in 1866. Freedom entailed peasants being able to own property, run their own commercial enterprises and marry who they wished.
- Nobles had to hand over a proportion or allotment of land to peasants. This was measured and allocated by official surveyors.
- The state provided compensation to landowners which was often based on valuations way above the market level.
- Peasants had to help pay for the compensation through redemption payments (that is, repayments of loans that allowed peasants to make the compensation). These were to be paid over a 49-year period at six per cent interest. Legal rights to the land were only confirmed after the last payment was made. An alternative was for peasants to continue to work on the land of a noble for so many days in a year to compensate for their own land allocations.
- The administration of redemption payments was carried out by the village council of elders (the *mir*). This group also ensured that land could not be sold on before the final redemption payment had been made.

There was considerable opposition to the statute from landowners although the compensation clauses did much to allay their fears. In the long term though, the reform caused much unrest among the peasants and the nobility:

- Generally, peasants were allocated poorer quality land. They also received less, on average, than they had been farming before emancipation.
- Many peasants struggled to earn enough from the land to meet redemption payments. Financial difficulties were made worse by the necessity to pay rural poll taxes.
- Peasants were not totally free in so far as they had to answer to the *mir*. Decisions about what was to be produced and how crops were to be cultivated had to be made by the village elders. It was also the responsibility of the *mir* to ensure that the principle of **subsistence farming** was adhered to. As a result, more able peasant farmers had no incentive to produce surpluses and were reluctant to invest to improve the land.
- The nobility had been struggling to maintain their large estates before emancipation. Many had taken out large loans to help cover day-to-day costs. The revenue from redemption payments tended to be diverted to repay debts. If this failed estates were broken up and sold off. Thus, by 1905, the land owned by the nobility had been reduced by about 40 per cent.

Key term

Subsistence farming
Ensuring just enough was produced to keep members of a community fed over a given period.

Alexander III and agriculture

In 1891, during the reign of Alexander III there was a disastrous famine. The Tsar blamed this partly on poor farming techniques deployed by peasants. To encourage the spread of good practice a ministry of agriculture was established shortly after the famine. However, as the historian J.N. Westwood has pointed out, officials also claimed that rural troubles were due to the character of peasants. They were considered to be generally 'resentful, indolent, disrespectful, unruly and intoxicated'. The Tsar's solution to this problem was to employ a special kind of local official, the Land Captain, to keep discipline in rural areas.

The Stolypin reform

Rural unrest peaked during the years 1905–7. Nicholas II responded by instructing Stolypin, appointed as Prime Minister in 1906, to revamp government policy over land distribution. Stolypin's aim was to use land redistribution to build and strengthen the class of more able, educated and 'best' peasants. The hope was that they would then act as a role model for other peasants to follow as well as act as a force against the *mir*. To this end the Stolypin reform (or 'wager on the strong' as it was sometimes called) involved the following:

- Unused or poorly utilised land was made available to the Peasant Land Bank (established in 1883). Forward-looking peasants could then buy the land from the bank on favourable terms.
- Peasants who were still farming strips (small plots spread over two to three fields) due to the strength of the *mir* were given the right to **consolidate** their land into smallholdings (small farm units). Hereditary household plots were not affected by this and it was also stipulated that land could not be immediately sold on to non-peasants. These provisos were designed to ensure that the mainstay of the Russian rural economy became the small peasant farm run independently by peasants.

In reality, the plan backfired due to the following reasons:

- The process led to an expansion in the numbers joining the wealthier class of peasants who in theory would be more loyal to the Tsar. However, they were not totally satisfied with the stipulations of the Stolypin reform as they believed that the best land was still inaccessible to peasants.
- By 1914, about two million peasants left the village communes leaving some regions very short of rural labour. The First World War accelerated this trend. Such an exodus added to the challenge of keeping supplies of food going to the growing urban population.

Consolidate
The joining together of resources. In this context, smallholdings were granted that were equivalent to the area of the strips farmed under the old way of farming.

Key term

The Decree on Land

The Provisional Government did little to resolve land issues. During the July Days, peasants seized land by force. The Bolsheviks exploited this trend by promising 'Peace, Bread and Land'. By October 1917 the Bolsheviks had proclaimed that they were the party representing peasant and worker interests. Once they seized power they immediately issued their Decree on Land which aimed to ensure that the majority of peasants were kept onside. However, this did not stop the communists treating the peasants as an underclass in the same way that the tsars had done. War Communism (see page 108) was the prime example of the contempt shown for peasants, especially with the imposition of grain requisitioning.

War Communism and the *kulaks*

A major feature of War Communism was the forceful taking of grain from peasants who had supposedly hoarded surpluses. By this time Lenin had identified three types of peasant: the poor, the middling and the **kulak**. The latter were blamed for food shortages and were punished by having not only food but also seed corn and personal property confiscated. Committees of the village poor were set up with the sole aim of denouncing *kulaks* and, with the help of the *Cheka*, were used to 'unleash a class war'. In fact, although Lenin had changed his view about the importance of the peasants to the revolution, the latter were still viewed with disdain by the Bolsheviks. The consensus was that they were ignorant, backward and superstitious and worked against the interests of the proletariat. It was not surprising, therefore, that they became scapegoats for some of the economic problems experienced by the Bolsheviks in the years immediately following the revolution.

The NEP and the *kulaks*

When the NEP replaced War Communism, the attitude towards the *kulaks* changed. They started to be viewed as the 'more cultured and educated peasants'. Wealthier peasants seemed to grow in number and were more easily identifiable through official definition. In 1925, a *kulak* was a peasant who owned at least three cows (in 1928, the figure was increased to six). Despite being more tolerated, *kulaks* were still treated more severely than other rural folk. They suffered from higher taxes, were disenfranchised and their children were refused entry to state schools. But within the peasant class the *kulaks* were respected for being not being afraid to voice concerns about peasant working and living conditions. Here lies the real reason as to why the authorities were so intent on victimising the *kulaks*.

Collectivisation

Collectivisation refers to the process of bringing a number of small farm units together to form bigger farms. The idea was that peasants would then collaborate to produce as much food as

Key term

Kulaks
Peasants who accumulated wealth through producing a surplus of food and selling it at local markets. Under the tsars *kulaks* stood out and were disliked for being money-lenders. With the Bolsheviks it was never really clear as to who actually was a *kulak* as opposed to an ordinary peasant. However, Bolshevik leaders associated grain hoarding and therefore shortages with the *kulaks*. Needless to say, wealthier, more productive peasants were persecuted and blamed for the shortcomings of Bolshevik agricultural policy.

Social

possible to feed themselves and the growing urban proletariat. Farms would be managed so that land was utilised in the optimum way to ensure that nobody starved. This system was based on the belief that shortages were due mainly to surpluses being hoarded until they could be sold in markets at the highest possible prices. Such a practice was allowed under the NEP but Stalin came to view it as bourgeois and anti-revolutionary.

From the beginning, the Bolsheviks wanted to create collective farms but stalled as a result of resistance from peasants. Lenin urged the need for a gradual approach to collectivisation to be taken which would result in the creation of 'civilised cooperatives'. This was fine except that many considered it unacceptable during a food crisis. Thus, just before Stalin emerged as leader of Russia, only about three per cent of peasant farmers were working on a collective.

Mass collectivisation

The famine of 1927–8 prompted Stalin to push for mass collectivisation. He was more generally motivated by the wish to create 'socialism in the countryside'. In turn, this involved getting rid of the NEP, eradicating the so-called wealthier class of peasants (the *kulaks*) and marginalising 'rightists' who supported a more commercially based agricultural policy.

Stalin's collectivisation policy got underway in November 1929 and went hand in hand with 'the liquidation of the *kulaks* as a class'. Stalinists saw this as a 'class war in the countryside' that was

---

Dekulakisation

Under Stalin, collectivisation went hand-in-hand with dekulakisation. The treatment of *kulaks* during this period followed a similar pattern throughout Russia. Wealthier peasants were 'visited' by **Komsomols** and **plenipotentiaries**. *Kulak* houses would then be stripped bare in an attempt to locate hidden wealth. Clothing, food, fuel, furniture and other personal belongings were confiscated and sold or given away to other villagers. In anticipation, *kulaks* often sold their goods, slaughtered animals and even abandoned their homes to flee to the towns. If caught by the authorities, their fate depended on how they were categorised:

- 'Fortunate' *kulaks* were those who were reallocated land often of a very poor quality. They were then given unrealistic food production targets which they invariably failed to meet. The result was that they were deported to work camps in inhospitable places such as Siberia.
- Standard *kulaks* were simply robbed and sent straight to concentration camps where they tended to die fairly quickly.
- Malicious, ideological or 'sub'-*kulaks* (*zlostnye*) were those who actively opposed collectivisation. They either were transported immediately, again to concentration camps, or were more likely to be shot.

It is estimated that from the beginning of 1928 to the end of 1930, between one million and three million *kulak* families (6–18 million people) were deported. On top of this about 30,000 *kulaks* were shot. In this sense Stalin achieved his aim to 'liquidate the *kulaks*' as a class. But in many ways *kulaks* were a myth. The term was invented to provide an excuse to blame certain people for the failings of communist agricultural policies. Up to the end of the period there were always some peasant farmers who seemed to be more productive than others, simply because they were good at farming. To classify them as an élite group within the peasant class was very misleading.

Komsomols
Members of the youth organisation known as the Young Communist League.

Plenipotentiaries
Officials who had 'total' power at a local level.

Key terms

to be carried out quickly and systematically. Collectivisation was actually meant to be voluntary but, in reality, it usually occurred as follows:

- The principles of collectivisation were explained to villagers at special meetings organised by plenipotentiaries.
- A mixture of poorer peasants, Komsomols and politically aware workers were recruited to seek out wealthier peasants and denounce them as *kulaks*. This helped create a sense of fear within a community which subsequently made it much easier to encourage others to sign up to the collective programme. Other incentives were offered such as the prospect of working with a new tractor and combine harvester.
- The result was the formation of either ***Kolkhozy*** ('pure' collectives) or ***Sovkhozy*** (state collectives).

By March 1930 Stalin claimed that 58 per cent of all households had been collectivised which was a gross exaggeration. Nevertheless, 'mass collectivisation' had a dramatic effect as witnessed by widespread opposition from peasants and local officials. Such resistance often took the form of direct action as was the case at Bransk-oblast where peasants actually drove away a party of Komsomols who were insistent on commandeering the church bells. Resistance came in other forms such as migration. In Kazakhstan, collectivisation virtually destroyed the nomadic way of life. The peasants there reacted by moving out of the region into China. The population of Kazakhstan fell by 75 per cent within a few years.

Stalin blamed this kind of scenario on regional officials who he argued had become 'intoxicated with success'. By the end of March 1930, the pace of collectivisation slackened and Stalin coupled this with a proclamation allowing peasants to quit collectives they had recently signed up to. The inevitable mass exodus followed only to be quickly clamped down on by renewed pressure to collectivise by the end of the year.

Renewed collectivisation

The move back towards intensive collectivisation resulted in about 50 per cent of all peasants once again being brought together in *Kolkhozy*. By the end of 1937 the figure had increased to 93 per cent. In contrast to the first wave of collectives, peasants were now allowed to keep small plots of land. Also, blocks of 40 farms were organised through motor-tractor stations (MTS). As the title suggests, these were originally organisations through which tractors and other heavy equipment could be loaned to peasants. An MTS would be responsible for distributing seed, collecting grain, establishing levels of payment for produce and deciding on what produce farmers could keep for their own consumption.

The famine of 1932–4 disrupted the development of collectivisation (see pages 133–4). Partly as a result of this, a special charter was issued in 1935 to improve payments to farmers in the *Kolkhozy* and to give owners of small plots more

Key terms

Kolkhozy
A farm owned and partly organised by the state but worked on by peasant farmers not directly employed by the state. Members could own a house, a small plot of land and a few animals.

Sovkhozy
Farms owned by the state and worked on by state employees.

legal security. Interestingly, the small plots proved more productive than the collective farms especially when it came to supplying dairy goods.

By 1941, 98 per cent of all peasant households worked on collectives. Despite an improvement in conditions on collective farms they were still disliked by peasants.

There were a number of reasons for resistance:

- The traditional way of organising farming was valued by peasants. The abolition of the *mir* in 1930 was considered a major blow to village autonomy.
- Collectives deprived peasants of the right to make a little extra income which would keep them just above subsistence level. It also placed restrictions on the variety of crops that could be grown and other rural activities that had previously been tolerated and enjoyed.
- The 1932–4 famine confirmed to many that collectives were likely to contribute to food shortages rather than help relieve them. Many believed that as requisitioning (taking grain from peasants by force) was part of the collectivisation policy the famine was largely 'man made'.

Khrushchev's agricultural policies

Khrushchev showed a great interest in agriculture and professed to be something of an expert on all aspects of farming. One area Khrushchev focused on for improvement was the organisation of agricultural production. More emphasis was placed on increasing production through state farms. This was partly at the expense of smaller collective farms, many of which were merged. Other measures included the change in the role of the Ministry of Agriculture from being involved in planning and implementing policy to that of an advisory body and the abolition of MTS. However, the historian Geoffrey Hosking is probably correct in stating that Khrushchev 'never fully got to grips with the authoritarian and bureaucratic structure of agricultural administration, which offered producers few incentives to improve either output or productivity'.

The question of providing more incentives was addressed through raising the prices for state procurements (amounts of food taken directly by the state from farmers), reducing the actual amounts to be procured, reducing taxes placed on peasants and increasing the provision of electricity to more isolated rural areas. Some success was achieved although increases in the price of food angered urban dwellers. It was unfortunate that Khrushchev's main drive to increase the incentive to raise production preceded the disaster years of 1962 and 1963; bad weather resulted in a terrible harvest. Riots broke out in the countryside but more seriously in towns. The most notable incident was at the Budyenni Locomotive Works in Novocherkassk where the KGB ended up killing 23 protesters.

Virgin Land campaign

From the start of his rule, Khrushchev displayed a keenness to quickly increase the amounts of cereals produced. To this end, in 1954, he introduced the Virgin Land campaign. The aim of this was to increase the amount of land to be cultivated. This was not new; Stolypin had introduced the idea but dekulakisation had put a halt to the process. The results were as follows:

- In 1950, 96 million acres of land were given over to the production of wheat. By 1964, this had increased to 165 million acres.
- Urban dwellers started to feel that their food requirements were at last being adequately met.
- But, the approach to using the 'virgin soil' was flawed. The land was overused with little attention paid to crop rotation. The effect was a reduction in soil fertility. Also, little was done to counter soil erosion, a result of the virgin soil regions being arid, close to the central Asian desert and prone to wind storms. Generally, Khrushchev wanted his policies to be implemented speedily and, as a result, he cut corners. In the long term, productivity and production fell, the first major indication of which came in 1963. Many historians believe that the Virgin Land campaign was the main reason for Khrushchev's downfall in 1964.

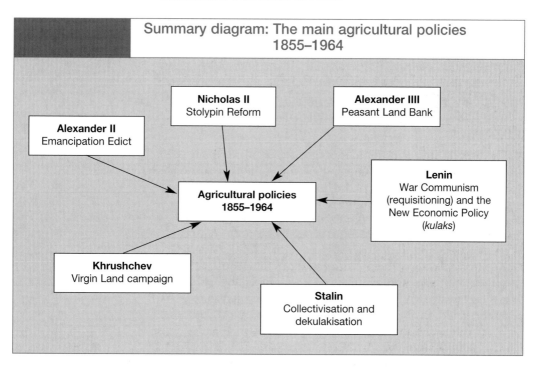

Summary diagram: The main agricultural policies 1855–1964

2 | The extent of social change

Population growth

The population of Russia grew significantly during the period in question. Much of this was due to a '**natural rate of growth**' although this was indirectly affected by the political, economic and social policies implemented by various regimes. Demographic change was also influenced more directly by measures designed to control birth rates and migration. The table below indicates how the population grew and includes separate figures for the urban population.

Table 3.4: The population of the Russian Empire and the USSR from 1858 to 1960

Year	Total (in millions)	Percentage in towns
1858	74	6
1870	86	11
1897	125	15
1913	166	18
1920	137	15
1926	147	18
1939	191	32
1950	178	39
1960	212	49

Key terms

Natural rate of growth
The relationship between birth rates and death rates and how this affected population growth. If the birth rate increased and the death rate fell the natural rate of growth would have been relatively high.

Census
An official count of the number of people in the population.

The first official **census** was not taken until 1897 and the figures before this time are, to some extent, 'guesstimates'. Even the official census material needs to be handled with caution due to the inconsistent methods used to collect data. The statistics also need to be considered in light of the fact that the extent of the Empire and Soviet Union changed significantly over the period.

With this in mind, a number of important trends can be observed:

- The biggest spurts in population growth occurred from 1870 to 1914 and during the inter-war period. In both cases this was due more to an increase in birth rates rather than a fall in death rates. Rising birth rates were stimulated by industrialisation (Witte's 'Great Spurt' and the Five-Year Plans); industrial work gave the prospect of more regular employment and, therefore, slightly higher levels of real income. Therefore, there was a tendency for people to marry earlier and have more children as it was affordable. This trend was especially strong given that industrialisation also created public health problems that resulted in rising mortality rates. Other influences that caused death rates to rise included wars and Stalin's purges.
- Unsurprisingly, industrialisation stimulated urbanisation. Increasing numbers of people moved to the big cities, especially St Petersburg and Moscow, in search of work. This had serious implications with respect to living standards and, more specifically, the availability of housing.

A number of government policies had a direct impact on demographics. Most of these were introduced during the period of communist rule:

- The Emancipation Edict of 1861 gave freedom to peasants to marry anyone they wished. However, **civil marriage** for peasants was not officially introduced until after the October Revolution of 1917. Ironically, this led to more families splitting up as 'official' divorce became an option. To counter this Stalin provided various financial incentives to 'strengthen' the family unit. This was considered to be especially important during the Second World War which demanded that the Russian people should maintain unity and a common purpose to defeat the enemy. Hence, in 1944 for example, the 'Distinctions to Mother Heroines' scheme was introduced whereby women, who at any one time had 10 or more children, were given substantial money rewards.
- In 1926 abortion was legalised. This seemed to result in a fall in the birth rate which promoted a revision of the law; abortion was only allowed if the life of the mother was thought to be threatened. Subsequently, the birth rate rose only to fall again after, in 1955, all restrictions on abortion were lifted.

In general, government policies on family planning were never clear or consistent except during times of crisis.

Changes in social structure

The structure of Russian society had a bearing on the policies of governments but equally ruling élites had an impact on the way social groups were organised. The hierarchical structure of Russian society was similar for the period up to the October 1917 Revolution, as shown in Box 3.1.

A number of features and developments are evident from Box 3.1:

- Russia was still a very rural-based society by the end of the nineteenth century. Over 80 per cent of the population was still dependent on agriculture. This meant that the Russian economy was still undeveloped and backwards; the other great European powers had a far greater proportion of their populations engaged in industrial activity.
- The distinction between traditional peasant and industrial worker was becoming blurred. Large numbers of peasants were moving towards cities and towns to take up employment in industry. An 'aristocracy of labour' among some peasant industrial workers emerged. These were individuals who developed special skills and offered their services as teams or *artels* as they were known.
- The rise of the middle classes was significant. Although small (numbering about two million in 1914) and divided (between the commercial and professional classes) this group presented an increasing threat to the monopoly of power enjoyed by the upper nobility and aristocracy.

The Tsar

The nobility (about two per cent of the population)

Aristocracy-included families that could trace their roots back to the original founders of the Russian state. Male members used the title of Prince or Grand Prince/Duke if related directly to the Tsar. The rest of the nobility was shaped by a table of ranks first introduced by Peter the Great, and which lasted until 1917:

- nobles of inherited title (barons, counts, etc.) – the lesser nobility
- nobles holding foreign titles
- nobles created by royal patent
- nobles who got the title by gaining rank in the bureaucracy
- nobles who gained an officer's commission.

The clergy and the 'middle classes'

The 1897 census revealed a burgeoning 'middle class' made up of the following:

- Christian priests
- non-noble bureaucrats
- 'honoured citizens' – those given special titles based on their duties and commitment to the Russian Empire
- merchants
- petty commercial classes.

The lower classes

The lower classes consisted mainly of peasants (still amounting to about 80 per cent of the population by the time of the First World War). But peasants were not a homogeneous group and, to an extent, this was revealed in the census. The different categories were as follows:

- peasants in rural areas, i.e. isolated in very scattered communities
- peasants in towns
- Cossacks – peasants from south-east Russia renowned for their horse-riding skills and who were given certain privileges for serving in the cavalry under the Tsar
- settlers
- foreigners
- others – there was little indication of what constituted 'others'.

Box 3.1: The structure of Russian society from 1855 to 1917.

- The nobility was in relative decline, due to the rise of the middle classes and profligacy. For decades, many of the nobility had lived beyond their means and had mortgaged property to pay off debts. When, in turn, repayments became difficult many sold big chunks of land to peasants. Thus, in total, by the mid-1870s, the gentry owned about 200 million acres but this fell to about 140 million acres with over 90 per cent of the reduction being accounted for by peasant purchases. Nevertheless, the hardcore nobility remained and it was that group that was most significant in ensuring the Tsar maintained autocratic rule.

Although the basic structure of society remained the same there were enough subtle changes to suggest that the way Russia was governed would also have to alter.

The social structure under communism

Under the communists there was, by definition, no class-based society. In theory, society consisted of workers who would eventually govern without the help of a cadre (a group of key officials). The reality was different. Soviet communism was characterised by a hierarchical bureaucracy led by a small élite which governed over the people. Even among workers there were status rankings. For example, some were considered technical experts and were often given privileges (as long as they continued to toe the party line). By the early 1930s, about 1.5 million workers had purportedly been promoted to managerial positions. Thus, there was more continuity than change in how society was organised under the tsars and the communists.

Education

Both the tsars and the communists attempted to expand the provision of education at all levels. Despite this, there were times when too much education, especially for the masses, was considered dangerous. Subsequently, there were periods when reform slowed down or where improvements were actually undone by a reversion to repression. Of particular note is the way in which some rulers used education to impose Russification (see Chapter 2 for details).

Throughout the period, schooling was available at elementary (primary) and secondary level, although free secondary schooling for all was only introduced during Khrushchev's time in power.

Elementary (primary) schools

Before 1864, provision of elementary schools was through wealthy, benevolent (kindly) individuals or the church. Parents paid fees for their children to attend and the curriculum centred around the three 'Rs' (reading, writing and arithmetic) with a fair bit of religious instruction thrown in. Pupil attendance was erratic and achievement poor as witnessed by the relatively low literacy rates. Prompted partly by the repercussions of the Emancipation Edict and also by the need to modernise, in 1864 Alexander II introduced a major education reform. He placed the responsibility for the administration and expansion of elementary education with school boards which in turn were run by the *Zemstva* (see page 43). This had an immediate impact in that the number of available school places, especially in more isolated places, rose and the quality and variety of provision also improved. The only drawback was that the composition of the boards was dominated by the clergy, nobility and government officials. Also, there was something of a dual system as the church still provided schools.

In 1870, some of the authority of the *Zemstva* was taken away by the Minister for Education, **Dmitri Tolstoy**. By 1877, the ministry had almost total control over what the *Zemstva* could do. Central government officials had authority over the appointment of teachers, the length of the school day and year, and quality checks by way of a new schools inspectorate.

Key figure

Dmitri Tolstoy 1823–89
Minister of Education from 1865 to 1880.

Under Nicholas II, the first *Duma* announced a plan for 'universal primary education' to be achieved by 1922 although the Great War and the 1917 revolutions put a stop to the plan. Nevertheless, expansion in the number of schools and pupils attending continued. Table 3.5 gives a good indication of the progress made.

The *Zemstva* clearly did a good job in providing more schools and provided a solid platform for the Bolsheviks to build on. The first commissar for education, Lunacharsky, had absolute control of all educational institutions. This included church schools which, in 1918, were handed over to local soviets to administer. Those responsible for schooling under Stalin carried out the aim of the first *Duma* by, in 1930, making attendance at primary school compulsory for all up to the age of 12. As a result another leap forward in the numbers attending occurred:

- 1929: eight million pupils were attending primary schools
- 1930: 18 million pupils were attending primary schools.

Under the communists, the primary school curriculum continued to revolve around developing basic literacy and numeracy skills. 'Extra' subjects were linked to the concept of revolution and the teaching of religious scriptures disappeared.

The expansion of provision was linked to a 'war on literacy' (the campaign to improve literacy levels) in general; it was quite usual for adults as well as young children to attend elementary schools with the aim of creating a more educated and capable workforce. The Stalinist system of primary education clearly suited the needs of the communists and remained in place until the end of the period.

Table 3.5: The approximate number of primary schools in Russia 1880–1914

1880	1896	1914
23,000	79,000	81,000

Secondary schools
The history of Russian secondary schooling was dominated by the debate over whether the traditional gymnasia (grammar schools) should be replaced with institutions that provided a mixture of academic and vocational subjects. All of the tsars retained the gymnasia, but modifications were made to the curriculum and to admissions procedures. Alexander II introduced a 'new code' for secondary schools which allowed for the continuation of traditional gymnasia provision alongside modern, 'real' gymnasia. The traditional gymnasia taught mainly Russian plus the classics (Latin and Greek) and games (physical education). In contrast the 'real' gymnasia taught subjects such as modern languages, science and mathematics, all of which were considered by some conservatives to engender a 'spirit of revolution'.

As a result of these reforms, the number of pupils attending secondary schools doubled from 1855 to 1865. The middle classes seemed to benefit significantly from the increase in places. The conservatives, epitomised by Dmitri Tolstoy, reacted by campaigning for universities to only accept pupils who attended the classic gymnasia; that is, children of the nobility. In fact Tolstoy manipulated the secondary school curriculum and university entrance examination system so that middle-class children were virtually excluded from progressing to tertiary education. Alexander III took the exclusion policy a step further by banning 'lower-class' children from attending secondary schools. Until the Bolsheviks came to power, secondary schooling remained the preserve of the élites in Russian society despite the inroads made by the middle classes.

The Bolsheviks scrapped the bourgeois gymnasia and replaced them with polytechnics, which were a bit like modern comprehensive schools. These schools placed heavy emphasis on skills development that would be directly related to a particular area of work. Not all party members agreed with this policy, and by the 1930s there was a return to a mixed provision of old-type grammar schools and purely vocational-based institutions. However, the greatest emphasis was placed on the development of vocational education especially when the Five-Year Plans were implemented. The figures showing the increase in secondary schools under Stalin therefore mainly reflect a growth in vocational education:

- 1931: 2.5 million pupils were attending secondary schools
- 1932: 6.9 million pupils were attending secondary schools.

Khrushchev reverted to secondary schools based on the polytechnic model. Other changes included the scrapping of all school fees (introduced by Stalin in 1939), the closing down of co-educational boarding schools, the creation of specialist academies and the spread of correspondence courses. Such progressive policies, though, were balanced by a number of restrictive measures including the rewriting of 'official' history books to reflect the disengagement from the Stalinist past.

Universities

Higher educational provision probably caused Russian leaders the most cause for concern. Universities were potentially the breeding grounds for opposition groups and it is of little surprise that students were clamped down on hard if they showed any sign of subversive activity. In 1861, for example, students from St Petersburg University were accused of sedition (anti-tsarist activity) and were punished by having a range of privileges withdrawn. Generally, though, leaders were keen to see universities grow and provide educated people who would enable Russia to enhance its world status.

A statute of 1863 reinstated a large degree of autonomy to universities. A special council for each of the existing eight universities governed the nature of teaching, publications by academics and student discipline. But, despite the statute, the Ministry of Education had the final say on what was to be taught and how it was to be taught.

Under Alexander III, university autonomy was chipped away at. For example, elections to the university councils were scrapped and replaced by an appointment system and a more rigorous inspection process was introduced. Nevertheless, the universities continued to flourish. By the end of the nineteenth century there were nine institutions catering for about 16,500 students.

The importance of Moscow University

Nearly a quarter of Russia's students were placed at the University of Moscow which typified the university set-up. At Moscow, there were four departments:

- law
- medicine
- physics and mathematics
- history and philology.

Students attended lectures and submitted written papers to be discussed with tutors and/or other students. Women had very limited opportunity to attend, and poorer students found life very difficult as there was only limited financial help from tsarist governments. Students belonged to a variety of student societies and the student council. The focus of extracurricular activity was invariably current affairs or aspects of high culture. When meetings got out of hand and became linked to demonstrations, the authorities became very oppressive. Whips were used to disperse unruly student groups and arbitrary expulsions were commonplace. Repression of students reached new levels under Stolypin with all non-academic meetings in all universities being made illegal.

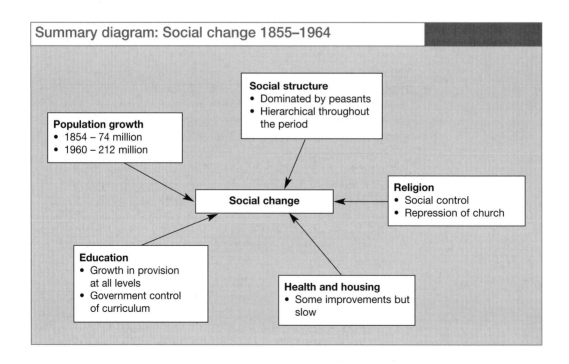

Summary diagram: Social change 1855–1964

Social structure
- Dominated by peasants
- Hierarchical throughout the period

Population growth
- 1854 – 74 million
- 1960 – 212 million

Social change

Religion
- Social control
- Repression of church

Education
- Growth in provision at all levels
- Government control of curriculum

Health and housing
- Some improvements but slow

Essay focus

Essay 1, paragraph 4, on page 142 makes good use of material on education to illustrate how some benefits accrued to workers under the communists. This is linked clearly to a thematic approach with education discussed under the heading of social change and opportunity. Essay 2, paragraph 6, on page 146 also makes reference to education but the comments are rather terse and do not add much to the quality of the response.

Key question
To what extent was there very little improvement in the living and working conditions of peasants and workers in the period from 1855 to 1964?

3 | Living and working conditions of rural and urban people

Housing
Urban housing
By the end of the nineteenth century, about 15 per cent of the Russian population lived in towns and cities compared with 80 per cent in Britain and 40 per cent in the USA. Only 19 cities had more than 100,000 inhabitants. St Petersburg (1.25 million) and Moscow (one million) were by far the largest cities.

Much of the detailed information we have about urban living conditions comes from the census, although the first of these was not carried out until 1897. Urbanisation continued at a rapid rate after 1897. For example, by 1914 the populations of the two main cities and others, such as Riga and Kiev, almost doubled. The main result of rapid urbanisation was an increase in public health problems. Housing was generally erected quickly and on the cheap. By modern standards, buildings were of a poor quality with inadequate drainage, water supplies and sanitation. Demand for reasonable accommodation at affordable rents always outstripped supply. This led to overcrowding and the inevitable spread of diseases such as cholera. A spin-off of this, according to the historian Hans Rogger, was that the 'brutishness of the working man's life tended to make him difficult and explosive'.

At the start of the First World War, in 1914, there were over 1000 towns containing about two million buildings. Over half of all housing was constructed from wood and therefore prone to fire damage. Homes and streets were mostly lit by kerosene lamps; only 74 towns had access to electricity and 35 to gas. Around 200 had piped water and 38 a sewerage system. But even where facilities were fairly widespread, disease still multiplied. Cholera was especially rife in St Petersburg (about 100,000 deaths in 1910) even though its citizens experienced living conditions marginally better than elsewhere. Conditions in this city were further improved with the installation of a sewerage system in 1911, showing that politicians were willing to act when situations became really desperate. Also, cholera outbreaks always provoked a positive reaction to reform as the disease affected all classes in society.

Factories were nearly always located on the edge of cities. As transport links were slow to develop, it became necessary to provide special worker housing on site. Worker 'barracks' were hastily built and were invariably overcrowded and insanitary. Shift systems resulted in workers (and their families) sharing bunk beds. In small-scale enterprises, workers usually slept in the workshop. Skilled workers were better off as they could afford to rent private rooms, but on the whole factory workers experienced some of the worst living conditions found anywhere in Russia.

The Decree on Peace (see page 38), issued after the Bolsheviks seized power, partly focused on what the party intended to do about property, including housing. Dwellings in towns and cities were to be wrested from private owners and handed over to the proletariat. To ensure this was done fairly, the redistribution was placed in the hands of the soviets. Some improvement occurred as a result but this was short lived.

During Stalin's rule, housing conditions deteriorated. Overcrowding once more became the norm. In Moscow in the mid-1930s, for example, 25 per cent of the population was living in one room that was shared between two or more households. A further 25 per cent lived in communal dormitories. Furthermore, about five per cent lived in a bathroom, kitchen, corridor or hallway. The result was that living space had fallen from 8.5 m^2 in 1905 to 5.8 m^2 by 1935. The Stalinist policy was to allocate space rather than rooms to individuals and families. Even when some were lucky to get their own room in one of the new communist high-rise **tenements**, bathrooms and kitchens would be shared. Outside observers were shocked and surprised at the low priority given to housing in a country being built on socialist principles. The communists responded to criticisms by stating that sacrifices had to be made in the short term to enable the Russian economy to expand. Generally, most social projects were put on hold so that attention could be focused on achieving the aims of the Five-Year Plans.

The Second World War resulted in swathes of Russia becoming depopulated and over 25 million Russians being made homeless. Stalin made some attempt to address the problem, but it was Khrushchev who launched a housing programme of huge proportions. Between 1955 and 1964 the housing stock doubled and the principles behind communal living were abandoned. One result was that the population were happy that at last some of their aspirations were met. A more worrying development was that some benefited more than others through the emergence of **housing cooperatives**. These benefited better off professionals who could afford to pay deposits on new cooperative housing (usually 15–30 per cent of the purchasing price) and make loan repayments at reasonable rates of interest. Finally, by the end of the period, the authorities sensed that living standards were improving as more people wanted to stay in the comfort of their homes rather than attend political meetings.

Tenements
Similar to blocks of flats.

Housing cooperatives
Organisations formed by employees who belonged to the same work enterprise or professional union. They were given first pickings over new state housing as long as they could meet government-set prices.

Key terms

Rural housing

For the majority of the period, housing for the 'average' peasant remained the same. It consisted of a single-room wooden hut (*izbas*) heated by an oven which also served as a sleeping platform. Such accommodation was invariably overcrowded especially given that animals were also housed in the hut. The nature of hut building varied from region to region but generally such accommodation was poor by modern standards. It was cold, damp and grubby and added to the misery of the peasants. However, it was at least cheap to construct and once erected peasant families had control over how the accommodation could be used.

Under Stalin there was a change to this situation for some peasants with the construction of 'special' housing blocks located on the periphery of collective farms. Under Khrushchev, the plan was to take this idea further to construct self-contained 'agro-towns'. As with the tenements for urban workers rural housing was built quickly and cheaply and was subsequently of a poor standard. They became very overcrowded and residents found themselves subject to the public health problems experienced in the towns and cities. Displaced *kulaks* suffered even worse conditions. When forced from their properties they were usually dumped in barracks or given tent accommodation in a field. Overall, little was done by any Russian leader during the period to aid improvements in rural housing.

Food and famine

The staple food for all Russians throughout the period was grain, especially rye. Buckwheat was also popular, being used to make dumplings and pancakes. Cereals were often eaten with meat dishes, although in many areas there was a scarcity of animals. Fish was consumed in large quantities in regions that had a coastline or where there were bountiful lakes. More significant than the consumption of meat was that of vegetables. Potatoes, turnips, beetroot, cabbage, garlic and onions were grown and eaten all over Russia. Fruit was also produced, especially apples, pears and plums and cherries were a speciality in the area of Vladmir. People living close to woodlands had the added bonus of being able to gather mushrooms and berries. In terms of drink, ale, mead, tea and, of course, vodka were preferred. Overall, it would appear that the Russian diet was relatively rich and varied and that, given the emphasis placed on agriculture, there was little need for the Russian people to go short of food.

The reality was that the whole of the period was characterised by intermittent food shortages and full-blown famines. This was due to a number of reasons:

• There was a tendency towards monoculture (in this case, an over-reliance on grain).
• The restrictive practices of the *mir*. For example, the insistence of the *mir* on the growing of certain crops.

- Severe weather conditions in particular years.
- Government policies (grain requisitioning and collectivisation).

Even before 1855, food shortages had consistently caused governments concern. When Alexander II came to the throne he was worried that if shortages continued to occur there would be widespread social unrest. To this end, in 1864, he placed the *Zemstva* in charge of drawing up emergency measures to deal with famines. This still did not prevent people starving and dying from hunger in large numbers. There were a number of famines before the First World War but by far the most severe was that of 1891.

The famine of 1891

A major challenge for the *Zemstva* happened in 1891 when adverse weather resulted in half the provinces of Russia suffering from food shortages that were unprecedented. The provincial governments appeared to cope very well but the famine, made worse by outbreaks of cholera and typhus, still resulted in about 350,000 deaths. Some blamed central government for this. Vyshnergradsky, the Finance Minister, had raised the tax on consumer goods which meant that the population had to pay more for everyday items. Peasants appeared to sell off any surpluses of grain they had stored to cope with the inflated prices. Therefore, the shortage of food due to poor harvests was exacerbated. Alexander III tried to counter criticisms by banning exports of grain, setting up a Special Committee on Famine Relief and funding emergency help from two 'extraordinary' lotteries. For most this was too little too late and it provided an added incentive to join one of the revolutionary groups emerging at the time.

The First World War

During the first three years of the First World War there were good harvests although those in towns and cities did not necessarily reap the benefits. Bread queues of eight hours or longer became the norm (later leading to the view that the 'revolution started in the bread queue'). Some peasants hoarded grain and/or fed their animals (rather than slaughter them early, which critics argued needed to be done in times of crisis). An inadequate transport infrastructure also made accessing food difficult.

The Russian people hoped that with the fall of the Tsar and the ending of the war there would be greater access to food. However, their hopes were dashed due to a continuation of problems linked to the availability of land and how it was farmed.

Food crisis of 1918

By 1918 another food crisis loomed. Peasants had continued to hoard and valuable agricultural land had been lost as a result of the Treaty of Brest-Litovsk (see page 38). The Bolsheviks responded to this by introducing grain requisitioning. This was the practice of taking food and grain surpluses from some peasants and redistributing it among those who were in greatest need. Most of the redistributed foodstuff went to the towns and cities.

Kulaks were blamed for the shortages and subsequently persecuted. Peasants reacted angrily by resorting to violent protest, refusing to sign up to collectives and by resisting the demand to create surplus supplies of grain. By 1920, the *Cheka* and the Red Army had been instructed to seize all food supplies for redistribution and not simply surpluses. More violent reaction occurred and by the end of 1921 the countryside was in a state of utter chaos. All of this coincided with another severe famine.

The famine of 1921

Although the Bolshevik policies towards the immediate post-war food crisis contributed to the famine, droughts followed by severe winters in 1920–1 also had a dramatic effect. Ukrainian food production fell by 20 per cent during this time. Due to an almost complete shutdown of the Russian railway system, which emanated from the Civil War, it was extremely difficult to transport produce over even moderately long distances. It was also virtually impossible for urban dwellers to travel to where there might have been food supplies. The end result was a death toll of over five million. The crisis was also characterised by rumours of bodysnatching and cannibalism. Like Alexander III before him, and Stalin at a later date, Lenin was partly blamed for the famine as he was slow in his response and reluctant to accept aid from the **American Relief Administration**. In fact, any kind of charitable aid was treated with suspicion and there were instances where members of relief agencies were arrested by the *Cheka* and exiled.

Stability in the countryside by the mid-1920s

By the mid-1920s stability had been restored to the countryside. There were decent harvests in 1926 and 1927 but in 1928, food shortages reappeared. Much of this was due to the weather although peasants had also reduced the amount of land sown. The finger of blame was pointed at the *kulaks* and once again requisitioning was resorted to. In 1928, treatment of wealthier peasants worsened with the introduction of the Urals-Siberian method. Under this scheme villagers were encouraged to reveal grain hoarders and those who showed bourgeois tendencies in exchange for rewards.

The famine of 1932–4

A combination of the effects of the first phase of collectivisation and poor harvests due to terrible weather conditions led to the most disastrous famine of the whole period. Although the number of deaths resulting from starvation and disease was similar to that for the 1921 famine, many more suffered as a result of repression by the Stalinist regime:

- The death penalty was imposed for stealing grain (even though the grain might have legally belonged to the accused).

Key term

American Relief Administration
A US relief mission to aid Europe, including Russia, after the First World War. The director of the organisation was Herbert Hoover, future president.

- Peasants who ate their own seed corn were shot along with those sent to guard it.
- Discussion of the grain crisis was banned; this was a necessity as Stalin publicly denied a food problem existed.
- Severe restrictions were also placed on those who wanted to move around to look for food.
- The reaction of some peasants did not seem to help. Animals were slaughtered in preference to handing them over to the authorities. A horse shortage ensued which slowed down the ploughing of fields. Cattle often froze to death on collectives that lacked big enough barns to house them.

By 1935 matters seemed to improve and food production increased slowly. However, on the eve of the Second World War it was unlikely that total food output had reached pre-First World War levels. Generally, the diet of workers in particular seemed to worsen under the communists. By the late 1930s, for example, the consumption of meat and fish had fallen by 80 per cent.

The Second World War and food supplies

During the Second World War, the policy towards collectivisation was relaxed. With the removal of restrictions on the size of private plots of land, food production rose. However, this was short lived as another famine took place in 1947. The pattern of poor harvests and associated food shortages continued during the rule of Khrushchev. Despite the Virgin Land campaign (see page 121) and improvements to the **state pricing mechanism** for agricultural produce, food still had to be imported. Critics at the time and since believed that adherence to a policy of subsidised 'socialised agriculture' simply led to inefficiency and a situation whereby the demand for food in Russia always outstripped the ability of Russian farmers to meet it.

State pricing mechanism
The government policy of providing official prices for goods and services.

Key term

Essay focus

Look at Essay 1, paragraph 2 on page 142. The student has made use of material on workers' diets to support the argument. Students often assume rather simplistically that the availability and variety of food was only of concern to the rural population. One of the key points concerning famines is that they were often exacerbated by requisitioning which was usually organised to meet the dietary needs of urban dwellers.

The nature of rural and urban work

Rural work

In general, work on the land was dictated by 'nature's clock'. Specific tasks had to be completed at certain times of the year. The success of peasant farmers was determined more by the quality of soil, the weather and their innate ability to farm rather than government policies.

Nevertheless, the emancipation of serfs, the appointment of Land Captains, grain requisitioning, collectivisation and the

Virgin Land campaign all influenced conditions under which peasants worked. Agricultural work obviously involves hard physical labour but at least before the Bolshevik takeover peasants were able to control the pace at which they worked and how much they produced. The only restrictions outside of those provided by nature were those imposed by the *mir* (see page 115). For most peasants, the main aim was to produce as much as possible so that they could feed their families, pay off debts and save a little for a rainy day. It is quite incorrect to assume that the Russian agricultural system before communism was simply based on achieving subsistence levels. To achieve a surplus, peasants worked most days of the week from dawn to dusk and often under harsh climatic conditions. There was still time for festivities; holy days (holidays) often coincided with celebrations linked to particular seasons.

Under the communists the nature of rural work changed. How much was produced and the methods used were dictated by central government policy. Collectivisation resulted in the requirement that peasants worked cooperatively and to set targets, most of which were seldom achieved. Investment was made in new agricultural techniques and technology to boost productivity. The tractor was heralded as a major breakthrough, although it was utilised with mixed levels of success. Overall, work for peasants under communist rule was far more regulated, and individuals who did not toe the party line were liable to be punished severely (see pages 117–20).

Urban work

Those who worked in towns and cities were employed in either the service industry or manufacturing. The worst conditions were present in factories, although most of these, along with other heavy industry (for example, mines, steel plants and engineering works), were located on the edge of conurbations. As there was no factory inspectorate until 1882, working conditions for many industrial workers especially those employed in textiles were dangerous and unhealthy. Even when inspectors were introduced, they were largely ineffectual as they were too few in number and had limited powers of enforcement. Thus, for example, despite factory legislation of 1882 banning the employment of children under the age of 12, it was possible for employers to continue to use child labour as they were unlikely to be found out.

In fact the introduction in February 1920 of *Rabkrin* (the Workers' and Peasants' Inspectorate) under the communists was a backward step as this body became a talking shop rather than one that enforced industrial law. Hours were long by modern standards, pay was relatively low and the enforcement of the 'new work discipline' done harshly.

The use of fines (often 10 per cent of wages) as punishment for petty wrongdoings was especially disliked by workers. Workers were also threatened by being 'purged' especially if they were considered to be anti-revolutionary. Officials sometimes claimed that certain workers were intent on disrupting production by damaging machinery ('wrecking') or purposely working slowly so as to prevent the implementation of the Five-Year Plans. Furthermore, women and children were treated more severely than men. It took some time for all of this to change.

By the end of the nineteenth century, laws were being introduced that governed the length of the working day. But hours still fluctuated across the period depending who was ruling. It is worth noting that there were particular times when excessively long hours were accepted as necessary by all concerned such as during periods of war. Table 3.6 summarises the trend in working hours. Note that some of the figures represent what happened directly after legislation was passed. Where 'the norm' is stated this means the average working day imposed by employers. Sometimes employers under the tsars found loopholes in the law and pushed workers to work longer than the statutory hours. Under the communists, working hours were strictly controlled by the state.

By Western standards, industrial wages were low during the whole period, although it is difficult to provide details as accurate statistical evidence is lacking. Women received less then men on average even when they were employed in the same work. Low pay was partly offset by the introduction in 1903 (adapted in 1912) of a **workers' insurance system** and, under the communists, by **bonus schemes**. The latter was popularised through the Stakhanovite movement (see page 89) and some workers did very well out of this. From the beginning to the end of the first Five-Year Plan (1928–32) though real wages fell by 50 per cent. They rose again after this time but it was not until 1954 that they started to reach the levels of the early 1920s. Wage differentials increased substantially under Stalin as a result of the

Workers' insurance system
Insurance against being injured in the workplace. Other schemes, against ill-health, old age and unemployment, were also introduced through the 1924 and 1936 constitutions.

Bonus schemes
Where extra payments were made to workers for exceeding individual production targets.

Table 3.6: Trends in working hours in Russia 1896–1958

Year	Hours	Comment
1896	11-hour working day (10 hours on Saturday). This was fixed by law	Workers were not obliged to work on Sundays. Small workshops were not covered
1914	9–10-hour working day was the norm	Statutory holidays had been introduced by this time
1917	8-hour working day was the norm. This was a result of a decree made by the Provisional Government	Bolsheviks quickly brought in laws to improve working conditions to illustrate that they were the workers' party
1932	10–12-hour working day was the norm	Stalin claimed the demands of the first Five-Year Plan meant workers had to endure a longer working day
1939	7-hour working day was the norm	Workers were rewarded for their efforts in implementing the Five-Year Plans
1940	8-hour working day was the norm	This was due to the war. Holidays were also disallowed
1958	7-hour working day was the norm	Khrushchev wanted to move away from the oppressive Stalinist years. The 7-hour day remained to the end of the period

piece rate payments. Some workers were paid more than others simply because they produced more. The piece rate system was meant to provide an incentive to workers to be more productive.

Essay focus

Consideration of the changing statutory requirements for the length of the working day for those employed in industry pays dividends when trying to evaluate how urban workers were treated. From the beginning to the end there was a decline from an 11-hour plus to a seven-hour working day. This indicates a clear improvement in conditions over the long run. Both Essays 1 and 2 on pages 142–4 and 145–7 make reference to hours but needed to be clearer about how they changed over the whole period.

Summary diagram: Changes to rural and urban living and working conditions

Conditions	Tsars	Communists
Rural housing	Wooden huts – idealised by folk literature but cold and damp	Remained the same but some move towards agro-towns
Urban housing	Relatively poor with respect to quantity and quality. Public health problems	Characterised by overcrowding but some improvement under Khrushchev
Rural work	Governed by 'nature's clock'; some improvements through reforms but control by *mir*	Governed by political regime through collectivisation (although less so under Khrushchev)
Urban work	Poor conditions (long hours, low pay, strict discipline) but some reforms aided improvement	Similar poor conditions but hours much lower by end of period. Workers prone to being purged under Stalin especially if considered to be 'wreckers' (saboteurs)

---

4 | Civil rights

Limitations on personal, political and religious freedom

Civil rights refer to the rights citizens have to the personal freedom to speak, think and act. This freedom is usually associated with the law, politics and religion. Details on the limitations on many of these rights, especially legal and political, have been covered in other sections of this book. This section will therefore focus mainly on religious freedom. As a generalisation, poorer Russians had far fewer rights than the wealthy throughout the period. However, under Stalin even members of the ruling élite were likely to lose their basic rights through being purged.

Personal freedoms

Both the tsars and communists were adept at controlling the personal freedoms of individuals by using the legal system, the police ('normal' and secret), the armed forces, propaganda and censorship. These have all been discussed in Chapter 2. Generally, the people were allowed to exercise their free will as long as it did not conflict with the interests of autocracy and totalitarian rule. When a more liberal climate was created it was often short lived or countered by a string of repressive measures.

Political freedoms

The basic political rights that supposedly existed in the democracies of the West were never apparent in Russia at any time during the period under consideration. On occasion, individuals were allowed to belong to political parties and trade unions and some were even allowed to vote (see Chapter 1). But the key point to be made is that such political rights were never universal or consistently granted. As with personal freedoms, whenever leaders felt their authority was being challenged by political activity from below, they reacted with repressive measures. The only exception was during the time of the Provisional Government when a more tolerant approach was adopted towards grass-roots political activism.

Religious freedoms

Orthodox and Non-Orthodox religion remained under state control across the period. The Orthodox Church was important to the tsars as it acted as a useful form of **social control**. Many of the clergy, such as the highly regarded Father John of Kronstadt, were happy to support autocracy even though they championed the plight of the poor. The church actually relied on governments for money and the encouragement given to the people to attend services. Even when Pobedonostsev tightened control over the activities of senior clergy very few dissented. Under the communists, religion was considered the **'opium of the people'**. Immediately after the 1917 revolution it appeared that the church would be left to its own devices. But, in response to the Orthodox Church bringing back **patriarchy**, the Bolsheviks made the 'Decree on the Separation of the Church from the State and School from the Church'.

This placed severe restrictions on the activities of the church including the withdrawal of state subsidies and the prevention of religious groups from possessing property (including icons). During the Civil War many churches were closed and their property was confiscated. Anti-religious pressure groups designed to promote atheism were encouraged to form, most notably the League of the Militant Godless (1925). The only concession under Lenin was the appointment of a church spokesperson. The first person to hold this post was Metropolitan Sergei although he was only favoured because he preached for conciliation between the state and the church. Stalin continued to close churches and many of the clergy suffered during the Great Terror (see page 84) of the late 1930s. According to the historian Walter G. Moss, by 1938 there were only 16 working Orthodox churches, compared with 224 in 1930, and the number of clergy had been reduced by 60 per cent.

Khrushchev also had little time for religion and believed that to speed up the full implementation of communism religious prejudices had to be eradicated. To this end the 22nd Party Congress of 1961 introduced a new 'moral code' which was essentially a substitute for the Bible.

The main beliefs that fell under the heading of non-Orthodox were those of the **Old Believers**, **Sectarians**, Catholics, Protestants, Jews, Muslims and Buddhists. Although there were times when there was a relaxed attitude towards these groups most leaders either encouraged conversion to the Orthodox Church or resorted to restriction of practice. Thus, for example, a law of 1883 gave Old Believers the right to meet in their houses of prayer but banned any public promotion of their beliefs. Nicholas II modified this, in April 1905, and also allowed Orthodox believers to convert to other Christian denominations. But in 1910, the rights of the non-Orthodox were again restricted with the increasingly popular Baptists being hardest hit. During the communist period most sects were forced to operate 'underground'.

Minority religious groups were targeted during the Second World War as they were associated, usually incorrectly, with collaborating with the enemy. After the war, non-Orthodox believers suffered a similar fate to those of Orthodox leanings. An official anti-religious campaign launched in 1958 meant that religious activity of any kind was under scrutiny unless it was conducted in an 'official place'.

In conclusion, religion was never banned as such, but it was very difficult for believers of any kind to carry on their practice without being scrutinised by the authorities. Nevertheless, it was not until 1958 that religion was considered officially to be unscientific and therefore to the detriment of the well-being of the people.

Key terms

Old Believers
Those who believed in the most traditional form of the Russian Orthodox Church. They also thought that they were more Russian than other Russians.

Sectarians
Anyone who belonged to a group that held extreme, and often unusual, religious views.

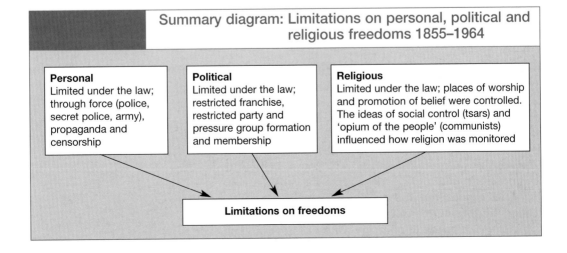

Summary diagram: Limitations on personal, political and religious freedoms 1855–1964

Personal
Limited under the law; through force (police, secret police, army), propaganda and censorship

Political
Limited under the law; restricted franchise, restricted party and pressure group formation and membership

Religious
Limited under the law; places of worship and promotion of belief were controlled. The ideas of social control (tsars) and 'opium of the people' (communists) influenced how religion was monitored

Limitations on freedoms

5 | Conclusion

The dictatorial regimes of the tsars and the communists had both positive and negative effects on the economy and society of the Russian Empire and the Soviet Union. The impact varied according to time and place. Having said this a common theme that runs through the period was the wish by all leaders to industrialise to a level that was comparable to what was happening in the West.

The 'Great Spurt', the New Economic Policy and the Five-Year Plans were all designed to boost heavy industry and increase the rate of economic growth. In this respect they all succeeded although the rates of growth were not consistent and generally lagged behind those of Western economies. For the tsars, industrialisation was important in order to ensure that Russia retained its status as one of the Great Powers. Wars such as the Crimean War and the First World War demonstrated how far behind Russia was technologically. The communists were also concerned with world status especially after the Second World War and, as with the tsars, they were also aware of the need to prioritise heavy industry so that the military would be fully equipped to defend the homeland. What all dictatorial regimes seemed less concerned about was sharing some of the fruits of economic growth among the bulk of the population. Most of the available indicators point, at best, to a slowly rising standard of living for the masses over the whole period. There were particular times when the people found themselves less well off than before. Rapid urbanisation was characterised by a multitude of public health problems which most governments struggled to deal with or even chose to ignore.

The agricultural sector always played second fiddle to the needs of industry. Reforms occurred that were designed to increase production and productivity but only to ensure that workers were adequately fed. Famines, which affected rural folk the most, were common and were often fuelled by requisitioning. Problems relating to land ownership were never tackled effectively by any leader during the period. As a result peasants were left impoverished and lacking some of the most basic civil rights.

Social policies also lacked consistency and oscillated from reforms that benefited many to repression that spread terror. Overall, there was real progress in the field of education with respect to the number of schools made available, the spread of universities, compulsory attendance, the rising school leaving age and the decrease in illiteracy. Acting as a check against this were restrictions placed on the curriculum, Russification and the use of schools, especially by the communists, as a form of social control. Help for families, the sick and the elderly was never systematically offered. Insurance schemes were very slow in being introduced and never seemed to cover more than the most basic needs. Religious groups were tolerated especially under the tsars but all leaders were keen to ensure that Orthodox and non-Orthodox Churches were made to obey the whims of government.

Changes in regimes undoubtedly altered the functioning of the economy and the impact this had on social change. However, the common aim to industrialise Russia and increase economic growth was largely achieved during the period. The downside to this, even when accounting for some of the problems linked to measurement, was that living standards never seemed to reach levels that ordinary Russians found acceptable.

Further questions for debate

1 Explain why the pace and extent of industrialisation were much greater under the communists than the tsars.

2 To what extent did Russian leaders make changes to agricultural policies only to serve the needs of industry?

3 To what extent were peasants continuously treated with contempt and inhumanity during the period from 1855 to 1964?

4 Assess the reasons for fluctuations in living standards of urban dwellers during the period from 1855 to 1964.

5 'There was never any prospect of Russian people gaining full civil rights during the period from 1855 to 1964.' How far do you agree with this view?

Advice on answering essay questions on assessing the extent of change and continuity with respect to how peasants and workers were treated

The treatment of peasants and workers by rulers is a popular topic with examiners who set questions. Such questions demand that the student completes two principal tasks. One is to compare and contrast the fortunes of the urban working classes under different political regimes. It is important to be clear about the term 'urban working classes'. It refers to manual workers who laboured in factories, mines, workshops, etc. in the towns and cities of Russia. Although there were workers who had different skill levels and therefore different degrees of status across the period, they were distinct from rural workers. However, it would be appropriate to point out that peasants often became workers by finding employment in the factories, mines and workshops located in urban areas. This was especially true during times of famine.

The second task for the student is to make an assessment of the degree of change and continuity in the way in which workers were treated. The very best answers should adopt a thematic framework (economic, political, social, etc.) that blends in judgement about the relative importance of the different forms of treatment meted out to workers. A narrative, chronological approach can be used but it then becomes less easy to show explicitly patterns of change and continuity.

Read each of the following essays carefully. Each essay was written in one hour and without the use of notes. Note any strengths and weaknesses and compare your views with those of the assessor. Marks should be awarded for each of the two assessment objectives described in the tables at the end of the book (see pages 192–3).

Essay 1: Assess the view that the urban working classes of Russia were treated worse by the communist rulers than by the tsars in the period from 1855 to 1964

1 When assessing the view that the urban class of Russia was treated worse by the communist rulers than the tsars during 1855–1964 it is important to consider a number of key areas. These include the social conditions of the working class, the political rights available to the working class, their economic freedom and rights, and lastly, the use of terror on the working class.

2 Socially, one can point to the very poor living standards suffered by the working class under the communists. By 1935 living space had decreased from 8.5 m^2 (1905 level) to only 5.8 m^2 per person. The workers' diet had also rapidly worsened, only eating one-fifth of the meat and fish eaten in 1905. A worker's wage was a third of what it had been when Lenin first introduced communism to Russia in 1918, and with the introduction of fees for education in 1939 Stalin ensured that the working classes had little access to education.

3 Under the tsars, although living conditions were undoubtedly poor, with Hans Rogger quoting that the 'brutishness of the working man's life tended to make him difficult and explosive', tsarist rulers, especially in the latter stages of Alexander III's reign and Nicholas II, showed increasing commitment to care for the welfare of the urban working classes. This is shown through the introduction of a decree in 1882 forbidding the labour of children under 12 years and in 1904 Nicholas followed this reforming nature with the introduction of factory inspections and the limiting of working hours. By 1917 the working week consisted of 50–60 hours with a maximum eight-hour day. Stolypin's initiative to install a sewerage system in St Petersburg in 1911 after 100,000 deaths from cholera in 1910 also suggests that the tsars were becoming increasingly concerned for the welfare of their people. All of this indicates that the working classes were treated reasonably well by the tsars even if this was simply to keep them happy and prevent them from rebelling.

4 However, there were unprecedented opportunities for the workers under the communists. Free and compulsory education up until the age of 12 was introduced in 1930. By this time about 18 million children attended primary schools although they were also made open to adults. A communist 'war on literacy' resulted in a substantial reduction in illiteracy. In Petrograd illiteracy went down to 18 per cent in females and four per cent in males. The communists also enshrined the workers' rights in the 1924 and 1936 constitutions, and ensured the promotion of 1.5 million workers to managerial positions in the early 1930s. Another communist social reform providing opportunity was Khrushchev's housing policy. From 1955 to 1964 the housing stock doubled and the principles of communal living, much despised by urban dwellers, were abandoned. This, when compared to the opportunities under the tsars would suggest that the workers were not treated worse under the communists.

---

1 This is a clear start that indicates the mini-themes that are to be discussed in the main part of the essay.

2 A relevant comment is made here about changing social conditions. It is well supported with factual detail.

3 A very solid analytical point is made here about the way in which the tsars attempted to treat workers favourably when it came to working conditions. It is clear that the candidate is sticking closely to the thematic approach outlined in the introduction.

4 A good level of ability to compare and contrast is revealed here. A good deal of supporting material is synthesised to support the key observation.

5 A strong argument is put forward here and, once again, it is quite well supported although the comment about elections during the Stalinist era is rather vague.

5 Politically, there is not as much scope to suggest that the workers were treated worse under the tsars than the communists. Lenin's view that the workers were in control of the government at the beginning of 1918 appeared null and void when, after 41.5 million out of 80 million voted to elect a constituent assembly within two days it was closed. Any attempts at staging elections to any representative body after this were rather farcical. Although universal suffrage and the use of the secret ballot were evident, results were announced before voting began and candidates were pulled from 'official' communist lists. Under Stalin the centralisation towards a one-party state became increasingly apparent. However, Khrushchev destalinised and handed over some authority to the Politburo. Thus there was something of a thaw in totalitarianism by 1964.

6 A good attempt is made here to sustain a comparative approach and make evaluative comment. Sections 5 and 6 together display a good level of synoptic ability.

6 With the tsars, especially both Alexander II and Alexander III, there is little evidence to find for suggesting a vast array of political rights for the workers. However, under Nicholas there was some change with the development of trade unions in 1905 (such as that run by Father Gapon) and then the creation of a *Duma* in the October Manifesto of 1905. The latter involved multi-party elections although the workers' influence was narrowed due to the limiting of the franchise in a 1907 electoral law. Nevertheless, the system allowed for the election of radical groups into the assembly. The continued action of the *Duma* throughout Nicholas' reign helps to support the suggestion that, considering the communists claimed to be a 'worker's government', with the workers forming the vanguard of the proletariat, they were in fact treated worse under the communists than the tsars.

7 This is a thrusting, detailed comment on the use of terror under the communists. There is clear indication in the opening sentence that a compare and contrast structure is still in place.

7 The use of terror is heavily apparent under both regimes, ranging from the Third Section under Alexander II, the Statute of State Security in 1881 under Alexander III, the *Okhrana* under Nicholas, the *Cheka* under Lenin and the NKGB under Stalin. All the above rulers undoubtedly used terror as a method to control the workers. However, the scale of this terror is much greater under the communists than that under the tsars. This point is best illustrated by Stalin signing the death certificates of 6600 prisoners in 1945 in one day; this was more than the tsars had killed in 100 years. Both Lenin and Stalin saw terror as a vital component of their method of governing, with Stalin taking its scale to a new level. The use of internal passports and the continual threat of being accused of sabotage, as is illustrated by the 1928 trial of 50 engineers from a factory who were charged with plotting against Stalin, are clear examples of the terror state inflicted on the urban working classes by a government which claimed to be a 'workers' government'. Khrushchev moved away from this approach to a degree by getting rid of *Gulags* and freeing political prisoners. Nevertheless, he did not hesitate to resort to repression when necessary.

8 The tsars were not much better in their restrained use of terror against the workers with the Third Section under both Alexander II and Alexander III arresting workers for poor discipline and either sending them to Siberia, or the House of Preliminary Detention in St Petersburg. Under Nicholas the suspicion and hostility shown against the workers through incidents such as the Lena goldfield shootings in 1912 provided evidence for continuity between tsarist authority and those such as the crushing of the Kronstadt mutiny in 1921 under Lenin. The scale between the two regimes however, must be used as the deciding factor in concluding that the urban working classes were treated worse by the communist rulers than the tsars.

> 8 This paragraph strengthens the argument adopted by the candidate over the scale of repression used by the communists. It is carefully linked to a judgement about how the treatment of workers started to change post-1917.

9 Economically, the fact that, under the communists, urban unemployment was near zero per cent at a time when there was Western recession helps to portray the huge economic opportunities encountered by the workers during the communist period. The constitutions of 1924 and 1936 enshrined the workers' right to work but also ensured them age, health and unemployment insurance. Over 1.5 million workers were elevated to senior managerial positions with women having nearly as great economic opportunities as men. Women made up 40 per cent of the medical profession, with 60 per cent of all undergraduates also being women. With the introduction of wage differentials in the late 1930s, skilled urban workers were able to benefit from higher wages and become part of the newly formed communist élite. However, the workers as under the tsars were taxed heavily through indirect taxes. Under the tsars, up to 48 per cent of wages were paid in kind, something that soon began to emerge under Lenin where the impact of War Communism caused inflation to rise to a million per cent. The tsars provided little economic opportunities when compared with the communists with promotion opportunities low, and indirect taxes high. The economic grievances suffered under the tsars, especially the impact of First World War resulted in eight-hour bread queues, and eventually the 1917 Revolution. The mantra 'revolution started in the bread queue' appears very apposite here. This would therefore suggest that economically, the urban working classes suffered, and were treated worse by the tsars than the communists.

> 9 Some balanced analysis is offered here with discussion of the economic conditions experienced by workers. Although the commentary is very full, some points are possibly exaggerated, for example, 'million per cent inflation' and others lack a bit of clarity, for example, 'age insurance'. However, the range of material used shows that the student has read widely. A fair bit of skill has been used to synthesise and apply a good amount of knowledge.

10 In conclusion, in both periods, workers had long lists of grievances. These were a result of the use of terror, abuses in the social, economic and political sectors of life, the imposition of forced labour and internal passports. The diversification of industry under Khrushchev, although signalling a rise in consumer goods for the workers, as well as a rise in living standards, did not produce results great enough to compensate for the harm caused by Lenin and Stalin's rule. Overall, the communists treated the working class far worse, in terms of scale of repression, than the tsars during the period 1855–1964.

> 10 A rather clumsy ending with comment about Khrushchev bolted on. However, a clear judgement is made that is in line with the main part of the text.

> **Assessment for Essay 1**
>
> Uses a wide range of accurate, detailed and relevant evidence. Accurate and confident use of appropriate historical terminology. Answer is clearly structured and mostly coherent. **[Level IA: 18 marks out of 20]**
>
> Shows a good understanding of key concepts relevant to the question set. Good synthesis and synoptic assessment of the whole period using mini-themes. Answer is consistently analytical with developed and substantiated explanations. The ending could have been more effectively structured. **[Level IA: 37 marks out of 40]**
>
> The overall mark of 55 would take this into the A* bracket. The ending could have been more effectively structured and detracts slightly from the overall quality of the response.

Essay 2: Assess the view that the urban working classes of Russia were treated worse by the communist rulers than by the tsars in the period from 1855 to 1964

1 There were times when the communists treated the urban working classes far worse than the tsars did such as during the rule of Stalin. But there were also occasions when the tsars carried out policies that benefited working people such as reducing working hours.

2 During the time of Alexander II the urban working classes hardly existed so there was logically not an issue about how they were treated. One of the effects of the freeing of serfs was that many fled to the towns and cities looking for work in factories. This started urbanisation which in turn led to public health problems such as the spread of cholera. In this way Alexander II carried out a reform that was not helpful to the urban working class. His father, though, showed more interest in developing Russia's industry and creating more jobs. He employed Witte to push industrialisation forwards including the expansion of the Trans-Siberian railway. But like the other tsars, when workers complained about conditions, he was not afraid to use the police and army to arrest them and send them to prison.

3 Nicholas II carried on his father's economic policies thus creating more regular and better paid work for those employed in industry. He introduced factory inspectors and, by 1917, the average working day had been reduced to eight hours. Better education was also introduced for the children of workers. However, urban living conditions got worse and little was done to solve the problem of the spread of disease. Workers either lived in overcrowded blocks of flats or barracks. The average flat housed 16 people and only about 30 per cent of the houses in the main cities had running water. The supply of food was erratic especially during times of famine such as in 1922. Most people had to make do with cabbage soup. Nicholas also repressed worker strikes and protests. The best example of this was on Bloody Sunday 1905 when peaceful protesters were shot at by the imperial guard as they marched on the Winter Palace. Even when Nicholas carried out reforms to help workers through his October Manifesto he soon went back on them. In theory the *Duma* allowed the

Margin annotations

1 The introduction shows an awareness of change and continuity but is rather vague. There needed to be more indication of the line of argument that is to be adopted.

2 There is some useful analytical comment here although there is also drift towards describing how workers were treated. The student has obviously opted to cover each period of rule chronologically which is probably not the best approach to use.

3 This is very descriptive and some of the material is a bit superfluous (e.g. cabbage soup). But the factual material about accommodation is very full and relevant.

voice of the workers to be heard but by the time of the fourth *Duma* it was dominated by supporters loyal to the tsar. All of the political groups that claimed to represent worker interests, such as the SRs and SDs were clamped down on. Thus, some things seemed to improve for workers during the reign of Nicholas II but on balance urban dwellers were treated poorly.

4 The Provisional Government did not exist long enough to have much of an impact on the urban working class. The Petrograd Soviet had more effect as it helped campaign for higher wages and better working conditions. Generally, it was effective in organising workers politically and helping to overthrow a regime that was unwilling to help working people.

> 4 A thin section which continues the narrative approach.

5 When the Bolsheviks seized control they promised that Russia would eventually be ruled by the proletariat. However, the first thing they did was disband the Constituent Assembly which was democratically elected and which consisted of individuals who were intent on improving conditions for urban people. This was similar to how Nicholas II manipulated the *Duma*. Urban people were then badly affected by the Civil War as they were asked to work excessively long hours to produce munitions for the Red Army. There were again food shortages due to War Communism although things changed with the introduction of the NEP. Some workers became Nepmen and made quite a bit out of selling a range of consumer goods.

> 5 The candidate has maintained a certain level of focus on the exact demands of the question. There is also a decent attempt to provide some comparative analysis and evaluation.

6 The hardest time for the urban working class was under Stalin. The Five-Year Plans resulted in increased working hours and lower pay. Production targets were set which were virtually impossible to meet. When workers failed to do so they were either fined or sacked. New accommodation was built for workers but it was worse than ever. Some families ended up living in the hallways and bathrooms of single apartments which they shared with others. Education improved as more schools were built. The only problem with this was that the curriculum was very restricted. All children had to learn about communism and how wonderful Stalin was. Workers who complained were badly treated as they had been with the tsars and Lenin. Those who were accused of being saboteurs or wreckers were very harshly dealt with. Rebel workers were purged either by being exiled to salt mines in Siberia or executed. Some workers did well under Stalin especially if they increased their own productivity levels. The Stakhanovites were given substantial financial rewards and medals for exceeding production targets. They were set up as heroes for others to follow. Generally, workers who remained loyal to the party were rewarded with promotion and better living conditions. It could also be argued that Stalin benefitted workers by ensuring that Russia was ready to fight and defeat Germany during the First World War. If Germany had won, the Russian people would have been treated horrendously.

> 6 Quite a reasonable knowledge and understanding of the treatment of workers by Stalin is displayed but the content could have been used more effectively if a synoptic approach had been adopted.

7 A fair summary of the policies of Khrushchev towards urban workers but, once again, with little attempt to link this with the actions of other rulers.

7 Conditions improved for urban dwellers during the rule of Khrushchev. He doubled the amount of housing and reduced overcrowding, although the Five-Year Plans were continued, targets were more realistic and workers were not bullied as much to achieve them. Education and health care improved although there were still not many consumer items around as the emphasis continued to be on producing goods for the military. Destalinisation resulted in less oppression of working people although they still had to obey the party line. One negative development was the escalation of the Cold War. Khrushchev's brinkmanship policy nearly took Russia into a nuclear war. This meant that Russian people often lived in a state of fear just as they had done in the earlier periods of communist rule.

8 This is quite a solid conclusion. There is a fair attempt to make a judgement that is congruent with the rest of the essay.

8 The urban working classes were treated worse by the communists especially Stalin, who took repression to new heights. However, there were times, such as in 1905 when the tsars were just as nasty towards workers. Of course, the irony is that the communists were meant to create an ideal society for urban workers but they failed miserably.

Assessment for Essay 2

Where evidence is used it is accurate and relevant. The response is mostly well organised and written in a clear, legible manner. **[Level III: 13 marks out of 20]**

There is some attempt to provide a balanced, analytical response but a fair bit of the explanation is unevenly developed. Also, some of the support provided is a bit thin and general. **[Level III: 24 marks out of 40]**

The overall mark is 37 which is a middling to low C. The candidate has made a reasonable attempt to deal with the concept of change and continuity and to remain focused on the exact demands of the question. But, there is a lack of some supporting material and some comments needed explaining more fully. The essay would have benefited from a framework that revolved around mini-themes. This would have allowed for more rigorous comparison and a response that clearly showed an ability to write synoptically.

4 War and Revolution and the Development of Government

OVERVIEW

This chapter focuses on how a number of different wars affected the structure and function of Russian governments throughout the period. To understand the consequences of wars, it is helpful to understand how they came about in the first place and how they developed. However, examination questions on this issue will always centre on the impact of wars on government.

Another general point to make is that where wars prompted economic and social change, this often had a knock-on effect for governments. For example, wars always disrupted patterns of economic growth which meant that politicians then had to devise strategies to get the economy back on track. Thus, it is important to consider how wars impacted on the economy and society and not just directly on politics and government.

From 1855 to 1964, Russians were involved in eight different wars; these are covered in the chapter chronologically as follows:

- The Crimean War 1853–6
- The Russo-Turkish War 1877–8
- The Russo-Japanese War 1904–5
- The First World War 1914–18
- The Russian Revolution 1917
- The Russian Civil War 1917–21
- The Second World War 1939–45
- The Cold War 1947–64

Note making

Make your notes using the headings and sub-headings. Ensure that you focus mainly on the impact of the wars. Nearer to the final examination, it would be a good idea to condense your notes further in the form of a table (wars listed on one side with corresponding boxes for economic, social and political effects).

Key question
What were the consequences of the Crimean War for the development of Russian government?

Key terms

Ottoman Turks
Those who were part of the dynasty originally founded by Osman (c1300) which governed the Turkish Empire until 1922.

Great Powers
Britain, France, Russia, Germany (Prussia before 1871) and Austria-Hungary before 1914.

Eastern Question
The issues that arose over the decline of the Turkish Ottoman Empire.

Straits
The stretch of sea from the Dardanelles into the Bosporus.

Sultan
Muslim head of the Ottoman Empire.

Principalities
Territories ruled over by a member of a royal family, usually a prince.

Protectorates
States that were temporarily protected by another, usually more powerful state.

Legiticism
Policy based on the idea that what was being done was right and just in the eyes of the majority.

1 | The Crimean War 1853–6

The Crimean War was fought between Russia and the **Ottoman Turks** with the latter supported by France and Britain. As with all the wars during the period, an understanding of the origins of the conflict help explain how it impinged on the development of government. Note that the first section on origins goes back to look at events in the 1820s. Although this book covers the period from 1855 to 1964, it is relevant, with the Crimean War, to consider events that precede the start of the war. It would otherwise be very difficult to make any judgement about the relative importance of the war.

Long-term origins

Russia, along with the other **Great Powers**, was concerned to resolve the **Eastern Question** in a way that best preserved its economic and political interests. A number of events illustrated how worried Russian tsars were over the crumbling Ottoman Empire (that is, the Eastern Question):

- In 1827 Russia, along with Britain and France, decided to support an agreement with Turkey to allow the Greeks to govern themselves (Greece had been part of the Ottoman Empire). The **Sultan** (ruler) of Turkey was reluctant to stick to the agreement which resulted in the Battle of Navarino Bay. Russian, British and French naval squadrons combined to defeat the Sultan's naval fleet. After this, Tsar Nicholas I did a deal with the Sultan (under the Akkermann Convention) that allowed Russian merchant shipping easier access through the **Straits** and the Turkish seas. Two months later the Sultan reneged on the agreement and a full-blown war between Russia and Turkey ensued. After major Russian victories in the Balkans and Caucasus, the Treaty of Adrianople was signed.
- The Treaty of Adrianople (1829) stipulated the following:
  - the Sultan had to honour the Akkermann agreements
  - territory in the Caucasus and mouth of the Danube on the Black Sea was ceded to Russia
  - the Danubian **principalities** of Moldavia and Wallachia (both occupied by Russia during the war) were to be recognised as temporary Russian **protectorates**.
- The war against Turkey had bothered Nicholas I as he believed it contradicted the concept of **legiticism** that underpinned his foreign policy. Partly to make up for this, in 1833 he decided to help the Ottomans in a struggle against Egyptian rebels led by Mehmet Ali. Russian efforts were rewarded through the Treaty of Unkiar Skelesi.
- The Treaty of Unkiar Skelesi (1833) resulted in:
  - Turkey agreeing to close the Straits, during time of conflict, to foreign warships. It was also implied (although not clearly stated) that Russian warships would be allowed to enter the Bosporus and, thus, the heart of the Ottoman Empire. The historian Walter G. Moss believes this was the first attempt

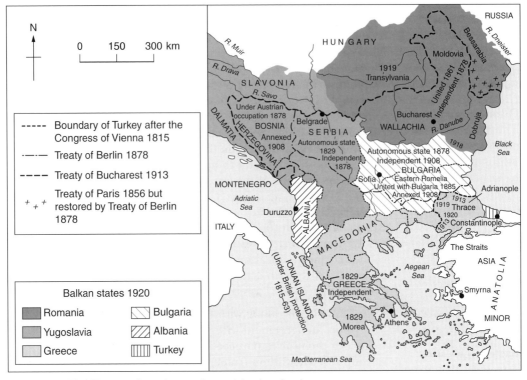

Figure 4.1: The Eastern Question and countries involved.

by Russia to 'transform the Turkish core area into a Russian protectorate'
- in return Russia agreed to support Turkey if it was attacked by another of the world powers.
- A further revolt by Mehmet Ali culminated in the signing of the Straits Convention (1841). This, partly as a result of pressure from the other Great Powers, weakened Russia's arrangements with the Turks:
  - all of the major European powers conceded that Turkey should ban all foreign warships from entering the Straits during periods of international tension
  - to clarify the confusion over the 1833 agreement, Russian warships were banned from the Dardanelles and the Bosporus.

Although this aggrieved Nicholas I, he knew Russia was not really in a position to go to war with any of the other European powers. He therefore proceeded to use diplomacy to ensure that Russia's interests in the East were preserved.

Short-term origins
By the middle of the nineteenth century, a dispute between Russia and France arose over Orthodox Christian and Catholic rights and duties in the Holy Lands, which were part of the Ottoman Empire. Arguments over this issue escalated and sparked the beginning of the Crimean War:

- Before the squabble erupted, Russia had persuaded the Sultan to allow special privileges to be granted to Orthodox Christians in the Holy Lands. This was considered fair as Orthodox Christians represented a majority in the region and contributed much to the local economy.
- This arrangement was challenged, in 1851, by Charles Louis Napoleon, the first President of the French Republic and Emperor of France from 1852 to 1870. He stated that, according to a rather obscure treaty of 1740, the French had a moral obligation to be the sole protectors of Christians in the Holy Lands. This sudden renewal of claim was made as a result of the French leader's desire to win back support from prominent members of the French Catholic Church.
- Late in 1852, the Sultan agreed that Catholics should be consulted over the restoration of the **Holy Sepulchre** in Jerusalem and were to be given access to Bethlehem's Church of the Nativity.
- Nicholas I was understandably annoyed by the French intervention and sent Prince A.S. Menshikov to Constantinople to obtain confirmation of Russia's 'superior' rights in the Holy Land. The Turks were very worried by Menshikov's claims about the numbers of Christians and amount of territory that needed to be controlled by Russia and therefore refused his demands.
- In July 1853, Nicholas retaliated by sending troops into the principalities of Moldavia and Wallachia. Requests from the Turks, British and French were made for Nicholas to backtrack but he refused. Turkey then declared war on Russia (October 1853) and the British and French sent fleets to the Dardanelles, formally declaring war on Russia themselves in March 1854. Nicholas then changed his mind and withdrew forces from the principalities, in August 1854, in an attempt to appease his European rivals. His actions came too late and by October the Siege of Sevastopol (the main port in the Crimea) was well under way.

Key term

Holy Sepulchre
The cave outside Jerusalem in which the body of Christ is believed to have lain between his burial and Resurrection.

The origins of the war say much about the Tsar's concern to preserve Russia's status as one of the Great Powers. It was important for Nicholas to stand up to the British and French so that the Russian people maintained faith in the Romanovs and, hence, autocracy. But the background to the war also showed that Nicholas had many reservations about taking on the other powers; he was not confident that Russia had the right economic and social infrastructure to win a major conflict. The implication was that the Russian government would have to make some radical changes if Russia was to maintain its standing in the world.

The impact of the war
General
The poor showing of the Russian military during the war coupled with the stipulations of the Treaty of Paris led to public discussion about the future of the Russian Empire. A significant number of Russians, especially those known as Slavophiles, questioned how

The course of the Crimean War: main events

- November 1853: The Russians destroyed the Turkish fleet at Sinope. The sinking of part of the Turkish fleet was a response to a major Turkish attack on Russian forces positioned in Wallachia. Over 4000 Turks were killed and the incident sparked intense protest from Britain and France.
- January 1854: Both the British and French navies were positioned in the Black Sea by this date. However, British politicians, despite public pressure, were still intent on averting a full-blown war.
- February 1854: Britain and France sent Russia an ultimatum to withdraw from the principalities, which was ignored. The British and French now felt obliged to commit to war.
- March 1854: British and French declared war on Russia and gave support to Turks.
- August 1854: Under pressure from the threat that Austria might join the war on the side of the British and French, Russia decided to pull out of the Principalities. Austria proceeded to make peace proposals (the 'Four Points') but these were not accepted by the Tsar until November 1854. By that time Britain showed a willingness to prolong the war to impose further damage on Russia and force the Tsar to make greater concessions over access to the Black Sea.
- September 1854: Britain and France invaded the Crimea. However, they were slow to attack the key Crimean port of Sevastopol. This allowed Russian forces to regroup within the port which inevitably led to a siege. The Battle of Alma was the first major confrontation of the Crimean campaign. It was noteworthy due to the fact that the Russians lost 6000 troops and were using outmoded weaponry (Russian guns were captured that dated back to 1799). Other notable battles occurred at Inkerman and Balaclava but they failed to achieve a breakthrough for any of the forces concerned.
- February 1855: Nicholas I died of pneumonia. He was replaced by his son Alexander II.
- October 1854–September 1855: The Siege of Sevastopol. This was a long, drawn-out affair mainly due to adverse winter weather conditions, the fortifications of Sevastopol and the resilience of the Russian defenders. But by August 1856 the Russians were suffering from 2000 to 3000 casualties daily. After a series of severe artillery bombardments in the late summer of 1856, the Russians eventually surrendered. The strategic importance of the port meant that surrender was a major setback for the Russians
- September 1855–January 1856: The war petered out during this period. Austria renewed threats to join the war and Russia eventually agreed to peace talks based on the original 'Four Points' plan (see above).
- March 1856: Treaty of Paris was agreed.

great Russia really was. Many argued that Russia's status as a great world power had been severely damaged.

Casualties

According to the historian Alan Farmer, 'the Crimean War involved far heavier casualties than any other European war fought between 1815 and 1914. Between 650,000 and 750,000 are thought to have died. Britain lost 22,000, France 90,000, Russia 450,000 and Turkey about 150,000. Only one in five lost their lives in battle: most died of disease.'

The Treaty of Paris, March 1856

This resulted in the following:

- The duty to protect Christian subjects in the Ottoman Empire was handed over to the other European powers.

- Russia gave up its claim to act as the protector of the principalities.
- Russia had to agree to hand a substantial chunk of Bessarabia (part of the South-West Russian empire) to Moldavia.
- Most importantly, Russia was prohibited from maintaining a fleet in the Black Sea and had to remove all naval fortifications along the Black Sea coastline. Given the logistical importance of this to Russia, such a measure was humiliating.

The treaty obviously highlighted the weak position Russia found itself in. As the historian Geoffrey Hosking has argued, 'at a stroke Russia ceased to be a leading guarantor of the *status quo* and became a revisionist power, dedicated to regaining sovereign power over its own coastline'. Ironically, the seemingly harsh terms of the treaty illustrated how fearful the other European powers were of the **Great Russian Bear** and that the military weaknesses revealed in the war might easily be remedied.

The war had an indirect impact on the development of Russian government in that it appeared to act as a catalyst for a number of significant economic, social and political reforms. A more direct impact came in the changes to the way in which localities were governed although this was linked to the major social reform of Alexander II's reign, the emancipation of the serfs.

Key term

Great Russian Bear
A term used by the West to describe the perceived military threat posed by Russia.

The emancipation of the serfs

The Crimean War supposedly, in comparison to the other combatants, revealed Russia to be backward and underdeveloped. This was especially true when it came to transport, communications and the use of technology in general. Industrialisation had taken root in Russia but it was progressing at a much slower rate than in Britain and France. For many Slavophiles and Westernisers, the root cause of this stagnation was the continued existence of serfdom. The Slavophile, Samarin, claimed that: 'We are defeated not by the external forces of the Western alliance, but by our own internal weaknesses … stagnation of thought, depression of productive forces, the rift between government and people, disunity between the social classes, and the enslavement of one of them to another … prevent the government from deploying all the means available to it … and mobilising the strength of the nation.' This was a sentiment that Alexander II sympathised with and it encouraged him to 'reform from above'.

Whether the Tsar would have abolished serfdom regardless of the war is open to conjecture but it is worth noting that Nicholas I had considered the idea but rejected it as it would have led to 'an even more ruinous evil'. Also, it was some time after the war that the edict was actually made, suggesting that other considerations had to be taken before the reform could be enacted (see pages 114–21). As serfdom had underpinned the way in which Russian society was structured, organised and administered, it was natural that the abolition of it would lead to some change in the way Russia was to be governed.

Reform of local government

The emancipation of the serfs resulted in a reduced political role for the nobility at local level (see pages 114–21). The creation of the *Zemstva* filled the gap but was also significant in that members of local government now had to be elected. Although this element of democracy was watered down by the fact that there were property qualifications attached to voting, it gave some indication that tsars might be prepared to lessen their autocratic grip. In the longer run though, when the *Zemstva* started to flex their muscles (see pages 43–4), the tsarist regime returned to repression to quieten them.

Reform of the military

If Russia was to maintain its world status, it was crucial that a modernisation of the military had to occur. At the start of the war, the Russian army consisted of about one million men made up mostly from peasants. To instil order, harsh discipline was enforced including the notorious 'running of the gauntlet', a punishment which involved running through a tunnel of soldiers who would beat the miscreant with wooden clubs.

Accommodation was poor which had the knock-on effect of diseases spreading; it is estimated that from 1833 to 1855, about one million soldiers died through ill-health. Coupled with the lack of decent clothing and equipment (including weapons), this meant that the morale of Russian troops was low. Leo Tolstoy summed up the situation towards the end of the war when he said that 'we have no army, we have a horde of slaves cowed by discipline, ordered about by thieves and slave traders'. It was no wonder, therefore, that many figures in the tsarist regime demanded reforms to be made.

From 1862 to 1874, a string of military reforms were enacted under the guidance of **Dmitrii Milyutin**. Using the Prussian military system as a model, Milyutin reduced service in the army to 15 years, modernised training and provided rigorous instruction for officers. The result was a far more professional army and one that was more in line with that of Western rivals. Also of importance to the government was the fact that it now had an army that, in theory, could be relied on to help maintain civil order at home as well as fight wars overseas.

> **Dmitrii Milyutin 1816–1912**
> Military reformer and War Minister (1861–81).
>
> **Key figure**

Other reforms

During the reign of Alexander II there were other key reforms most notably in the field of education and the church. However, it would be difficult to link the origins of these changes to the Crimean War. One economic development of note that was undoubtedly stimulated by the conflict was the expansion of the railway system. The war had revealed how slowly Russia had been to mobilise resources compared with the enemy. Thus, railway development became a priority. Using foreign loans, nearly two billion roubles were spent on constructing over 20,000 kilometres of track from 1861 to 1878. In a relatively short space of time, Russia had a transport system that boosted its ability to deal with the logistical problems of expanding, protecting and maintaining an empire.

The changes and most of the reforms of Alexander II's period of rule undoubtedly appear to be linked to the Crimean War. But, it is still important to consider whether such changes would have occurred without the war. Also, although Russia seemed to enter a more liberal phase of government post-Crimea, autocracy remained firmly in place.

Key question
How valid is the view that the Russo-Turkish War had a limited impact on the development of Russian government?

2 | The Russo-Turkish War 1877–8

Long-term origins

By the 1870s Russia was finding difficulty in maintaining friendly relations with Austria. Both had an interest in the Balkans and, more generally, the Eastern Question. Austria was especially concerned at the increase in Slav nationalism which appeared to be seriously destabilising the Ottoman Empire. The Austro-Hungarian Empire had a significant Slavic population and there was a fear that they would be influenced by what was happening in other Slavic communities. Russian interest in the Balkans revolved around religious issues (that is, the need to protect Orthodox Christians living in the region) and the strategic importance of the Black Sea and Mediterranean.

The 1870s also witnessed a rise in Russian nationalism and **pan-Slavism**. One of the main influences was the Slavonic Benevolent Committee (SBC) led by **M.P. Pogodin**. Some very prominent members of the Russian intelligentsia belonged to this body including Dostoevsky, Fadeev, Aksakov and Ignatiev. By 1877 it had over 1000 committed members but was probably more significant in terms of the pressure it was exerting on senior politicians to adopt a foreign policy that focused on uniting Slav peoples.

Key term

Pan-Slavism
The movement to unite all Slavic peoples as one nation.

Key figure

M.P. Pogodin 1800–75
A well-known and highly respected professor of Russian history.

Short-term origins

In the middle of 1875 Herzegovina, closely followed by Bosnia, rebelled against the Ottomans. By the spring of 1876 they were joined by Bulgaria and, in the summer, Serbia and Montenegro actually declared war on Turkey. A Russian-influenced plan to stop the crisis escalating was presented to the warring parties. Land, tax and religious reforms were promised to the Balkan states (to be administered by Turkey) but this package was unacceptable to the other Western states especially Britain. The British Prime Minister, Disraeli, was wary of Russia trying to manipulate a situation to benefit its own interests. The plan was never implemented and the war raged on.

The Russian people continued to provide support for their Slav compatriots. Pressure on the Russian government to take more direct action grew from different quarters. The SBC, the Orthodox Church, the military and individuals such as Dmitri Tolstoy all campaigned for the Tsar to be more belligerent. Connected to this was the Ignatiev initiative which resulted in the

Russian ambassador in Constantinople intonating to the Serbs that they could rely on Russian military support if the war intensified.

By the autumn of 1876 it was evident that the Serbs were losing the war. Russia threatened to attack Turkey unless a truce was called. Their wish was granted and a six-week armistice was granted.

After the armistice had finished, Turkey returned to taking an aggressive stance against the Serbs. Mostly as a result of Russian public opinion, Alexander II declared war on Turkey in April 1877. The decision was aided by Austria agreeing to remain neutral as long as they could have jurisdiction over Herzegovina and Bosnia. The war was welcomed by Russian intellectuals particularly the radicals and liberals. They saw the war as an opportunity to release fellow Slavs from the tyranny of an imperialist oppressor.

The course of the Russo-Turkish War: main events
- Russian forces faced difficulties in the early stages of the war especially in Bulgaria and the Caucasus. Nevertheless, despite experiencing thousands of casualties, the army advanced
- It is worth noting that the army was still in a period of transition after the Milyutin reforms. Weaknesses that had been apparent in the Crimean War had not been fully eradicated.
- There were two exceptions to the above. The engineer section of the army shone; they were crucial to the successful crossing of the Danube and to the capture of Plevna. The Russian navy was also very successful in using steam-powered vessels to destroy the Turkish fleet.
- Early in 1878 Turkey agreed to an armistice.

The impact of the war
In March 1879, the Treaty of San Stefano was signed between Russia and Turkey. It stipulated the following:

- Russia was to regain South Bessarabia which it had lost during the Crimean War.
- Russia also made substantial territorial gains in the Caucasus.
- Turkey was forced to pay a **war indemnity** to Russia.
- Recognition was given to the independence of Serbia, Montenegro and Romania. Serbia and Montenegro also made their own territorial gains.
- Turkey was served the task of carrying out reforms to benefit Herzegovina and Bosnia.
- A 'large' Bulgaria was established.

War indemnity A sum of money paid by one nation to another as a result of losing a war.

Key term

Unfortunately for Russia, the conditions of the treaty offended and worried Austria-Hungary and Britain. Russia feared that those who were upset might decide to provoke a bigger, more costly conflict over the Balkans. The Tsar therefore decided to accept an offer from the German Chancellor, Bismarck, to broker a bigger peace conference in Berlin. The Congress of Berlin was held in mid-1878. The following was decided:

- Russia was allowed to retain its right to South Bessarabia and kept gains in the Caucasus.

- Austria-Hungary was given the right to govern Herzegovina and Bosnia.
- Britain took over the administration of Cyprus to strengthen its interests and influence in the Balkans.
- Bulgaria became smaller.

Although Russia gained territory and money (from the indemnity) and saw the Ottoman Empire further weakened, Russian nationalists were very unhappy at what happened in Berlin. For the pan-Slavic supporters in particular, the concessions made to Austria-Hungary and Britain were unacceptable. They saw this as amounting to a loss of world status. Alexander II found it very difficult to deal with the unrest that this created and some historians have argued that this one event was responsible for his assassination in 1884.

3 | The Russo-Japanese War 1904–5

Long-term origins

In 1894, Japan fought a limited war against China with the aim of gaining territory already under Chinese control. Japan won and was 'rewarded' by obtaining land around Port Arthur together with a war indemnity. Russia and the other Great Powers were worried that Japan might expand further to threaten their own economic interests in the east. Using skilful diplomacy, the Great Powers were able, in a fairly short space of time, to persuade Japan to return Port Arthur to the Chinese. But the situation was further complicated by the fact that Russia gave money to China to pay off its war debts and that China was compliant in allowing Russia to construct the Chinese Eastern Railway across Manchuria (therefore expanding Russian influence in the area).

In 1897 Germany invaded Kiaochow, in eastern China, and the other Great Powers demanded a share of the spoils. France became more active in the south and Britain looked to consolidate interests in central China. Russia was wary of the Western Europeans expanding their influence in this way.

Russia was able to negotiate a 25-year lease of Port Arthur from China and turned it into a naval base. The latter was then joined to the Chinese Eastern Railway via a branch line. Japan obviously felt threatened by this turn of events as the influence of the Great Powers increasingly started to impinge on Japan's own sphere of interest. In particular, Port Arthur was strategically placed and gave the Russians great scope for controlling the seas between China and Japan.

The Chinese grew angry at the incursions of the Great Powers into its territory. Unrest in China grew resulted in the **Boxer Rebellion**. As the Russians started supporting the Western Europeans during this time (despite reservations about their intentions in China), especially with the help of the navy based at Port Arthur, a mini-war between Russia and China broke out. Russia easily defeated the Chinese but, as a result of Japanese

Key question
How far did the Russo-Japanese war differ from the wars that preceded 1904 with respect to the impact on the development of Russian government?

Key term

Boxer Rebellion
A seven-week siege of foreign embassies in Peking by Chinese rebels.

intervention, Russia backed down from insisting on too severe a peace treaty. In fact, Russia agreed to withdraw forces from Manchuria by 1903. Russian leaders seemed happy enough with the military victory which they believed showed that their forces were superior to any oriental army.

Russia and Japan continued to reveal an interest in occupying and controlling Korea. Some historians have argued that Japan was willing to work a trade-off that would have allowed Russia to stay in Manchuria while Japan took over Korea. However, it is not clear as to what exactly the Russian government wanted. Some ministers, such as Plevhe, Minister for the Interior, seemed to be pushing for an outright war with Japan to settle disagreements once and for all. This would have had the added bonus of deflecting the attention of the Russian public away from mounting social problems. Others, worrying mainly about financial cost and lack of preparedness, were against a war. They included **Kuropatkin** and **Lamsdorff**; there is more disagreement over the stance of Witte who held, at this time, the important position of Minister of Finance.

Japanese attempts at diplomacy over the Korean issue were rebuffed by the St Petersburg administration. Partly as a result, Japan, in 1902, formulated an alliance with Britain. As France was an ally of Britain, the French were unlikely to take sides with Russia if a war between Russia and Japan was to break out.

Short-term origins

Russia reneged on its promise to withdraw troops from Manchuria which angered the Japanese. In February 1903 Japan retaliated by launching a night attack on the Pacific Squadron at

A.N. Kuropatkin 1848–1925
Military reformer and War Minister (1898–1904)

V.N. Lamsdorff 1841–1907
One of Nicholas II's most valued ministers (Foreign Minister 1900–5).

Key figures

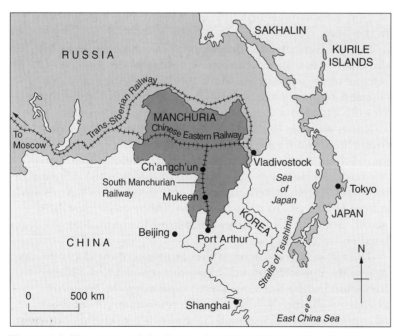

Figure 4.2: The course of the Russo-Japanese War and the countries involved.

Port Arthur. This escapade was something of a shambles but it did result in damage to three Russian ships. It also seemed to have a negative effect on Russian morale.

Japan then proceeded to blockade Port Arthur. Preparations were made by both parties for a major sea battle to occur.

The course of the Russo-Japanese War: main events

- Battle of Yalu. The Japanese moved north from Korea to confront Russia in southern Manchuria. Outnumbered by about three to one, Russian forces were well beaten. This was an enormous shock to the Tsar and the other Great Powers.
- The siege of Port Arthur continued, isolating about 60,000 Russian troops. In December 1905, the port eventually surrendered.
- May 1905: Rozhestvensky's Baltic Squadron, on its way to relieve Port Arthur, came up against Admiral Togo's fleet at Tsushima Straits. This proved to be another terrible defeat for Russia and emphasised the technological superiority of the Japanese navy.
- 1905: The final straw for Russia came with a humiliating defeat at Mukden. This prompted peace talks and the signing of a treaty.

The impact of the war
General

Similar to the Crimean War, the disastrous outcome of the Russo-Japanese war led to doubts being expressed about the ability of the Tsar to maintain Russia's world status and concerns about the efficacy of autocracy in general. Also, in comparison to the Crimean War, the conflict with Japan was followed by significant reform. This was because the Russo-Japanese War seemed to spark far more social unrest in the Russian homeland which in turn influenced the nature of the reforms enacted by Nicholas II.

The Treaty of Portsmouth, August 1905
This resulted in the following:

- Russia was forced to withdraw from Port Arthur, south Sakhalin and south Manchuria.
- Russian leaders had to acknowledge Japanese sovereignty in Korea.

Reforms
The war revealed that Russian military leaders had a lack of knowledge, understanding and skill in dealing with an enemy that, on paper, was vastly inferior. The Russian public associated military incompetence of this order with the Tsar himself; this appeared to fuel discontent at home rather than extinguish it, which had been one of the key aims of the war. In fact some historians believe that the social unrest that occurred in 1905 was tantamount to a revolution. Thus, Nicholas II, rather reluctantly, introduced an element of democracy to Russia by setting up the *Duma* (see page 30). The hope was that the public would be convinced that the Tsar was willing to become more accountable for his actions and those of his advisers. It is unlikely that this would have happened without the war as the Tsar was a staunch

adherent of 'autocracy, orthodoxy and nationalism'. This is reinforced by the fact that in a very short space of time the powers of the *Duma* were greatly diminished.

Despite the expansion of Russia's rail network since the Crimean War, the Russo-Japanese conflict revealed serious communication and transport weaknesses. The Trans-Siberian railway, still unfinished, had failed to solve the logistical problem of getting troops and supplies to war zones quickly and efficiently. The result was further investment in the transport infrastructure and, more generally, in industry. Ironically, such developments also led to rapid urbanisation and mounting public health problems. Poor working and living conditions produced an increasingly discontented populace; reforms were enacted with the promise of raising living standards but they appeared to do the reverse.

Summary diagram: Similarities and differences in the effects of the Crimean, Russo-Turkish and Russo-Japanese wars on the development of Russian government

Similarities	Differences
• Russia lost to enemies that, on paper, they should have defeated • The Russian people were critical of leaders and took to the streets to protest • The wars all led to programmes of reform • Some of the reforms were designed to change the way Russia was governed but autocracy remained in place after each conflict • The wars were costly but not as damaging to the economy as later wars proved to be	• The Crimean War was different from the others in that Russia had to fight Britain and France as well as Turkey • The level of social unrest that followed the Russo-Japanese War was much higher than that which led on from the other two wars. Some historians go as far as to say the protests of 1905 constituted a revolution • The Russo-Turkish War had the least significant impact on the development of Russian government

---

4 | The First World War 1914–18

Long-term origins

For most of the nineteenth century Russian foreign policy was dependent on the maintenance of friendly relations with **Prussia** and Austria-Hungary. This fell apart when the unified Germany under Wilhelm II failed to renew the Reinsurance Treaty of 1887 (a treaty between Russia and Germany whereby both parties agreed not to support a third party with whom either might fall into conflict). Russia was then pushed to seek new allies and subsequently formed an alliance, in 1894, with France. This was logical given that the other great European power, Britain, remained wary of Russian designs.

Relations with France were further strengthened after the Russo-Japanese War as Russia actively sought allies in case further

Key question
To what extent was the First World War the most important turning point in the development of Russian government from 1855 to 1964?

Prussia
Important Germanic state before the unification of Germany in 1871.

Key term

Balkan Wars of 1912–13
These came in two phases. First, the Balkan League went to war against Turkey with the hope of getting the Turks to withdraw from Macedonia so that the latter could be divided up among League members. The Turks were defeated and signed an armistice in December 1912. Second, immediately after the armistice, Bulgaria claimed that it was being cheated out of territory handed over by the Turks by another member of the League, Serbia. Bulgaria then attacked Serbia. Greece, Romania and Turkey went to the aid of the Serbs and the Bulgarian forces were defeated. Bulgaria was forced to hand over all of the gains made during the first war.

Balkan League
An alliance, put together between the spring and autumn of 1912, between Serbia, Bulgaria, Greece and Montenegro.

conflicts with Japan occurred. Given the cordial nature of relations between France and Britain, it was not long before France, Britain and Russia joined together to form an alliance (the Triple Entente) to counter the threat of the growing partnership between Austria and Germany (the Central Powers). As the latter were stronger, in a military sense, than Russia, some historians have argued that the Triple Entente was not the best arrangement for the Tsar to agree to.

The continued break-up of the Ottoman Empire worsened the relationship between Austria-Hungary and Russia. Both had an interest in the Eastern Question, with Austria-Hungary looking to protect its own empire from Balkan nationalist influence and Russia seeking to support Slavic Balkan states when necessary. In 1908, Russia made a deal with Austria-Hungary that once again allowed Russian shipping free movement through the Straits (see the map on page 150) in exchange for Russian support for the Austrian annexation of Bosnia-Herzegovina. Two problems arose from this. First, Serbia believed that Bosnia-Herzegovina was Serbian and that, as a Slavic country, its claims deserved support from compatriot Slavs (especially Russia). Second, the other European powers rejected the idea of allowing Russia easy access through the Straits. On top of this, Germany reacted by stating that it would support Austria-Hungary if the so-called Annexation Crisis got out of hand. The tsarist regime felt humiliated by and helpless at the German response; Russia was simply not prepared enough to take on the Central Powers and win.

The **Balkan Wars of 1912–13** were also a disappointment to Russia. The hope had been that the **Balkan League** would deal a serious blow to the prestige and status of Austria-Hungary but instead they squabbled over gains made from the Turks. Bulgaria, in particular, was weakened by this episode; this was serious for Russia as Bulgaria was seen as the Slav state most in line with Russian thinking and planning.

The Balkans crisis was significant in that it illustrated that Russia was not in a position to dictate how serious conflicts between the European powers could be resolved. It once more revealed a degree of political and military impotence which angered people at home and did not bode well if disagreements over the Balkans escalated.

Short-term origins

In June 1914, Archduke Franz Ferdinand of Austria-Hungary was assassinated by Gabriel Princip, a member of a Serbian nationalist group. From this point in time it was virtually impossible for Russia not to get involved in a disagreement that was likely to grow into a much bigger conflict. Russia had an obligation to protect Serbia, a fellow Slavic state, against possible Austrian retaliation. There was also the prospect that the incident would galvanise Austria-Hungary into using a war against Serbia as a springboard for making other gains in the Balkans which would have been detrimental to Russian interests. Thus, it was not surprising that, when Austria-Hungary declared war on Serbia in July 1914, Russia reacted by issuing a **mobilisation order**.

Mobilisation caused a dilemma for Russian politicians and military leaders. A partial mobilisation, in defence of the Slavic countries in the south-west, would have left Russia vulnerable to attack by Germany in the west. As the Russian railway system was still inadequate in that links to the west were undeveloped, it would have been very difficult, at short notice, to move troops to defend against German incursion. On the other hand, there were those who argued that full mobilisation was too antagonistic and that Russia might find itself embroiled in a war on a scale that was catastrophic.

The full mobilisation order of 30 July was designed to act as a deterrent but it did not prevent both Germany (1 August) and Austria-Hungary (5 August) from declaring war on Russia. This was quickly followed by the implementation of the German **Schlieffen Plan** and further built on by the establishment of an **Eastern Front**. This rapid escalation of the conflict was what the bulk of Russian leaders had feared the most.

The course of the First World War: main events

- August and September 1914: An initial Russian victory at Gumbinnen was followed by disastrous defeats at Tannenberg and the Masurian Lakes.
- February 1915: Russian forces were pushed back from East Prussia but in March managed to take Memel.
- August 1915: Nicholas II took personal command of the Russian forces much to the consternation of many of his advisers. The Russian retreat was temporarily halted but by September Nicholas was forced to abandon Vilna.
- February 1916: A glimmer of hope emerged as Russian troops took Ezerum from the Ottomans.
- June 1916: The Brusilov Offensive was launched with the intention of gaining lost ground and appeasing discontent that was spreading at home. There was some initial success but the Germans easily snuffed out the threat.
- June and July 1917: An all-out attack on Austrian forces was made but by the end of July the Russians were once more in retreat.
- August 1917: Russia withdrew from the strategically important port of Riga in Latvia.
- December 1917: Peace talks at Brest-Litovsk resulted in the signing of a treaty (1918). Trotsky claimed that the conditions amounted to a *diktat* (see page 38).

Casualties

Russian casualties for the whole war of the were around eight million, including 1.7 million dead and 2.4 million captured.

The impact of the war

A useful way of analysing the impact of the First World War on Russian government is to consider two schools of thought; one is the so-called 'optimist' school, the other the 'pessimist' school.

The optimists

The optimists argue that tsarism and autocracy, by definition, were extremely resilient to the forces of change. It needed a

Key terms

Mobilisation order
The order by the government for the military to be organised to go to war. A part mobilisation refers to some of the military being prepared for a limited conflict (that is, against a relatively small state). Full mobilisation means that all of the military would be in a state of readiness to go to war.

Schlieffen Plan
The plan put together in 1905 by the Chief of the German General Staff, General Count Alfred Von Schlieffen (1833–1913), to act as a blueprint for a German attack in the West.

Eastern Front
Where the German and Austrian-Hungarian forces met the Russian forces in Eastern Europe.

dramatic and unique event to completely change the nature of Russian government. The First World War fitted the bill perfectly. The optimists claim that Russia was never able to get to grips with the demands of the world's first industrial war (that is, the first large-scale war to be fought using the products of industrialisation) and it was inevitable that the Russian people would point the finger of blame towards those who led them into the conflict. Furthermore, without the war, the Tsar would have coped with the demands for further constitutional reform and, gradually, changes to government would have occurred which would quieten the critics. This was already a trend that had started, particularly from 1905 onwards, and there was little reason to believe that further progress would not be made.

The optimist line of thought about the impact of the war is neat and cogent. Military failures resulted in economic pressures which in turn impacted on the daily lives of Russians on the **Home Front**. The consequence was that impetus was given to levels of social unrest not witnessed before. The scale and degree of coordination of protest were such that the authorities could not cope and only a drastic change in government averted a state of anarchy. For the optimists, the formation of the Provisional Government was not a disaster and was not necessarily doomed to fail; it was the continuation of the war that meant the new regime struggled to establish its authority. If Russia had pulled out of the war in March 1917, then maybe the Provisional Government would have succeeded with the added possibility of the reinstatement of the Tsar to create a constitutional monarchy.

It is important to look at the components of this argument in more detail.

Military failures

Military historians seem to agree that the best chance of Russian military success was at the start of the war. But the terrible defeats at Tannenberg and Masurian Lakes meant that the morale of the Russian troops was severely dented. Russian soldiers had actually fought well but they were let down by the poor strategic decision-making of Generals Samsonov and Rennenkampf. The Russians lost twice as many troops as the enemy during these early campaigns and the hope at home that Russia would score an early victory waned.

By the end of 1915, Stavka, the command centre for the Russian army, blamed lack of military progress on a 'shells crisis'. The implication of this was that industry was struggling to keep up with the demands of the army and, therefore, workers had to put much more effort into increasing munitions production. The truth of the matter was that industry was already working near to full capacity. As the historian Norman Stone has argued, the problem was not that there was a deficit of munitions but it was more a case that military administrators did not have the ability to cope with the logistical challenges posed by the war. This was made worse by communication and transport problems (similar to those that existed in the Crimean and Russo-Japanese Wars). It

Key term

Home Front
This refers to what was happening domestically during the war – what kind of wartime work civilians were involved in.

was not surprising that stockpiling of supplies occurred; piles of foodstuffs rotted away and, at Archangel (in northern Russia), the mountains of hardware were so great that they started to sink into the ground!

Further defeats and the subsequent Great Retreat in 1915 (see page 162) prompted Nicholas II to take the rather shocking and unprecedented step of taking personal control of the armed forces. By early 1916 it looked as though Russian military prospects had picked up. However, the Tsar's decision to leave the capital (renamed Petrograd at the start of the war) left a political vacuum. The Tsarina, Alexandra, was left as a temporary *de facto* ruler. This was not popular with the *Duma* and supporters of the Tsar partly due to Alexandra's German background but also because of her 'friendship' with Rasputin (see page 33). All of this resulted in mounting criticism of Nicholas and a window of opportunity for those who wanted to push for a more liberal political set up.

Although Russia's war effort seemed to improve throughout 1916, the failure of the Brusilov offensive and the emergence of **attrition warfare** gave indication that the Tsar was not capable of bringing the conflict to a satisfactory end. By the time the Tsar was forced to abdicate, it was not inevitable that Russia would be defeated by Germany. Nevertheless, the domestic upheaval that proceeded throughout 1917 meant that the war was unlikely to turn in Russia's favour and the Bolshevik decision to withdraw from the conflict in 1918 was, for many, sensible and logical. Not all agreed with this; patriots (mainly conservatives and supporters of the Tsar) and a host of others of various political persuasions wanted a continuation of the war to the bitter end. This further supports the view of the optimists that the impact of the war was crucial in determining the development of Russian government.

Economic and social factors

The financial burden of the war was huge, although this only became apparent from the middle of 1916 onwards. The total cost was in the region of three billion roubles which far exceeded levels of government expenditure during peacetime. In 1913, for example, government expenditure was about 1.5 billion roubles. The cost was partly met through borrowing (foreign loans, **War Bonds**), increases in tax (income, excess profits) and printing more money. Such measures worked to an extent; for most of the war, enough money was invested in Russian industry to enable it to meet the projected demands of the military. It also meant that Russian workers were fully employed and received a regular and slightly higher income than usual. However, the latter was offset by rampant inflation, the inevitable consequence of an increase in the circulation of money. Prices had risen 400 per cent by 1917, and, as is always the case with inflation, those on fixed incomes suffered greatly.

Even if peasants and workers were able to at least maintain a decent level of real income, the likelihood of being able to spend it on even the bare necessities reduced as the war progressed.

Key terms

Attrition warfare
Where no progress is made by either side during a war but where both sides continue to wear each other down until one gives way.

War Bonds
Government savings certificates issued during wartime to the public with a promised fixed rate of return after the war. They had the important psychological impact of making people feel that they were making a valid contribution to the war effort.

This was especially the case after 1916 with respect to food supplies. Throughout the war period, the average output of cereals was a fair bit higher than it had been during the first decade of the twentieth century. But, a rapidly rising population, food requisitioning by the army, a fall in the availability of fertilisers and transport problems all worked together to create food shortages. Some historians have pointed out that this was largely a regional problem; those in Petrograd suffered more than others, with, for example their bread ration falling 25 per cent in the first three months of 1916. But regional variation is not particularly important as the social unrest that resulted from high prices and shortages gathered momentum in the places where it was likely to have the greatest impact – the growing towns and cities in the west of Russia.

For the optimists, adverse wartime conditions on such a scale had never existed before. It was not surprising that such unique circumstances united those who suffered the most hardship to challenge the ruling élite and demand a far more representative form of government.

Political consequences

Military weaknesses and mounting economic problems gave fuel to the critics of the Tsar. Under pressure from military advisers, the progressive bloc in the *Duma* (see page 33), friends and relatives, Nicholas decided to abdicate from the throne. Romanov rule was replaced by the unelected Provisional Government. Optimists believe that the continuation of the war made it impossible for the temporary government to deal with the burning issues of land reform, the modernisation of industry and the call for a constituent assembly. Thus, the war gave an opportunity to revolutionaries to overthrow the government completely and install their own form of direct rule. As the historian Stephen Lee has pointed out, the war was obviously '… a turning point – which actually turned twice'.

The pessimists

The pessimists argue against the First World War being a significant turning point for the following reasons:

- The Tsar had been struggling for some time to deal with the demands for a constitutional government. The *Duma* had developed a progressive bloc before the war; this was acknowledged by Nicholas II which was why he restricted the composition and freedoms of the *Duma*. Generally, Nicholas had proved to be an incompetent leader and it was only a matter of time before a serious challenge was made to depose him. The war is seen by pessimists as an event that simply speeded up his demise.
- The rise of the working classes as a distinct form of opposition to autocracy had also built up over time. It went hand in hand with large-scale industrialisation and urbanisation, which could be traced back at least to Witte's 'Great Spurt' (see pages 105–6).

Greater working-class consciousness was reinforced by the legalisation of political parties that represented their interests, the growth of trade unions and the setting up of soviets. Again, the war accelerated these trends and was not responsible for the emergence of working-class agitation.

The pessimists' view is clearly one that sympathises with the efforts of the working classes to gain greater concessions and freedoms over a long period. It is a pro-Bolshevik standpoint but fails to fully explain why, given the failure of the July Days (see pages 35–6), the Bolsheviks were able to fully seize power in October 1917. This could not simply have been the inevitable consequence of class struggle that had been going on for some time.

> **Essay focus**
>
> Look at Essay 1, paragraphs 4–6 on pages 189–90. This is a very good example of how to compare and contrast synthesised historical material. An approach has been adopted which has resulted in a well-structured, carefully supported argument. The student will undoubtedly have summarised his or her notes before the examination in table or chart format. Using such a summary allows for easy identification of similarities and differences between events.

5 | The Russian Revolution 1917

The origins, course and consequences of the revolution have been discussed at some length in Chapter 1. However, it is worth, at this place in the book, making some further general points about the conflict:

Key question
How does the revolution compare with the other wars with respect to the impact on the development of Russian government?

- The revolution can hardly be described as a war; the final overthrow of the Provisional Government and the short-lived Constituent Assembly was achieved with very little force and bloodshed.
- The origins of the revolution are obviously quite complex. It is still useful to consider the causes of the conflict in the traditional way (that is, long term and short term). What triggered the final takeover by the Bolsheviks is probably the most contentious part of the story and is inextricably tied up with the impact of the First World War.
- It is reasonable to argue that the course of the revolution ran from March 1917 until October, although some would argue that it is important to include the initial attempts by the Bolsheviks to consolidate power. This would mean that the revolution merges into the Civil War.
- The impact of the revolution at first glance seems obvious. The Bolshevik seizure of power was truly revolutionary in that it put an end to hundreds of years of autocratic rule by the Romanovs. The promise, at the time, was that autocracy would be replaced initially by the dictatorship of the proletariat which

would eventually give way to a stateless society, that is, communism. If this had succeeded, then the consequences of the revolution would have been truly momentous, not just for Russia but probably for the rest of the world. But, for a variety of reasons, the dictatorship *of* the proletariat was transformed into a situation whereby Lenin dictated *to* the proletariat, and the rest of Russian society. Dictatorship under Stalin, akin to that which emerged in other parts of Europe during the inter-war period, became a form of totalitarianism. It could be argued that this was an extreme form of autocracy. It is no wonder that this has led to claims that the tsars were simply replaced with red tsars; leaders that were different in appearance and background but almost identical in terms of how they went about their business. This would mean that the revolution, in conjunction with the First World War and the Civil War, did not really result in major changes to the governance of Russia even though the events themselves appeared dramatic.

> ## Essay focus
>
> Look at Essay 1, paragraphs 2 and 3 on page 185, which discuss the impact of the First World War on Russian government. This is a clear illustration of how to use materials synoptically. Notice how the student has provided a balanced account of the war by incorporating comment on different approaches adopted by historians.

Key question
Did the Civil War help or hinder the development of Russian government?

6 | The Russian Civil War 1917–21

Origins

The origins of the war can be traced to Russia's involvement in the First World War and the Russian Revolution. What this also indicates is that the Civil War, indirectly, was the result of a culmination of events that led to the other two wars mentioned above. This makes using the long- and short-term framework for analysing wars inappropriate in the case of the Civil War; it does not have a distinct, separate set of causes as the other wars do.

The Bolsheviks' seizure of power in October 1917 sparked chaos throughout what was still the Russian Empire. Different political and regional groups reacted according to their individual wants and needs; some saw the October Revolution as an opportunity to launch a counter-offensive against the Bolsheviks while others moved to attempt to gain long-awaited independence from Russian central government. The one single event that probably signalled the start of the war was Kerensky's Petrograd offensive (see page 168). This was suppressed with relative ease but other shows of resistance proved more challenging. The fact that the Civil War lasted over four years gives testament to the scale and magnitude of the forces that were determined to overthrow Lenin and his comrades.

The course of the Russian Civil War: main events

- November 1917: Kerensky's and General Krasnov's counter-offensive was brought to a halt.
- Spring 1918: Opposition from Cossacks in the region of the Don and the Urals was nullified.
- April 1918: Having defeated General Kornilov's volunteer army, Lenin proclaimed that the war was about to end. Foreign intervention occurred in this month when British marines were sent to support those opposing the Bolsheviks.
- May 1918: The Czech Legion on its way back to Vladivostock revolted and became a focus for those who wanted to add extra military muscle to their efforts against the Red Army. The Socialist Revolutionaries (SRs), in particular, were keen to ally with the Czechs.
- July 1918: The Tsar and most of his family were executed by the *Cheka* at Ekaterinburg.
- August 1918: Trotsky signalled his intent in ensuring the cohesiveness of the Red Army by executing deserters. The Bolsheviks became concerned at the arrival of more foreign troops, this time from the USA.
- September 1918: The Directory government emerged at Ufa. It was made up primarily of SRs and Czechs. By this time, opposition fighting forces were known as the White armies.
- November 1918: Admiral Kolchak announced himself as Supreme Ruler (of the White armies).
- December 1918 to the end of 1920: White armies fought against the Reds. The Red Army, based mainly in Moscow, initially soaked up attacks from the Whites from all directions. From October 1919 onwards, the Red Armies scored notable victories over the Whites (for example, against General Deniken, leader of the White Volunteer Army, at Orel and General Yudenich, leader of White forces made up of prisoners of war released by Germany, at Petrograd). By the depth of winter the Red Army had started to advance. In January 1920, Admiral Kolchak resigned (and was subsequently executed by the Bolsheviks). Certain regions such as the Ukraine also demanded to be freed from central control as they believed they should be allowed to develop a separate national identity. These regions constituted the nationalist forces that were an extra thorn in the side of the Reds. By February there were signs that the resistance from the nationalists was receding (for example, Estonia signed a peace agreement with *Sovnarkom*).
- April 1921: Polish armed forces attacked Russia and reached as far as Kiev in the east. Russian forces counter-attacked and pushed the Poles back to Warsaw. Another counter-attack in August, this time by Poland, resulted in the Red Army retreating. The Russo-Polish conflict eventually came to a halt in October 1920 when the Treaty of Riga was signed.
- November 1921: Red forces drove out the last of the White troops from southern Russia.
- Throughout 1921, groups of armed peasants formed to oppose the Bolsheviks. They were known as the Green armies. Their aim was to gain more freedoms from Bolshevik leaders.

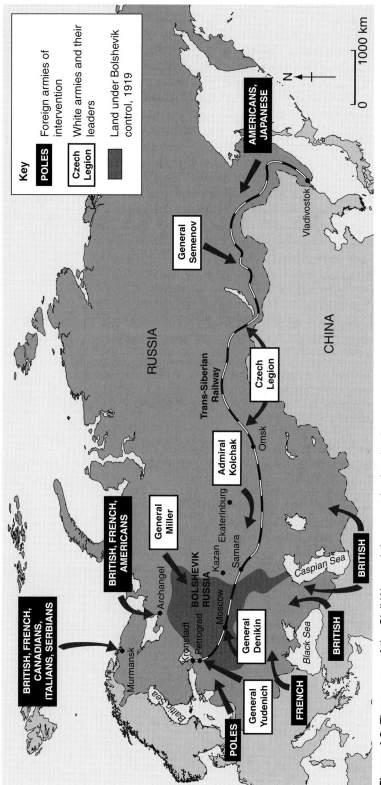

Figure 4.3: The course of the Civil War and the countries involved.

The effects of the Civil War on the development of Russian government

Defeat in the Polish campaign brought a similar kind of humiliation to the Bolsheviks as the Crimean War and Russo-Japanese War did to the tsars. Once again, a Russian army was defeated by another army, which on paper, was vastly inferior. Coupled with this, foreign intervention during the war on behalf of the Whites and a general mistrust of the Bolsheviks by Western European governments put Lenin on the defensive. Although Comintern and the concept of 'world revolution' were not abandoned, the Bolshevik government moved towards a foreign policy centred around developing peaceful relations.

The war influenced the nature of Russian government in so far as victory had been achieved through a particular kind of discipline, administration and management. The post-war communist government consisted of men who had served in the Red Army, the *Cheka* and other bodies. This experience was carried over into the running of the new Russia. The emphasis was on orderliness, trustworthiness, comradeship and loyalty to the party.

The militaristic approach to government is well illustrated by the introduction of War Communism (see page 109). The effects of this along with the actions of the *Cheka* caused divisions within the party and a move away from the use of 'terror' to control the populace. The New Economic Policy (see pages 109–10) was introduced to bring stability to government even though it appeared to be in contradiction of all that the communists stood for.

It is also fair to say that the war led to power being even more centralised than before. Power revolved around the Politburo and Orgburo. This meant that these very tightly knit party sub-committees became the main organs of government.

> ### Essay focus
>
> Look at Essay 2, paragraph 5 on page 190. Although the student has adopted a chronological framework to answer the question, the paragraph on the Civil War illustrates how events can be analysed and evaluated, rather than simply described. A clear judgement is made here about the impact of the war on Russian politics and government.

Summary diagram: The effects of the wars of 1914–21 on the development of Russian government

First World War
- Heavy military losses
- Shells crisis
- Tsar in command of the military
- Overlap with Russian Revolution
- Peace treaty signed with Germany before end of war

↕

Russian Revolution
- Strikes and protests in February 1917
- Installation of the Provisional Government
- Overthrow of Provisional Government in October 1917 by the Bolsheviks
- Overthrow of Constituent Assembly
- Overlap with Civil War

↕

Civil War
- Reds vs Whites and Greens
- War Communism and the *Cheka*
- New Economic Policy replaced War Communism
- Victory for Reds but no success over Poland
- Militarism of war shaped nature of post-war government

---

7 | The Second World War 1939–45

Long-term origins

Russia's involvement in the lead-up to the Second World War can be dated to Hitler's accession to power in 1933. Despite the wariness of the Third Reich towards building strong relations with Russia, the **Treaty of Berlin** was renewed and diplomatic visits continued. However, the Nazi regime remained anti-communist.

By the end of 1933, however, a change in relations occurred as Russia became increasingly concerned about indications that Germany intended to expand into other territories. This was made worse in January 1934 when Germany signed a non-aggression pact with Poland. Poland bordered Russia and the implication was that Germany and Poland would somehow form an alliance to invade Russia. In May 1934, Russia responded by ending all Polish and Baltic non-aggression treaties. This was to signal its intent to fight back against its East European neighbours if they collaborated with Germany. To add to mounting tensions, in September 1934, Russia was admitted to the **League of Nations** just as Germany and Japan opted out.

In 1935, a German–Soviet trade agreement was formulated (in another attempt to improve relations) only to be countered by

Key question
Why did the Second World War not affect the nature and function of Russian government as much as the First World War?

Key terms

Treaty of Berlin
Germany and Russia agreed to remain neutral if either was attacked by a third power.

League of Nations
An international body set up in 1919 to keep international peace through the settlement of disputes by arbitration.

mutual defence treaties with France and Czechoslovakia (May 1935) and a united fascist stance taken by the Seventh Comintern Congress (July 1935).

The Spanish Civil War (1936) was something of a turning point for the development of Russian government in the way it affected relations with the other international powers. Stalin's decision to support the Spanish government against the republican rebel Franco was, in itself, not an issue. The dilemma for the Russian leader was in deciding on the type and scale of support to be offered. In the end it consisted of the following:

• the NKVD provided military and technical advisers
• backing was given to the setting up of anti-fascist International Brigades
• disloyal Spanish leftists were discredited.

The limited nature of the support had the effect of, on the one hand, not causing too much of a backlash from Hitler (who was supporting Franco) and, on the other, preventing a quick victory for Franco and, therefore, a potential strengthening of Western fascism. Despite Russia's attempt not to upset Germany too much, Hitler still moved forward to form an Anti-Comintern alliance in conjunction with Italy and Japan.

In the light of the *Anschluss* **of Austria**, in 1938, Stalin pushed the view that Germany was increasingly a challenge to Russian security. The *Anschluss* strengthened German forces and resources and confirmed to Russia that Germany was prepared to march into other countries and take them over. This perceived threat was heightened by mounting anti-Soviet feeling in Britain and France due to knowledge of Stalin's 'purges' (see page 84) and his anti-appeasement stance. On top of this, the **Munich Peace Conference** of September 1938 excluded Russia and Czechoslovakia. It was no wonder, then, that Stalin proceeded to do deals with Nazi Germany; by the end of 1938 revamped trade agreements were in place, Russia had watered down its commitments in Spain and attacks in the Russian media against Germany virtually disappeared. Stalin justified his policy of dealing directly and firmly with Hitler to the Russian nation by pointing out that **appeasement** was failing, a war had almost started, and that Russia was industrially strong enough to resist invasion. The historian Adam Ulam has suggested that this policy amounted to a message from Stalin to Hitler along the lines of 'We don't need you, but you may need us; if so you had better hurry up.' Others, such as the historian Walter G. Moss, believe that Stalin's policy simply provided choice and flexibility; Russia could ally with the Nazis or continue to seek a deal with the West.

By the end of 1938 a pact between Russia and Germany became more likely. Hitler's invasion of the **Sudetenland** prompted a promise from France and Britain to help Poland. The importance of this was that in theory, Hitler now faced a war on two fronts (west and east) and therefore was pressured to go to Stalin to make a pact. In August 1939, the famous Nazi–Soviet non-aggression pact was made. Russia and Germany both agreed

***Anschluss* of Austria**
The union of Germany and Austria that was officially announced on 13 March 1938.

Munich Peace Conference
A meeting between Germany, Italy, France and Britain that resulted in Germany being allowed to occupy the Sudetenland as long as it guaranteed not to go into the rest of Czechoslovakia.

Appeasement
Foreign policy based on coming to a mutual agreement to resolve disputes, usually through the making of concessions.

Sudetenland
An area in Czechoslovakia in 1938 that contained about three million Germans.

Key figures

Vycheslav Molotov 1890–1986
The Prime Minister of Russia (1930–40) and Foreign Affairs Commissar (1939–49).

Joachim von Ribbentrop 1893–1946
Originally a wine salesman but rose to become German Foreign Minister from 1938 to 1945.

to stay neutral if either was the victim of 'belligerent action by a third power'. Behind the scenes, **Molotov** and **von Ribbentrop** signed a top secret protocol. Under this agreement, Lithuania and west Poland, Latvia, Estonia, Finland and Bessarabia were placed under Soviet influence.

The reaction to this was mixed. There was some opposition from those outside the Politburo who viewed it as a dastardly deal with the fascists. The core of the Russian leadership though hailed it as a success as it provided time to prepare for a hypothetical invasion by Germany and/or Japan.

Short-term origins

After Germany invaded Poland on 1 September 1939, France and Britain declared war on Germany. However, due to the Nazi–Soviet Pact, the period from September 1939 to 1941 was viewed as one of neutrality in Russia.

Neutrality did not prevent Russia from taking further moves to protect itself against attack. Soviet troops were sent to eastern

Key term

Scorched earth policy
Stalin ordered that all material objects of worth should be destroyed as the Russian forces retreated to stop them falling into the hands of the enemy.

The course of the Second World War: main events

- July 1941: In response to the implementation of Operation Barbarossa, Stalin ordered a **scorched earth policy** to be put in place. However, German forces moved forward with speed.
- September 1941: Kiev was taken and Leningrad encircled. The siege of Leningrad by the German army lasted for two years; the city was completely cut off from the rest of Russia.
- October 1941: The main attack on Moscow was launched. German forces were held at bay as they struggled to cope with severe winter weather. By December, the Russians had started a counter-offensive. Stalin ordered Russia to be defended 'to the last drop of blood'.
- May 1942: German troops moved away from Moscow and focused on attempting to take control of the oilfields in the Caucasus. To be sure of succeeding, the German army under General von Paulus had to take Stalingrad.
- August 1942: The Battle of Stalingrad started. Von Paulus had some initial success in surrounding the city. Gunfights on the streets of Stalingrad ensued. But, by the beginning of 1943, Soviet forces had launched a counter-offensive. In February the German army was forced to surrender at Stalingrad. However, the battle was infamous in that there were about 1.1 million Soviet casualties and around 500,000 deaths.
- July 1943: A major Russian victory at Kursk occurred. This involved the 'greatest tank battle in history' and signalled the start of a continuous German retreat. It was clear that the Germans had overstretched their resources, having tried to launch an invasion along a military front that ran about 2000 miles from north to south.
- November 1943: Kiev was retaken.
- January 1944: The siege of Leningrad ended but only after citizens endured wide-scale starvation resulting in around one million deaths.
- June 1944: The full Russian counter-offensive was launched with the intention of pushing the German army back to its homeland. Warsaw was soon captured by the Russians (January 1945), swiftly followed by Vienna (April 1945). The Red Army pushed on through Germany. The Battle of Berlin (April–May 1945) resulted in defeat for the entire German forces. Germany surrendered in May 1945.

Casualties

Over 27 million Russians lost their lives during the war.

Poland with the intention of protecting the Ukraine and Belarus.
The Baltic States were persuaded to allow the stationing of Soviet
troops on their soil to act as a line of defence for Petrograd and
Leningrad. Finland refused a similar demand, resulting in the
Winter War (November 1939 to March 1940). The significance of
this for the Russian government was that war once again
highlighted military weaknesses; there were somewhere near
50,000 Soviet deaths as a result of this very limited military
conflict. Nevertheless, Finland ceded border space to the
Russians and this set a precedent for the Baltic States to be forced
to become part of the USSR by the summer of 1940. Dissidents
within newly occupied territory were brutally dealt with, as
illustrated by the **Katyn Forest massacre**.

Wariness of possible German invasion grew again by the spring
of 1940. Stalin's response to the Nazi defeat of Denmark,
Norway, the Netherlands, Belgium and France was to state that
Hitler would move on to 'beat our brains in'. With the signing of
the **Tripartite Pact** in September 1940 and the German failure to
win the **Battle of Britain**, it appeared that an attack on Russia was
imminent.

In December 1940 approval was given by Hitler for Operation
Barbarossa, an all-out attack on Russia. Before it was launched
(planned for 15 May 1941), Russia managed to sign a pact with
Japan mainly in the hope of buying more time. Germany, in
theory, would have been wary of attacking Russia if the latter had
Japan on its side. On 22 June 1941, the attack finally started.

The effects of the war on the development of Russian government
Social effects

The human cost of the war to the government was enormous.
Over 27 million Russians were killed. Civilians constituted two-
thirds of this total; one million alone died during the siege of
Leningrad and there were 1.1 million casualties as a result of the
battle of Stalingrad. Politicians in the post-war years were thus
faced with the problem of a shortage of all types of labour which
was essential if Russia was to move successfully into the new
technological age.

During the war five million prisoners were taken by the
Germans. A significant number switched sides; the historian
Anthony Beevor has indicated that around 50,000 Russian
citizens fought on the side of Germany at the Battle of Stalingrad.
Stalin viewed all prisoners of war as traitors and if they managed
to return home they were treated harshly. Despite the patriotic
fervour that was whipped up, there was still desertion from the
armed ranks. About 13,000 deserters were shot.

During the counter-offensive and march on Berlin, Russian
troops reportedly raped over two million women. When
challenged over the behaviour of the typical Russian soldier
Stalin allegedly retorted with 'what is so awful about his having
fun with a woman?'

Katyn Forest massacre
The execution of
around 5000 Polish
officers by the Red
Army in the forest
of Katyn, Smolensk,
on the eve of the
German invasion.

Tripartite Pact
A military alliance
between Germany,
Italy and Japan.

Battle of Britain
An aerial battle
between Germany
and Britain that
took place from
12 August to 30
September 1940.

Stalin's treatment of prisoners of war, deserters and non-Russian women did little to enhance the relations with the allies both during wartime conferences and afterwards, when proposals for economic aid and reconstruction were discussed.

Economic effects

The government had a huge challenge in addressing the damage to the industrial and rural infrastructure. Much physical damage was caused both by the German military through shelling and by Stalin's scorched earth policy. Factories, production plants, mines, dams, roads, bridges and the railway were all badly affected. Such physical damage was made worse by the fact that during the war many industrial enterprises had to be relocated to the Urals, Volga basin and central Asia to be protected. However, these were not necessarily the best areas for the organisation of efficient and effective production. Also, many factories had to be reconverted from munitions production back to their original function. All of this was a costly business, especially given that the government ran a command economy and was therefore responsible for all industrial enterprise.

The Soviet government's reconstruction programme revolved around a fourth Five-Year Plan (1946–50). The specific aim of this was to get the Soviet economy back to growth levels achieved immediately before the war. The plan would then be followed by two others which would accelerate the development of heavy industry. As with the first three Five-Year Plans (see pages 110–13), the production of consumer goods was neglected. Interestingly, the targets set by the fourth plan were achieved after three years, way ahead of schedule. This was due to a number of reasons including the availability of 'free' labour (up to four million prisoners of war, Soviet prisoners and conscript labour), unilateral trade agreements (agreements that only favoured Russia), external financial aid (from the **United Nations**, USA in the form of **lend–lease**, Britain and Sweden) and, most significantly, the commitment of the Russian people. Ordinary Russian workers continued to labour for excessively long hours and under very challenging conditions to increase production and productivity in all of the staple industries.

There were a number of weaknesses in Stalin's post-war economic strategy though. The biggest flop was his continuation of 'gargantuan' projects. Great amounts of capital were ploughed into schemes such as the Volga–Don canal but with very little economic return. In the short run, agriculture also suffered, mainly through neglect. The war years had seen a reversion to a kind of small-scale ownership of land plots and a crumbling of some collective farms. Those who accrued private plots were soon hit by exorbitant taxes. The collectives suffered from shortages of labour and materials. The inevitable consequence was a famine in 1947 (see page 134) and rural unrest. Khrushchev, as Minister for Agriculture, attempted to resolve some of the problems through farm amalgamation (joining farms together to make bigger farm

Key terms

United Nations
An organisation that formally came into being in June 1945 that was designed to maintain world peace.

Lend–lease
The US Congress passed an act in March 1941 that allowed the president to lend or lease equipment to countries 'whose defence the president deems vital to the defence of the USA'.

units to share costs and raise production), but this had a limited impact.

Political effects
Impact on the structure of government
The war had very little impact on the structure of government. During the conflict, Stalin became the chairman of the State Defence Committee which had absolute control over the lives of Soviet citizens. He also took the role of Supreme Commander of the Military, just as Nicholas II had done during the First World War. The difference was that Stalin actually took advice from his advisers and even relied on others, deemed to be military experts, to make key strategic decisions. In fact, it would be incorrect to assume that the government became even more totalitarian. That would have been difficult given the high degree of control already in place. Besides, all governments of those countries directly involved in the war passed measures that gave them total authority. Unsurprisingly, until his death, Stalin retained the two key political posts in Russia; those of head of government (he actually took the premiership from Molotov during the war) and party secretary.

The Politburo
The composition of the Politburo also remained roughly the same. In 1948, the prominent members included Stalin, Molotov, Voroshilov, Kaganovich, Mikoyan, Andreyev and Khrushchev. All of these characters were part of the Politburo in existence 10 years earlier.

Party membership
Despite the extremely high number of war casualties, the numbers joining the Communist Party actually increased during the war from 3.76 million in 1941 to 5.8 million in 1945. Much of this rise was due to additions from the military who were rewarded for their gallantry with official party membership. By the time of the 19th Party Congress, called in 1952 (for the first time in 13 years), party numbers had declined although this did not seem to affect the main function of the party. It continued as an administrative tool especially when it came to economic affairs.

The NKVD
The NKVD was very active during and after the war. It was involved in the policing of prisons and the deportation of national minorities while the conflict ensued. The secret police were particularly harsh on Balkans, Chechens, Karachans and Crimean Tartars, all of whom were accused of collaborating with the Nazis. After the conflict, the NKVD reverted to purging the party and other groups of dissidents. Of special note was their involvement in the resolution of the **Leningrad affair** which resulted in over 200 supporters of **Zhdanov** being purged.

A.A. Zhdanov 1896–1948
An important member of the Politburo from 1935 to 1948.

Key figure

Leningrad affair
A purge of the friends and colleagues of Zhdanov after his death in 1948.

Key term

Grand Alliance
The wartime alliance of Britain, France, Russia and the USA.

Foreign policy

Soviet foreign policy was significantly affected by the war. By joining the **Grand Alliance**, Stalin believed that he placed Russia in a very strong bargaining position over making territorial gains. His main objective was to keep the frontiers established under the Nazi–Soviet Pact. The wartime conferences at Tehran (November–December 1943) and Yalta (February 1945) confirmed Russia's claims. Poland was forced to concede most of the Ukraine, Belarus and Lithuania to Russia but gained some German territory as recompense.

The more crucial point about this agreement was the addendum that Stalin was to be allowed to influence the nature of government in these areas, that is, to insist that they were ruled by communist regimes. As the Red Army pushed the German forces back they naturally occupied a string of other Eastern European countries (including Czechoslovakia, Hungary and parts of the Balkans).

As early as October 1944, the British Prime Minister Churchill agreed that Russia could maintain these areas as a 'sphere of influence' after the war. For Stalin, this was critical in helping maintain a physical barrier between the West and the western Russian border land. Others in the West viewed the Russian territorial gains as the start of a Soviet expansionism with the

Figure 4.4: Russian territorial gains as a result of the Second World War.

long-term intention of promoting communism throughout the whole of Europe. Churchill was to later refer to the barrier as an **Iron Curtain**; some claim that this point marked the start of the Cold War.

War against Japan
Stalin's agreement to enter the war against Japan was rewarded with further territorial concessions. Russia was given the **Kurile Islands and South Sakhalin**. Coupled with the Eastern European land, this meant that the Soviet Union had gained responsibility for a further 24 million people.

The issue of post-war Germany
The issue of what should happen to Germany after the war ended up causing the Soviet leadership difficulties. Germany as a whole, but also Berlin in particular, was divided into zones which were to be occupied by the allies until a stable German government could be set up. Russia had jurisdiction over the Eastern zones but there was mutual suspicion and tensions between the occupying forces right from the start. The **Berlin Blockade** of 1948 and the erection of the **Berlin Wall** worsened relations between Russia and the West. The result of this was that the key problem of unifying Germany was never resolved until communism started to collapse throughout Europe over 40 years later.

8 | The Cold War 1947–64

Definition
The Cold War, according to the historian Chris Cook, is the term given to the 'protracted state of tension between countries falling short of actual warfare'. 'Actual warfare' refers to physical combat: 'hot' war. Ironically, some of the most notable features of the Cold War related to 'hot' wars, for example, in Korea (1950–3) and Vietnam (1946–54 and 1961–75). The Soviet Union did not play any direct role in the 'hot' conflicts; it appeared more concerned to win the ideological battle.

The words 'Cold War' were made popular from 1947 onwards by the US journalist Walter Lippmann. The term seems to have been used by US politicians when the Truman Doctrine was announced in March 1947 (see page 180) and also during discussions over the implementation of the Marshall Plan in the summer of 1947 (see page 180).

Long-term causes of the war
Ideology
Probably the main cause of the war concerned the conflicting political ideologies held by the main players. The regimes of both Stalin and Khrushchev were based on Marxism–Leninism which espoused state control of the means of distribution, production and exchange on behalf of the Russian people. In turn, state control amounted to a dictatorship, with no element of

Key terms

Iron Curtain
An imaginary border between Russian-dominated East and West Europe.

Kurile Islands and South Sakhalin
The Kurile Islands in Russia's Sakhalin Oblast region, are a volcanic archipelago that stretches approximately 1300 km north-east from Hokkaido, Japan, to Kamchatka, Russia, separating the Sea of Okhotsk from the North Pacific Ocean.

Key question
'Of all the wars that Russia was involved in from 1855 to 1964 the Cold War had the greatest impact on the development of Russian government.' How far do you agree with this view?

Key terms

Berlin Blockade
In June 1948 the Western powers combined to introduce a new currency in the zones under their control. Russia saw this as an attempt to show how capitalism could bring prosperity to Berlin (a new currency meant a lowering of inflation and more spending power) and retaliated by blocking all communication links with the western part of the city. The blockade was eventually lifted in May 1949.

Berlin Wall
A wall erected in 1961 by Russia in Berlin to formally separate the east from the west. The aim was to stop people escaping to the Western zones.

democracy. This was, of course, diametrically opposed to the ideologies that predominated in the West. The USA stood for liberal democracy and free-market capitalism; to the Soviet Union this meant a bourgeois system similar to that which had emerged in tsarist Russia.

Immediately after the Second World War, during a speech in February 1946 to the Supreme Soviet, Stalin blamed the conflict on the 'monopoly capitalism' of the West (that is, the profit-making motives that dominated the economies of Western Europe). This was identical to the claims made by Lenin about what he believed to be the root cause of the First World War. For Stalin, the outcome of the Second World War was a success as it emphasised the strength of the Soviet economy and system of government. According to the Soviet leader, without the discipline and collaboration engendered by a communist system of government the Nazis would never have been defeated.

The Soviet war victory became a justification for the Soviet 'way' to be consolidated (mainly through new Five-Year Plans) and promoted. But this did not mean that Stalin and Khrushchev were intent on expansionism. The Russian leaders seemed to recognise that they would not be able to govern a state that could compete on equal terms with the USA in the developing world free market. Therefore, the 'sphere of interest' in Eastern Europe that Russia valued so highly was as much for purposes of economic growth as it was for political stability. Western politicians did not seem to understand this or at least chose to ignore it.

Short-term causes of the war
US mistrust of the USSR
After 1946, US mistrust of the USSR grew swiftly. The main reasons for this were as follows:

- The association of Russia with a newly established communist regime in North Korea.
- The discovery of a communist spy network in Canada.
- The Kennan 'long telegram'.
- Churchill's Iron Curtain speech.

The latter two factors appeared to be especially influential.

The 'Kennan long' telegram
On 22 February 1946, George Kennan, a US diplomat, sent a lengthy telegram message to the European Division of the US State Department expressing his concerns about Soviet foreign policy. Kennan was an acknowledged expert on Soviet affairs, having been in constant contact with Russian dissidents who had managed to escape from Russia and set up base in Riga. Kennan believed that Russia was not a 'fit ally or associate, actual or potential' for the USA. The Soviets had aggressive tendencies based on 'basic inner Russian necessities' and a 'traditional instinctive sense of insecurity'. The result of this was a 'patient but deadly struggle for total destruction of a rival power. Never in

compacts or compromises with it.' The Soviet Union would do all it could to strengthen the Soviet bloc and challenge capitalism. Kennan argued that US concessions that might be made to Russia would not work. The only solution was to actively contain communism. Because of Kennan's expertise, his telegram had a significant impact on the thinking of senior US politicians.

Churchill's Iron Curtain speech

The speech was made on 5 March 1946 at Fulton, Missouri, USA. Churchill's views echoed those of Kennan. To purposefully create anxiety in the West, Churchill claimed that 'from Stettin in the Baltic to Trieste in the Adriatic, an iron curtain has descended across the continent'. The spread of Soviet influence had made it a military force to be feared. Churchill played on the idea that any country taken over by communism would result in a complete loss of freedoms for its people.

The Truman Doctrine

Another expression of fear of communism came in the form of the Truman Doctrine announced in March 1947. Referring to the prospect of communist governments being installed in Greece and Turkey, US President Truman declared that 'it must be the policy of the United States to support free peoples who are resisting subjugation by armed minorities or by outside pressures'. Soviet politicians were antagonised by this statement as they found it very threatening.

The Marshall Plan

The **Marshall Plan** for the economic recovery of Europe was presented by the USA in June 1947. It was rejected by the Soviet Foreign Minister, Molotov, as the Russians believed it was a scam to spread capitalism. Such a snub simply created further ill-feeling against the Soviet Union from the West.

Cominform

The Soviets responded to the above developments by setting up, in September 1947, the Communist Information Bureau (Cominform). The aim of this body was to reject the West's offer of financial help and to coordinate economic recovery for Eastern Europe through a programme of cooperation. Cominform was not a great success and it probably created more problems for the Eastern bloc countries than it solved. It also served to heighten tensions and, along with the Truman Doctrine and the Marshall Plan, marked the start of the Cold War.

The effects of the war on the development of Russian government

The Cold War had very little direct effect on the structure and function of Russia's government. However, destalinisation (see pages 24–8) was an attempt by Khrushchev to present Russia in a more positive light to the rest of the world. This was especially important at a time when the USA was determined to enforce its

Key term

Marshall Plan
A programme to help European recovery after the Second World War which was put forward by the US Secretary of State General George Marshall (1880–1959). He believed that the USA should 'assist in the return of normal economic health in the world without which there can be no political stability and no assured peace'.

The course of the Cold War: main events

- March 1947: The Truman Doctrine was announced; in the summer, the Marshall Plan for European economic recovery was unveiled.
- September 1947: Cominform was set up.
- June 1948: Start of the Berlin Blockade.
- April 1949: NATO (the North Atlantic Treaty Organisation) was founded. Members of this group agreed to support each other if they were attacked by an aggressor. Those who belonged were anti-communist and it was obvious that NATO was designed to combat the perceived threat from the Soviet Union.
- May 1949: End of the Berlin Blockade.
- June 1950: Korean War started.
- November 1952: The USA exploded its first hydrogen bomb.
- August 1953: The Soviet Union announced the explosion of its first hydrogen bomb (the test took place on 8 August).
- May 1955: The Warsaw Pact was formed. This involved the signing of a peace and security treaty by the Soviet Union, Albania, Bulgaria, Hungary, East Germany, Poland, Romania and Czechoslovakia.
- April 1956: Cominform was disbanded.
- October 1956: The Hungarian Revolution. This was a popular uprising in Hungary in 1956, following a speech by Soviet leader Nikita Khrushchev in which he attacked the period of Stalin's rule. Encouraged by the new freedom of debate and criticism, a rising tide of unrest and discontent in Hungary broke out into active fighting in October 1956. Rebels won the first phase of the revolution, and Imre Nagy became Prime Minister, agreeing to establish a multiparty system. On 1 November 1956, he declared Hungarian neutrality and appealed to the United Nations for support. Western powers failed to respond, and on 4 November the Soviet Union invaded Hungary to prevent the 'revolution' getting out of hand.
- November 1956: The Soviet Union cut off diplomatic relations with Israel and warned France and Britain about the consequences of their behaviour during the **Suez Crisis**; Russian leaders hinted at possible missile attack.
- October 1957: *Sputnik 1* was launched by Russia and signalled the start of the space race. *Sputnik 1* was the world's first artificial satellite; it was about the size of a beach ball (58 cm in diameter), weighed only 83.6 kg, and took about 98 minutes to orbit the Earth on its elliptical path. The launch led to new political, military, technological and scientific developments.
- September 1959: Khrushchev flew to the USA for the first time and held negotiations with President Eisenhower; demands over Berlin were withdrawn.
- May 1962: A US U-2 spy plane, piloted by Gary Powers, was shot down while flying over Russia. Khrushchev demanded an apology from Eisenhower.
- June 1961: Khrushchev demanded the demilitarisation of Berlin during negotiations with US President Kennedy in Vienna.
- August 1961: The construction of the Berlin Wall was started.
- September 1962–January 1963: The Cuban Missile Crisis. This was a major Cold War confrontation between the USA and the USSR. After the Bay of Pigs Invasion (in Cuba) by the USA, the USSR increased its support of Fidel Castro's Cuban regime. By the summer of 1962, Khrushchev secretly decided to install ballistic missiles in Cuba. When US reconnaissance flights revealed the secret construction of missile launching sites, President Kennedy publicly denounced the Soviet actions. In October 1962 Kennedy imposed a naval blockade on Cuba and said that any missile launched from Cuba would be met with a full-scale retaliatory attack by the USA against the USSR. On 24 October, Soviet ships carrying missiles to Cuba turned back to Russia. Khrushchev then agreed on 28 October to dismantle the missile sites. The crisis ended as suddenly as it had begun. The USA ended its blockade of Cuba on 20 November and promised not to go ahead with a planned invasion of the island.
- June–July 1963: Rapid deterioration in Sino-Soviet relations after China accused Soviet leaders of 'restoring capitalism' and abandoning Marxism.

Key term

Suez Crisis
The Suez Canal was nationalised by President Nasser in 1956. France and Britain, alarmed by Egypt's growing ties with communists, planned to take control of this important shipping route.

containment policy towards Russia. American politicians never wavered from trying to prove that communism was evil and would easily spread if allowed to. In this way, Khrushchev's political ideology was partly determined by the Cold War.

The nuclear arms race and space race were very expensive. Before 1964, the Russian government managed to cope but high levels of investment in heavy industry to meet military requirements were to the detriment of consumer industries. The knock-on effect was that living standards appeared much lower than in the West. Russian people were not afraid to express their discontent but, as was always the case, protests were ruthlessly dealt with.

A number of the 'hot spots' during the Cold War took Russia to the brink of a major military conflict with the USA. The Cuban Missile Crisis in particular showed that Russian politicians were not afraid to flex their muscles. This incident also showed that the Soviets were willing to back down to prevent disagreements getting out of hand. The USSR was not financially strong enough to participate in another full-blown war.

Key term

Containment policy
The policy of attempting to stop communism spreading throughout the world.

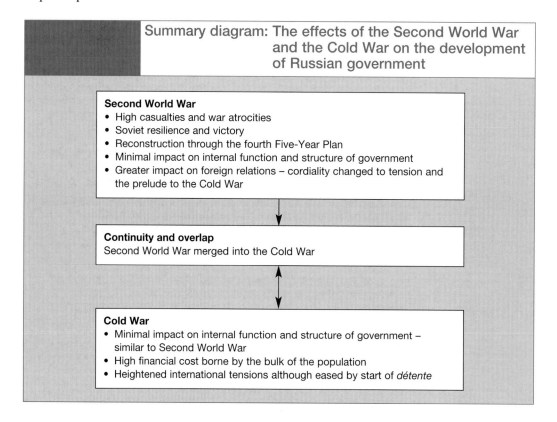

Summary diagram: The effects of the Second World War and the Cold War on the development of Russian government

Second World War
- High casualties and war atrocities
- Soviet resilience and victory
- Reconstruction through the fourth Five-Year Plan
- Minimal impact on internal function and structure of government
- Greater impact on foreign relations – cordiality changed to tension and the prelude to the Cold War

Continuity and overlap
Second World War merged into the Cold War

Cold War
- Minimal impact on internal function and structure of government – similar to Second World War
- High financial cost borne by the bulk of the population
- Heightened international tensions although eased by start of *détente*

Key question
Why did some wars have more of an impact on Russian government than others?

9 | Conclusion

Trotsky famously claimed that 'war is the locomotive of change'. In other words war was seen to act as a catalyst. However, this begs a number of questions. Did the wars during the period simply accelerate developments already underway or did they initiate change? For example, the Crimean War and the Russo-Japanese War seemed to lead to reforms that were already under consideration. On the other hand, the First World War, in conjunction with the Russian Revolution and Civil War, resulted in a fairly sudden and complete change in the way Russia was ruled.

Wars undoubtedly led to political change which was often linked to economic and social developments. On occasion, leaders committed Russia to wars in the hope that political, economic and social problems would somehow be resolved. Such action often backfired and resulted in Russian forces underestimating and being unprepared for the conflict they faced. In the case of the Crimean War, Russo-Japanese War and, to an extent, the First World War, there were dire consequences for rulers. The nature of autocracy was challenged, concessions had to be made and the First World War was a key factor in the fall of the Romanov dynasty. Russia fought in other wars due to changing international circumstance and a threat to internal security. Where this was the case, the Russian military was better prepared and more determined to win through. This was especially true of the Second World War (but not the case with the First World War) although research since 1991 has suggested that the centralised planning that happened under Stalin might have hindered Russia in its preparations.

Another way of looking at the effects of war is to focus on the type, nature and extent of military conflict. Some historians quite simply argue that limited wars (the Crimean War, Russo-Turkish War and Russo-Japanese War) had, by definition, a limited impact. The financial cost and human cost were less than in the **total wars** and the response of governments with respect to post-war reform and reconstruction was less far reaching. Revolution obviously resulted in a complete overhaul of the Russian political system, although some historians downplay the impact by claiming that one form of autocracy was simply replaced by another. Thus, it would appear that some wars had more of an impact than others depending on the nature of the war.

Wars clearly altered the way governments thought and behaved as revealed by policies in existence before and after the wars. However, whether policy change would have been enacted without war is a matter for conjecture. This is where the counter factual approach to historical study becomes useful. Perhaps the impact of wars in general on the development of Russian government has been exaggerated. Given that the nature of rule remained strictly authoritarian, this would certainly seem to be the case.

Key term

Total war
A war that had a more total and long-lasting impact on the whole nation.

Further questions for debate

1 How far did wars hinder the development of Russian government during the period from 1855 to 1964?

2 To what extent were total wars (the two world wars) far more important in the impact they had on Russian governments than any other wars that occurred in the period from 1855 to 1964?

3 'The importance of the First World War as a turning point in the development of Russian history has been vastly exaggerated.' How far do agree with this statement?

4 'The impact of war on the development of Russian government was never as significant as internal political change.' How far do you agree with this statement?

5 Assess the view that Russian governments always saw war as an opportunity to deflect attention from domestic economic and social problems during the period from 1855 to 1964.

Advice on answering essay questions on historical turning points

In the essays that follow, the focus of the question is on the assessment of the First World War as a turning point in the development of Russian government. You need to explain and analyse the importance of the other wars that preceded and succeeded the First World War to show change and continuity over time. You need to adopt a thematic approach to ensure that effective comparisons can be made and that you can make a judgement about relative importance.

Read each of the following essays carefully. Each essay was written in one hour and without the use of notes. Note any strengths and limitations and compare your views with those of the assessor. Marks should be awarded for each of the two assessment objectives described in the tables at the end of the book (see pages 192–3).

Essay 1: 'Out of all the wars that influenced the development of Russian government, the First World War was the most significant.' How far do you agree with this statement as it applies to the period from 1855 to 1964?

1 The First World War was undoubtedly important in that it was partly responsible for the fall of the Tsar and the overthrow of the Provisional Government. However, other wars were also important as they either prompted changes to the actual structure of government or prompted leaders to pass reforms which introduced greater freedoms for the Russian people. Some wars had very little impact simply because they were limited in scope and nature.

1 A straightforward introduction that gives some indication of the line of argument to be adopted. Maybe the student could have given a clearer indication of how he or she intended to measure the degree of change engendered by different wars given that the question is highlighting the way in which war can act as a turning point.

2 This is a very good synoptic analysis of the effects of the First World War on the development of Russian government. There is skilful discussion of a range of factors that are linked to the concept of consequence. Note that the student has quite rightly dealt with the war highlighted in the question in the first paragraph.

2 The First World War created significant political, economic and social changes. In turn, these undoubtedly had a significant impact on the development of Russian government. Militarily, the war was a disaster. Early on, defeats at Tannenberg and Masurian Lakes led to human losses twice as great as the enemy. The so-called 'shells crisis', the failure of the Brusilov offensive and the inept performance of Nicholas II as commander in chief of the armed forces reduced the morale of the Russian people and their faith in tsarism. The war was also an enormous economic burden. It cost somewhere in the region of 1.5 billion roubles which was financed mainly through taxation and borrowing. The resultant high levels of inflation reduced real incomes and living standards which further inflamed discontent with the government. A sense of unease also existed within the ruling élite which eventually led to the abdication of the Tsar. The Provisional Government, which replaced Nicholas II, had the unenviable problem of trying to mop up the problems left by the tsarist regime. Some of these, such as the effects of industrialisation and land distribution, had existed before the war but had not been dealt with effectively. It was not surprising that first Prince Lvov and then Kerensky both failed to take Russia successfully out of a crisis situation. The wartime situation proved conducive to the growth of organised opposition such as the Petrograd Soviet and the Bolsheviks. When these groups combined, firstly to oust the Kerensky government and then to force the disbandment of the Constituent Assembly in 1918, a major change in the course of Russian politics occurred. Given the differences, at least in theory, between tsarist autocracy and Bolshevik communism, the First World War obviously acted as a significant turning point. This is reinforced by the view of 'optimist' historians who argue that if the war had not happened then tsarism would have survived albeit in a modified form.

3 The importance of taking a longer term view of events before coming to a judgement about a single turning point is highlighted here.

3 However, other historians believe that a revolution was inevitable given developments before the war. Industrialisation had resulted in deteriorating living and working conditions for urban workers and rising social unrest. Radical pressure groups exploited this and started to chip away at the foundations of autocracy. The First World War simply provided the opportunity for tsarism to be bulldozed away completely. The other, more limited wars that happened from 1854 to 1917 all contributed to highlighting the deficiencies in Russian government that seemed to be incensing the masses.

4 A comparative approach has been cleverly adopted to illustrate similarities between three of the limited wars that Russia was involved in before 1914.

4 The Crimean War, the Russo-Turkish War and the Russo-Japanese War all had something in common; Russia struggled against enemies that on paper were inferior. As a result, the wars ended in treaties that provided terms unfavourable to Russia. Territory was lost (for example, Bessarabia to Moldavia under the Treaty of Paris) and international rights restricted (for example, the Treaty of Paris restricted access to the Black Sea; the Treaty of Portsmouth dismissed the prospect of Russian influence in Korea). Although the Congress of Berlin appeared to provide Russia with favourable terms

it made concessions to Austria-Hungary. The Russian public were angered by this as it reneged on the terms of the Treaty of San Stefano and made the Russian government appear weak. All in all, the wars before 1914 all seemed to lessen Russia's status as a major European power.

5 The pre-1914 wars led to reforms which affected the development of government. The Emancipation Edict forced changes to local government with the creation of *Zemstva*, to the way law and order was administered and to the organisation of the military. All of these developments appeared to create a more liberal way of governing although it has been pointed out that similar reforms had already been considered by Nicholas I; maybe the Crimean War simply acted as a catalyst. The Russo-Japanese War greatly influenced the creation of a more representative form of government in the form of the *Duma*. However, this was not as revolutionary as it first appeared as the Fundamental Laws of 1906 were used to restrict the power of the *Duma*. Thus, the wars were linked to what appeared to be major political, economic and social reforms although in reality the impact of such changes was rather limited. Unlike with the First World War, there was no fundamental change in the political ideology of rulers or to the structure and function of government.

5 The approach used in the previous paragraph has been continued with a clear focus on a mini-theme, i.e. reform. The candidate is clearly in control of the material.

6 Finally, the pre-1914 wars contrasted with the First World War in terms of cost, both human and financial. A lack of capital and manpower often restricted the ways in which Russian governments could implement reforms especially when it came to the economy. The difference with the First World War was that the scale of losses was far greater. This fits in with the theory put forward by historians such as Marwick who believe that the greater the level of participation by citizens in a war, the greater the impact. In this sense, the First World War was far more of a turning point than all of the military conflicts that preceded it.

6 Economic issues are effectively discussed with the inclusion of useful reference to the views of the historian Marwick. The themes paper does not require knowledge of relevant historiography but the candidate has displayed how it can be used as evidence to support an observation.

7 The First World War overlapped with and was tightly linked to the revolutionary war of 1917. The latter resulted in the overthrow of the Provisional Government and the democratically elected Constituent Assembly. The intention of the new government was to rule until a dictatorship of the proletariat could be achieved. But this never happened. Lenin and Stalin ruled as dictators in a way that was not dissimilar to the authoritarian rule of the tsars. Stalin took this a step further by introducing totalitarianism to Russia. Thus, it is questionable as to whether the revolution was genuinely revolutionary although it clearly had an important impact on the way Russians were governed.

7 This paragraph shows how one factor can be linked to another. A sound analytical comment about the significance of the revolution is made at the end.

8 A cogent and well-structured argument concerning the importance of the Civil War is made here. Again, clear links are made to wars discussed in previous sections.

8 The Civil War flowed from the two wars discussed above. It compared in effect with the pre-1914 wars in so far as the Bolsheviks failed to defeat a lesser enemy in the Poles and were therefore left humiliated. In contrast, and in conjunction with the revolution, the Civil War created a sense of mistrust among the international community. Britain, France and the USA in particular were appalled at the prospect of Bolshevism spreading. Their fears were confirmed when Lenin instructed the *Cheka* to enforce War Communism with a great deal of brutality. Despite a change to the more liberal New Economic Policy, the mistrust of the new Russia remained. The war had a more measurable impact on the structure of government. The Bolsheviks achieved success during the war through the highly disciplined Red Army and the strict administration and organisation implemented by Trotsky. The militaristic way of governing carried over into post-war life and was especially evident in the running of new government bodies such as the Orgburo and Politburo. Therefore, the impact of the Civil War was clearly significant but it would not have happened without the revolution and the First World War.

9 This paragraph displays an excellent level of ability to synthesise material while retaining relevance. A good range of supporting material has been used and a sound judgement is made at the end about the relative importance of the two wars being focused on.

9 Just as the First World War was linked with the revolution and the Civil War, the Second World War merged with the Cold War. The Great Patriotic War had very little direct impact on the structure of government. Stalin remained in sole control and the make-up of the Politburo was very much the same as it was before the war. Economically, the war was extremely costly although the US lend–lease programme was of great help in offsetting this. Over 27 million Russians lost their lives (compared with over nine million during the First World War). The industrial and transport infrastructure was damaged and Russian politicians also had to deal with the rising expectations for social reform from the Russian people. Stalin responded by continuing with his Five-Year Plans and clamping down any opposition to his reconstruction programme but without resorting to the levels of repression seen before the war. Wartime conferences at Yalta, Potsdam and Tehran revealed that the transition to a 'new' post-war world would be far from easy. The big questions concerned the future of Germany and Russia's territorial claims in the East and the role of the Western allies in keeping the peace. These were never resolved satisfactorily and, given the ideological differences between Russia and the West, it was almost inevitable that there would be conflict once the war finished. The tensions that arose between Russia and the USA were labelled the Cold War. It was characterised by a nuclear arms race, indirect involvement in 'hot' wars and events, for example, the Cuban Missile Crisis and economic sanctions. All of this had a financial cost to the Russian government but did not alter greatly the way Russia was run, although there was a move towards Peaceful Coexistence and *détente*, this was not new; Lenin had talked about more cordial relations being formed with the West decades before. However, Khrushchev's denouncement of the rule of Stalin could be seen as a product of the Cold War in that he was intent on

presenting a more positive image to the West so that tensions could be eased. On balance, both the Second World War and the Cold War did not appear to have the same dramatic effect as the First World War.

10 In conclusion, the First World War did have a very significant impact on Russian government as it fuelled the revolution which created a markedly different form of rule in contrast to that of the tsars. But, the causes of the revolution were deep seated and it is probably best to see the Great War as providing the right climate for it to ignite. The other wars of the period were less important in terms of consequence for government partly due to their type but also, in the case of the Second World War, because Russia was on the side of the victors.

10 A succinct end that makes a very clear judgement in favour of the First World War as having the greatest impact on the development of Russian government.

Assessment for Essay 1

Uses a wide range of accurate, detailed and relevant evidence. Accurate and confident use of appropriate historical terminology. Answer is clearly structured and mostly coherent. [**Level IA: 19 marks out of 20**]

Shows a good understanding of key concepts relevant to the question set. Good synthesis and synoptic assessment of the whole period. Answer is consistently analytical with developed and substantiated explanations. [**Level IA: 39 marks out of 40**]

The overall mark of 58 would take this into the A* bracket. If the answer has a weakness it lies in an assessment of the relative importance of factors. This, on balance, has been done implicitly.

Essay 2: 'Out of all the wars that influenced the development of Russian government, the First World War was the most significant.' How far do you agree with this statement as it applies to the period from 1855 to 1964?

1 The First World War was important in that it was responsible for the fall of the Tsar, the installation of the Provisional Government and the dramatic takeover of Russia by the Bolsheviks. However, there were other wars that could be considered turning points such as the Crimean War, the Russo-Japanese War, the Civil War, the Second World and, finally, the Cold War.

1 A reasonable start. There is little indication of the line of argument to be taken but the student shows an awareness of the need to discuss a range of wars.

2 The Crimean War of 1854–6 had an important impact on the development of Russian government in that it pushed the Tsar to make reforms. The war illustrated how backward Russia was compared with the rest of Europe and Alexander II therefore felt pressured to make changes that would modernise Russia and maintain its world status. The most important reform the Tsar introduced was the emancipation of the serfs in 1861. By freeing the peasants this had the knock-on effect of changes having to be made to the way society was governed, especially at a local level. Before the Emancipation Edict, local aristocracy were responsible for governance and administration in regions and their authority went unchallenged.

2 A chronological approach appears to have been adopted. It would have been better if the essay had started with an analysis of the First World War which would have allowed for a more comparative structure. Nevertheless, a decent attempt has been made to assess the impact of the Crimean War on Russian government.

The only person that they were responsible to was the Tsar. After the peasants were freed, they demanded more say in how regions were run and Alexander II responded to this by setting up the Zemstva or regional councils. Peasants could be elected to the Zemstva (although the councils were dominated by wealthier people) which meant that Russia became more democratic. Also, there were other reforms that were linked to the Emancipation Edict and that also affected the nature of government. They included those that changed the judicial system, the organisation of the military and the provision of education. Some historians have argued that the whole package of reforms had a negative impact on government as they allowed for the rise of opposition groups and the eventual assassination of the Tsar in 1881.

3 The chronological framework is continued. The paragraph makes some valid comment about the impact of the Russo-Japanese War although comparison with other wars is limited to the first sentence.

3 The Russo-Japanese War of 1904–5 was significant because as with the Crimean War, Russia struggled to beat an enemy that they should have dealt with easily. The Russian fleet was badly damaged at the Battle of Tsushima and which dented the morale of the navy. When the peace treaty was signed, Russia had to withdraw from Port Arthur, give up territory in East Asia and promise not to interfere in Korea. This was all very humiliating for the government and angered the Russian people. They couldn't understand how the might of the Russian military had lost to an unimportant Asian country. The anger of the people spilled over into a mini revolution. The Tsar responded by creating the Duma which allowed the population to have more say in the way the country was to be run. However, Nicholas clamped down on its powers and so it wasn't such a big change after all.

4/5 These paragraphs have merit in that they consist of a synthesis of a good range of relevant material. Some comments needed developing and, again, there was scope for including more comparative analysis. This is especially important given that the First World War is the war highlighted in the question.

4 As a result of the Russo-Japanese War, Nicholas II also instructed his ministers to speed up industrialisation and to continue to improve the railway system. Without this Russia would never have been able to compete in a major conflict with the other European powers. But even though this was mostly successful, Russia still struggled to cope with the First World War. During the first part of the war there were heavy defeats for the army at Tannenberg and the Masurian Lakes. The main reason for this was a shortage of munitions. Later, Nicholas took control of the armed forces and there was a decent attempt to launch a counter-attack offensive under General Brusilov. However, this failed and Nicholas was blamed for Russia's poor showing. He was forced to abdicate and was replaced by the Provisional Government. This was significant in that it was the first move towards a Constituent Assembly and the implementation of a democratic system of rule. But the Provisional Government was short lived. It struggled to cope with the pressure it was placed under by the Petrograd Soviet, offered little in the way of a solution to problems created by the war and failed to deal with land problems. It was no surprise that radicals took advantage of this situation and moved to overthrow the Provisional Government in October 1917.

5 Lenin and the Bolsheviks introduced a form of government based on communism which was very different from what had gone on before. Lenin decided to rule as a dictator until the people could take over. All land and wealth was to be shared out equally and everyone was to eventually be given the vote. In this way the First World War influenced the revolution which created a dramatic change to the way Russia was governed. In reality, things didn't work out how Lenin planned and rule by dictatorship remained until the fall of communism. Both Lenin and Stalin ruled with a rod of iron. Under Lenin, the *Cheka* was used to enforce War Communism and with Stalin, the governance of Russia was characterised by the Great Terror. Stalin used the secret police to purge opposition and create fear among the population so that they would obey Stalin without question. In many ways this totalitarian form of government was similar to autocracy under the tsars except that the level of repression was taken to new heights. Thus, it could be argued that the Russian Revolution did not lead to a totally new way of ruling.

6 The Civil War was not much of a turning point as it simply allowed the Bolsheviks to strengthen their power. They faced little organised opposition and the victory of the Red Army under Trotsky gave the Bolsheviks a mandate to rule how they wanted to. However, the war was very costly and disruptive which is why Lenin introduced War Communism. This was not popular and caused some divisions in the government. The New Economic Policy was brought in to replace War Communism and silence the critics but it simply led to divisions of a different sort. These party differences were exploited by Stalin after Lenin's death which allowed him to seize power. Therefore, the Civil War was significant in that it allowed Russia to eventually be ruled in a very repressive manner.

> 6 A fairly clear judgement is made about the importance of the Civil War even though the section is rather brief.

7 As Russia was successful during the Second World War there was no need for reforms and a change in the way Russia was governed. In fact, Stalin used victory to build the image of Russia as a strong and powerful nation ruled successfully by a communist regime. He expanded Russia's sphere of influence throughout Eastern Europe and committed Russia to the nuclear arms race. All of this gave Russia a much higher profile internationally. Khrushchev continued Russia's involvement in the so-called Cold War. Although there were a number of flashpoints that might have led to serious military conflicts with the USA, the Cold War had little impact on the internal workings of government.

> 7 The student has shown an awareness of the need to cover the whole period by providing a synopsis of the impact of the Second World War and the Cold War.

8 In conclusion, the First World War was important in that it provided the climate for radicals to overthrow the Provisional Government. However, the communists ruled in a way that was fairly similar to the tsars. In some ways the Russo-Japanese War was just as important in that it also led to a revolution that laid the foundation for the dramatic events of October 1917.

> 8 A judgement is reached in the conclusion that mostly follows on from what has been written in the main part of the answer. The comment about the Russo-Japanese War is a bit weak and needed expanding.

Assessment for Essay 2

Uses mostly accurate, detailed and relevant evidence, which demonstrates a competent command of the topic. Generally accurate use of historical terminology. Answer is structured and mostly coherent [**Level II: 14 marks out of 20**]

Sound understanding of key concepts relevant to analysis and mostly focused on the question set. The answer is something of a mixture of analysis and explanation but also description of events. Some of the analysis is uneven and there is a drift, in places, away from synthesising material. [**Level III: 25 marks out of 40**]

The overall mark of 39 would result in the award of a high grade C. The candidate has covered the whole period and has focused on discussing the importance of a range of wars on the development of Russian government. The chronological framework adopted means that the student has struggled to provide a comparative analysis of the impact of wars. Subsequently, a case for stating that one war was more important than another has not been forcefully made.

Mark Schemes for Assessing the Essays

How to use the mark schemes

Mark schemes are used by assessors and examiners to determine how best to categorise a candidate's work and ensure that the performance of thousands of candidates is marked to a high degree of accuracy and consistency. Few essays fall neatly into the mark levels. For example, some essays give a good overview but provide few supporting details, and some address the topic in general but not the question in particular. As a result, examiners seek to find the 'best fit' when applying the mark levels. Assessment

	AO1a Mark Scheme for Levels I, II, III and IV
Assessment Objectives	Recall, select and use historical knowledge appropriately, and communicate knowledge and understanding clearly and effectively.
Level IA **18–20 marks**	Uses a wide range of accurate, detailed and relevant evidence. Accurate and confident use of appropriate historical terminology. Answer is clearly structured and coherent; communicates accurately and legibly.
Level IB **16–17 marks**	Uses accurate, detailed and relevant evidence. Accurate use of a range of appropriate historical terminology. Answer is clearly structured and mostly coherent; writes accurately and legibly.
Level II **14–15 marks**	Uses mostly accurate, detailed and relevant evidence, which demonstrates a competent command of the topic. Generally accurate use of historical terminology. Answer is structured and mostly coherent; writing is legible and communication is generally clear.
Level III **12–13 marks**	Uses accurate and relevant evidence, which demonstrates some command of the topic but there may be some inaccuracy. Answer includes relevant historical terminology but this may not be extensive or always accurately used. Most of the answer is organised and structured; the answer is mostly legible and clearly communicated.
Level IV **10–11 marks**	There is deployment of relevant knowledge but level/accuracy of detail will vary; there may be some evidence that is tangential or irrelevant. Some unclear and/or under-developed and/or disorganised sections; mostly satisfactory level of communication.

Objective Ia assesses candidates' ability to use information relevantly, accurately and consistently to answer the question set. Assessment Objective Ib assesses their level of understanding and their ability to explain, analyse and synthesise key developments across the whole period. Synthesis is the most important skill in a synoptic exam and as a result carries most marks. When you read an essay, think about the two assessment objectives that are being tested. Decide which level best suits the overall quality of the essay and be positive, rewarding candidates for what they have done rather than penalising them for what they have failed to do. When you have decided upon the most appropriate level, start at the top of the mark band and work down until you reach the mark that best reflects the essay. The two marks will give you a final mark out of 60. Note that only the top four levels (out of seven) have been used to assess the essays in this book.

	AO1b Mark Scheme for Levels I, II, III and IV
Assessment Objectives	Demonstrates an understanding of the past through explanation and analysis, arriving at substantiated judgements of key concepts and of the relationships between key features of the period studied.
Level IA **36–40 marks**	Excellent understanding of key concepts relevant to the question set. Excellent synthesis and synoptic assessment of the whole period. Answer is consistently analytical with developed and substantiated explanations, some of which may be unexpected.
Level IB **32–35 marks**	Clear and accurate understanding of most key concepts relevant to analysis and to the question set. Answer is mostly consistently and relevantly analytical with mostly developed and substantiated explanations. Clear understanding of the significance of issues and synthesis of the whole period.
Level II **28–31 marks**	Mostly clear and accurate understanding of many key concepts relevant to analysis and to the topic. Clear understanding of the significance of most relevant issues in their historical context. Much of the answer is relevantly analytical and substantiated with detailed evidence but there may be some uneven judgements.
Level III **24–27 marks**	Sound understanding of key concepts relevant to analysis and mostly focused on the question set. Answers may be a mixture of analysis and explanation but also simple description of relevant material and narrative of relevant events, or answers may provide more consistent analysis but the quality will be uneven and its support often general or thin. There may only be a limited synthesis of the whole period.
Level IV **20–23 marks**	Understanding of key concepts relevant to analysis and the topic is variable but in general is satisfactory. Answers may be largely descriptive/narratives of events and links between this and analytical comments will typically be weak or unexplained or answers will mix passages of descriptive material with occasional explained analysis. Limited synoptic judgements of part of the period.

Select Reading List

Edward Acton, *Russia: The Tsarist and Soviet Legacy*, 2nd edition, Longman 1995.

Edward Acton and Tom Stableford, *The Soviet Union: A Documentary History, Volume 1, 1917–1940*, University of Exeter Press 2005.

Edward Acton and Tom Stableford, *The Soviet Union: A Documentary History, Volume 2, 1939–1991*, University of Exeter Press 2007.

Anne Applebaum. *Gulag: A History of Soviet Camps*, Penguin 2003.

Robert Conquest, *The Great Terror: A Reassessment*, Oxford University Press 1990.

Helen Dunmore, *The Siege*, Penguin 2002.

Orlando Figes, *A People's Tragedy: The Russian Revolution 1891–1924*, Jonathan Cape 1996.

Orlando Figes, *The Whisperers: Private Life in Stalin's Russia*, Penguin 2007.

Sheila Fitzpatrick, *Everyday Stalinism: Ordinary Life in Extraordinary Times: Soviet Russia in the 1930s*, Oxford University Press 1999.

Martin Gilbert, *The Routledge Atlas of Russian History*, 4th edn, Routledge 2007.

Vasily Grossman, *A Writer at War: With the Red Army 1941–45*, Pimlico 2006.

Geoffrey Hosking, *Russia and the Russians: From Earliest Times to 2001*, Penguin 2001.

Lindsey Hughes, *The Romanovs: Ruling Russia 1613–1917*, Hambledon Continuum 2008.

Catriona Kelly, *Comrade Pavlik: The Rise and Fall of a Soviet Boy Hero*, Granta Books 2005.

Michael Lynch, *Reaction and Revolution: Russia 1894–1924*, Hodder Murray 2005.

Catherine Merridale, *Ivan's War: The Red Army 1939–45*, Faber & Faber 2005.

Walter G. Moss, *A History of Russia. Volume I: To 1917*, 2nd edn, Anthem Press 2003.

Walter G. Moss, *A History of Russia. Volume II: Since 1855*, 2nd edn, Anthem Press 2005.

Peter Oxley, *Russia 1855–1991: From Tsars to Commissars*, Oxford University Press 2001.

Richard Pipes, *Russia Under the Old Regime*, Penguin 2005.

Christopher Read, *Lenin*, Routledge 2005.

Christopher Read (ed.), *The Stalin Years. A Reader*, Palgrave Macmillan 2005.

Simon Sebag Montefiore, *Stalin: The Court of the Red Tsar*, Phoenix 2004.

Victor Serge, *Memoirs of a Revolutionary*, University of Iowa Press 2002.

Robert Service, *A History of Modern Russia: From Nicholas II to Putin*, Penguin 2003.

Aleksandr Solzhenitsyn, *One Day in the Life of Ivan Denisovich*, Penguin 2000.

John Steinbeck, *A Russian Journal*, Penguin 2000.

Geoffrey Swain, *Russia's Civil War*, History Press 2008.

Ian D. Thatcher, *Trotsky*, Routledge 2003.

J.N. Westwood, *Endurance and Endeavour: Russian History 1812–2001*, 5th edn, Oxford University Press 2002.

Alan Wood, *The Origins of the Russian Revolution*, Methuen 1987.

Glossary

Agents provocateurs   Those who tempt others to commit a criminal act so that they can then be charged.

All-Russian Congress of Soviets   A meeting of delegates from soviets throughout Russia to decide on the policies to be adopted by the soviets.

American Relief Administration   A US relief mission to aid Europe, including Russia, after the First World War. The director of the organisation was Herbert Hoover, future president.

Anschluss of Austria   The union of Germany and Austria that was officially announced on 13 March 1938.

Anti-Semitic   To be prejudiced against Jews.

Appeasement   Foreign policy based on coming to a mutual agreement to resolve disputes, usually through the making of concessions.

April Theses   Lenin's outline of policies to be followed by the Bolsheviks after his return from exile in April 1917.

Armistice   An agreement to stop fighting.

Article 87   A section of the 1906 Fundamental Laws that allowed for proposed legislation to be submitted directly to the Tsar for his approval.

Attrition warfare   Where no progress is made by either side during a war but where both sides continue to wear each other down until one gives way.

Autocratic   To rule as an absolute sovereign using the power inherited from one's parents (and, in the case of the Tsars, granted by God. The Tsars believed that God had placed them on earth to rule autocratically.)

Balkan League   An alliance, put together between the spring and autumn of 1912, between Serbia, Bulgaria, Greece and Montenegro.

Balkan Wars of 1912–13   These came in two phases. First, the Balkan League went to war against Turkey with the hope of getting the Turks to withdraw from Macedonia so that the latter could be divided up among League members. The Turks were defeated and signed an armistice in December 1912. Second, immediately after the armistice, Bulgaria claimed that it was being cheated out of territory handed over by the Turks by another member of the League, Serbia. Bulgaria then attacked Serbia. Greece, Romania and Turkey went to the aid of the Serbs and the Bulgarian forces were defeated. Bulgaria was forced to hand over all of the gains made during the first war.

Battle of Britain   An aerial battle between Germany and Britain that took place from 12 August to 30 September 1940.

Belligerent countries   Those countries that had been directly involved in the First World War.

Berlin Blockade   In June 1948 the Western powers combined to introduce a new currency in the zones under their control. Russia saw this as an attempt to show how capitalism could bring prosperity to Berlin (a new currency meant a lowering of inflation and more spending power) and retaliated by blocking all communication links with the western part of the city. The blockade was eventually lifted in May 1949.

Berlin Wall   A wall erected in 1961 by Russia in Berlin to formally separate the east from the west. The aim was to stop people escaping to the Western zones.

Black Earth regions   The area from the south-western borderlands into Asiatic Russia.

Black Repartition   A vision held by peasants of a time when all land would be shared out equally.

Bloody Sunday   On 9 January 1905 a group of demonstrators marching on the Winter Palace, and led by Father Gapon, were shot at by soldiers. Over 200 people were killed and about 800 injured.

Bolsheviks   A breakaway RSDLP group who were the 'majority' (as labelled by Lenin).

Bonus schemes   Where extra payments were made to workers for exceeding individual production targets.

Boxer Rebellion   A seven-week siege of foreign embassies in Peking by Chinese rebels.

Break bulk   The carriage of low-value, high-density goods in large quantities. That is, heavy, bulky goods such as coal and iron ore.

Capitalist economy   An economy based on making as much profit as possible from industrial and commercial activity.

Census   An official count of the number of people in the population.

Central Committee   The chief decision-making group of the Russian Communist Party.

Civil marriage   Legal marriage whereby civilians are allowed to choose their partners.

Civil War   A war within a state between civilians holding opposing ideals.

Cold War   A state of tension and hostility between the Soviet bloc and Western powers after the Second World War. However, the hostility did not spill over into actual fighting between the two power blocs.

Collective leadership   Rule by a group whereby responsibilities are equally shared out.

Collectivisation   A communal system of farming whereby peasants shared resources to produce food which was then distributed to ensure that local populations were adequately fed. Surpluses were sent to urban populations.

Comintern   The Communist International body was established in March 1918 with the aim of spreading communism overseas.

Command economy   An economy that is controlled totally by the state.

Communist   A form of rule which allowed for the control, by the 'people', of the means of production, distribution and exchange.

Consolidate   The joining together of resources. In this context, smallholdings were granted that were equivalent to the area of the strips farmed under the old way of farming.

Constituent Assembly   An assembly of politicians that would be elected by the 'people'.

Constitutional government   A government that is organised and administered according to a set of written or unwritten rules.

Constitutional monarchy   A government that is organised and administered according to a set of written or unwritten rules (a constitution) but one that retains a monarch as a figurehead. In such a government, the monarch would relinquish autocratic power but would retain the right to veto legislation and policies deemed to be inappropriate.

Consumer industries   These included any industries producing goods and services for direct consumption by the population (for example, those producing clothing, ovens, cooking utensils, toys for children).

Containment policy   The policy of attempting to stop communism spreading throughout the world.

Council of Ministers   Senior politicians who drafted domestic policies.

Counterfactual argument   An argument based on what might have happened rather than on what actually did occur.

Cult of personality   The use of propaganda to build a positive image of a leader so that the population offer total obedience to that leader.

De facto   Rule as a matter of fact or circumstance rather than rule gained by legal means.

Dekulakisation   The eradication of the alleged wealthier class of Russian peasants known as *kulaks*.

Democratic centralism   Under the Bolsheviks, the people would agree to being led by a cadre (group of key personnel) based in Moscow, until a genuine workers' government could be put in place.

Destalinisation   The denunciation, by Khrushchev, of the policies of Stalin.

Détente   A relaxation in tensions between states during the period of the Cold War, although it is usually applied to the period from 1963 to the late 1970s.

Dialectical   The ongoing changes in society from one stage to another.

Dictatorship   Absolute rule, usually by one person, with no legal, political, economic or social restrictions.

Dictatorship of the proletariat   In theory, rule over the bourgeoisie by the workers. Lenin argued that before this could happen, workers would have to be ordered what to do by the Bolsheviks as they did not have the knowledge, understanding and skill to take full control of governing Russia.

Diktat   An order given by those in power; something that is non-negotiable.

Dissidents   Those who disagreed with the aims and procedures of the government.

Doctors' Plot   An announcement was made by the Stalinist regime in January 1953 concerning nine doctors who had worked alongside a US Jewish group to murder high-ranking Soviet officials. Seven of the doctors were Jews.

Duma   An elected imperial parliament but with a restricted franchise (only a narrow range of people could vote representatives on to the *Duma*).

Duopoly   Power in the hands of two people.

Eastern Front   Where the German and Austrian-Hungarian forces met the Russian forces in Eastern Europe.

Eastern Question   The issues that arose over the decline of the Turkish Ottoman Empire.

Economic autarky   When a country can provide all of the resources it needs without having to trade.

Emancipation of the serfs   An announcement in 1861 that peasants would be freed from being owned, like any other property, by wealthy landowners and the state.

Expansionist foreign policy   Foreign policy that involved the acquisition of territory from other countries (or sometimes expanding influence over such territory).

Factionalist   One who went about pursuing his or her own interests to the detriment of party unity.

First secretary of the party   The most important administrative officer in the Communist Party.

Five-Year Plans   These involved the setting of production targets to be achieved on a five-yearly cycle.

Free market   Any market free of restrictions such as taxes, tariffs, duties or quotas.

Fundamental Laws   Basic laws that reinforced the ideology underpinning tsarist rule.

Fundamental Laws of 1906   Regulations that reinforced the position of the Tsar. Law 5, for example, stated that 'Supreme Autocratic power belongs to the Emperor of all Russia'.

'Georgian Affair'   The mishandling of Georgian nationalism by Ordjonikidze, the Commissar for National Affairs in Georgia. His actions were defended by Stalin.

GNP per capita   Gross national product per head of the population. This is often used as a measure of living standards.

Gold standard   The fixing of a country's currency to a specific quantity (and therefore value) of gold.

Gosplan   A group originally set up in 1921 to plan for industrialisation and economic growth.

Government bonds   A way of investing in the government by buying bonds (loan certificates) and cashing them in at later date with interest.

Grand Alliance   The wartime alliance of Britain, France, Russia and the USA.

Great Patriotic War   The war against Nazi Germany from 1941 to 1945.

Great Powers   Britain, France, Russia, Germany (Prussia before 1871) and Austria-Hungary before 1914.

Great Purge   The period from 1936 to 1938 when thousands of people were arrested, convicted and executed for committing 'counter-revolutionary' crimes.

Great Russia   Also known as Muscovy, the old Russian principality that had Moscow at its centre.

Great Russian Bear   A term used by the West to describe the perceived military threat posed by Russia.

Great Terror   The period from 1936 to 1938 when the terrorisation of the Russian people reached a peak.

Green armies Mainly peasant groups who opposed Bolshevik rule.

Gulag A labour camp that was used mainly to house political dissidents and those suspected of being anti-communist.

Holy Sepulchre The cave outside Jerusalem in which the body of Christ is believed to have lain between his burial and Resurrection.

Home Front This refers to what was happening domestically during the war – what kind of wartime work civilians were involved in.

Housing cooperatives Organisations formed by employees who belonged to the same work enterprise or professional union. They were given first pickings over new state housing as long as they could meet government-set prices.

Ignatiev memorandum Nicholas Pavolich Ignatiev (1832–1908) was Russia's ambassador to Constantinople. In 1876, he sent a note to Serbian leaders, without official approval, saying that they could rely on Russian help if they declared war on Turkey.

In kind Payment other than by using money, such as the exchange of goods and services.

Incendiary Setting fire to rural property, usually farm buildings and hayricks.

Iron Curtain An imaginary border between Russian-dominated East and West Europe.

'July Days' A month of protests and strikes against the war and the ineffectual policies of the Provisional Government.

Justices of the Peace Landowners appointed as officials to maintain law and order at a local level. They worked in conjunction with the police.

Kadets The Constitutional Democrats, a liberal political group, founded in 1905.

Katyn Forest massacre The execution of around 5000 Polish officers by the Red Army in the forest of Katyn, Smolensk, on the eve of the German invasion.

Kolkhozy Farms owned and partly organised by the state but worked on by peasant farmers not directly employed by the state. Members could own a house, a small plot of land and a few animals.

Komsomols Members of the youth organisation known as the Young Communist League.

Kronstadt A Baltic naval base.

Kulaks Peasants who accumulated wealth through producing a surplus of food and selling it at local markets. Under the tsars *kulaks* stood out and were disliked for being money-lenders. With the Bolsheviks it was never really clear as to who actually was a *kulak* as opposed to an ordinary peasant. However, Bolshevik leaders associated grain hoarding and therefore shortages with the *kulaks*. Needless to say, wealthier, more productive peasants were persecuted and blamed for the shortcomings of Bolshevik agricultural policy.

Kurile Islands and South Sakhalin The Kurile Islands in Russia's Sakhalin Oblast region, are a volcanic archipelago that stretches approximately 1300 km north-east from Hokkaido, Japan, to Kamchatka, Russia, separating the Sea of Okhotsk from the North Pacific Ocean.

Labour camps Punishment camps where political opponents were set to hard labour. They were placed in the more inhospitable parts of Russia such as Siberia.

Labour Code Rules for the deployment and control of labour.

Labourists Those who were specifically interested in improving the working conditions of the proletariat.

Land and Liberty A pressure group consisting of intellectuals who believed it was important to live among peasants so as to get to understand their plight.

Land Captains Landowners who were appointed, from 1889 onwards, mainly to supervise the work of the regional councils or *Zemstva* that had been introduced by Alexander II.

Land to the Peasants A propaganda campaign that promised the land issue (a fairer distribution of land) would be resolved in favour of the peasants.

Leading cadres The 'top' members of the Communist Party responsible for organising and educating the masses.

League of Nations   An international body set up in 1919 to keep international peace through the settlement of disputes by arbitration.

Legiticism   Policy based on the idea that what was being done was right and just in the eyes of the majority.

Lend–lease   The US Congress passed an act in March 1941 that allowed the president to lend or lease equipment to countries 'whose defence the president deems vital to the defence of the USA'.

Lenin Enrolment   A campaign aimed to encourage peasants to officially join the Bolshevik Party.

Leningrad affair   A purge of the friends and colleagues of Zhdanov after his death in 1948.

Liberal democracy   A political ideology that promotes the right of the people to be able to be free to choose. This would include freedom to speak what one believed in and the freedom to choose a representative in government.

Liberals   Those who wanted changes to the political system but with the monarchy kept in place.

Light and consumer industries   Those industries that produced goods from primary products (coal, iron ore, other raw materials) to be consumed by the bulk of the population.

Liquidate the *kulaks* as a class   Stalin's policy to eliminate wealthier peasants (*kulaks*) as part of the class war in the countryside. *Kulaks* were considered to be bourgeois.

Marshall Plan   A programme to help European recovery after the Second World War which was put forward by the US Secretary of State General George Marshall (1880–1959). He believed that the USA should 'assist in the return of normal economic health in the world without which there can be no political stability and no assured peace'.

Marxism–Leninism   Lenin's interpretation of Marxism which argued that the move to worker control of the means of production, distribution and exchange could be speeded up.

Marxism–Leninism–Stalinism   Stalin's version of Marxism–Leninism.

Medele'ev tariff of 1891   Named after Dimitry Medele'ev who put together a 700-page book of tariffs (taxes) that should be applied to all imports of goods.

Megalomania   An individual's belief that they are very powerful and important.

Mensheviks   A breakaway RSDLP group who were the 'minority' (as labelled by Lenin).

Militarisation of labour   Workers were forced to work either as labourers or soldiers.

Mir   A group of elders who were responsible for governing the behaviour of members of rural communities or villages.

Mobilisation order   The order by the government for the military to be organised to go to war. A part mobilisation refers to some of the military being prepared for a limited conflict (that is, against a relatively small state). Full mobilisation means that all of the military would be in a state of readiness to go to war.

Monopoly concessions   Being given the right to be the only seller of a particular good.

Munich Peace Conference   A meeting between Germany, Italy, France and Britain that resulted in Germany being allowed to occupy the Sudetenland as long as it guaranteed not to go into the rest of Czechoslovakia.

National minorities   Ethnic groups that spread across the empire that were not of 'pure' Rus. They included, for example, Jews, Georgians and Ukrainians.

Nationalised   The state control of industry and commerce by taking ownership of the means of production, distribution and exchange of goods and services.

Natural rate of growth   The relationship between birth rates and death rates and how this affected population growth. If the birth rate increased and the death rate fell the natural rate of growth would have been relatively high.

Nepman   The 'new' type of businessman that emerged as a result of the NEP.

New Economic Policy   An economic policy that liberalised, to an extent, the operation of the Russian economy and one aimed to counter the adverse impact of War Communism. Thus, individuals were once more allowed to produce goods (including food) purely to make a profit.

New Soviet Man   The ideal Soviet citizen – one who was hard working, law abiding, moral and totally supportive of the Communist Party.

New work discipline   Factory owners introduced strict rules and regulations that were required for employees to work safely and efficiently with machines. This was especially important for recruits from the countryside who were used to working according to 'nature's clock'.

Nomenklatura   'Approved' officers, administrators and managers in the communist regime who possessed specialist skills.

October Manifesto   Nicholas II's blueprint for a new form of elective government that revolved around the *Duma*.

Octobrists   Supporters of the Tsar and, in particular, his proposals made in the October Manifesto.

Old Believers   Those who believed in the most traditional form of the Russian Orthodox Church. They also thought that they were more Russian than other Russians.

'Opium of the people'   The view that religion was like a drug that took people's minds off worrying about economic and social problems. It was coined by Karl Marx in *Contribution to the Critique of Hegel's Philosophy of Right* (1843–4).

Oppositionists   Those who opposed the communist revolution.

Orthodox and Non-Orthodox religion
Orthodox religion was the established and traditional beliefs of the Russian Orthodox Church, which had its roots in the Greek Orthodox Church. Non-orthodox refers to any set of beliefs that differed from those of the Russian Orthodox Church.

'Orthodoxy, Autocracy and Nationality'   The slogan used by the tsars and Pobedonostsev to justify and explain the conservative nature of tsarist rule.

Ottoman Turks   Those who were part of the dynasty originally founded by Osman (c1300) which governed the Turkish Empire until 1922.

Pale of Settlement   This was the region within which Jews were allowed to settle. From 1835, it included Lithuania, Poland and the south-western provinces (including the Ukraine).

Pan-Slavism   The movement to unite all Slavic peoples as one nation.

Paternalistic   Protecting the people.

Patriarchy   A male-dominated form of organisation and rule.

Peasant Land Bank   A bank especially set up by the government to allow peasants to borrow money at relatively cheap rates to allow the purchase of land.

Peasant vigilantism   Rural people taking the matter of law and order into their own hands.

People's Will   A terrorist group consisting of members of the educated classes who were upset by Alexander II's refusal to continue with his reform programme after the mid-1860s.

Petrograd   St Petersburg was renamed Petrograd in August 1914.

Petrograd Soviet   The Petrograd workers' council set up to campaign for workers' rights.

Plenipotentiaries   Officials who had 'total' power at a local level.

Pogrom   An organised massacre of Russian Jews.

Polish question   The question as to whether the Poles would be allowed self-rule.

Potemkin   A battleship on which a mutiny occurred. The incident was later made famous through the silent film *Battleship Potemkin* (1928).

Pravda   The key Bolshevik newspaper which was allowed to start publication again in 1917.

Presidium   A small group of ministers rather like the Cabinet in the UK political system.

Principalities   Territories ruled over by a member of a royal family, usually a prince.

Progressive Bloc   A group within the Fourth *Duma* consisting of members of the Kadets, Octobrists, Nationalists and Party of Progressives, who challenged the authority of Nicholas II.

Proletariat   A term used to describe those who worked in industry and lived in urban areas.

Protectorates   States that were temporarily protected by another, usually more powerful state.

Prussia   Important Germanic state before the unification of Germany in 1871.

Putilov works   The biggest private factory in Russia by the start of the twentieth century. It specialised in iron production and became very important during the First World War in providing artillery.

Rabkrin   The Workers' and Peasants' Inspectorate, a highly bureaucratic and overstaffed organisation.

Radicals   Those who wanted a complete overhaul of the political system including the abolition of the monarchy.

'Reaction'   Alexander III reacted to the liberal reforms put together by his father by reversing them and introducing more repressive measures.

Real wages   Wages after the impact of inflation is taken into account.

Red Army   The communist army that originally recruited mainly from the soviets and factory committees.

Red Guard   A general term to denote armed supporters of the Bolsheviks especially in the second half of 1917.

Red Terror   Fear engendered by the Bolsheviks through the threat of arrest, imprisonment, exile and/or execution.

Redemption payments   The repayment of loans that had to be taken out to purchase land that was redistributed after 1861.

Reds   A general term for those who actively supported the Bolsheviks during the Civil War.

Reparations   Payments of money that constitute compensation for the damage done during a war.

Revolutionary defensism   Defence and protection of everything achieved by the revolution of March 1917.

Russian Orthodox Church   A branch of Christianity that was very traditional and that was independent from outside authorities such as the papacy. It was used to teach the people to obey the Tsar as he was said to be anointed by God.

Russification   A policy aimed at transforming the different peoples of the Russian empire into 'pure' Rus (the supposedly original inhabitants of Russia).

Schlieffen Plan   The plan put together in 1905 by the Chief of the German General Staff, General Count Alfred Von Schlieffen (1833–1913), to act as a blueprint for a German attack in the West.

Scorched earth policy   Stalin ordered that all material objects of worth should be destroyed as the Russian forces retreated to stop them falling into the hands of the enemy.

Sectarians   Anyone who belonged to a group that held extreme, and often unusual, religious views.

Show trials   Trials of important political figures that were made open to the public.

Slavonic   Belonging to the Slav peoples. These peoples consisted mainly of Great Russians (Muscovites), Ukrainians and Cossacks, all of whom spoke the same Indo-European language.

Slavophiles   Those who believed that Orthodox Slavs were superior to Western Europeans.

Social control   Control, usually by politicians, of the beliefs, attitudes and actions of members of society through the careful organisation and administration of particular institutions, for example, education, religion, the media.

Socialist realism   The 'official' way of writing to reflect the heroic efforts of workers and peasants to ensure the success of communism.

Sovkhozy   Farms owned by the state and worked on by state employees.

Stakhanovite movement   Based on the extraordinary efforts of the Donbas miner, Alexei Stakhanov, who produced way above the normal quantity of coal per man-shift. He was turned, using propaganda, into a 'model' worker for others to copy. Those who did, creating a Stakhanovite movement, were given special rewards such as red carpets and holidays in Moscow.

State pricing mechanism   The government policy of providing official prices for goods and services.

Straits   The stretch of sea from the Dardanelles into the Bosporus.

Subsistence farming   Ensuring just enough was produced to keep members of a community fed over a given period.

Sudetenland   An area in Czechoslovakia in 1938 that contained about three million Germans.

Suez Crisis   The Suez Canal was nationalised by President Nasser in 1956. France and Britain, alarmed by Egypt's growing ties with communists, planned to take control of this important shipping route.

Sultan   Muslim head of the Ottoman Empire.

Supreme Soviet of the USSR   The main law-making body in Soviet government.

Synoptic   A general view or a summary of the whole picture.

Taxation exemptions   Being allowed to pay lower tax in return for lending money to the government.

Tenements   Similar to blocks of flats.

Total war   A war that had a more total and long-lasting impact on the whole nation.

Totalitarianism   A centralised form of dictatorial government that controls every aspect of the behaviour of the citizens of the state.

Treaty of Berlin   Germany and Russia agreed to remain neutral if either was attacked by a third power.

Tripartite Pact   A military alliance between Germany, Italy and Japan.

Tsar   The title given to the emperors of Russia.

United Nations   An organisation that formally came into being in June 1945 that was designed to maintain world peace.

Vanguard   In this context a leading group of people whose mission was to lay the base for a proletarian takeover of the governance of Russia.

Vera Zasulich case   Zasulich was a revolutionary who shot and wounded the governor of St Petersburg, General Trepov, in 1878. Trepov was considered to be a tyrant of the highest order who thought nothing of flogging political prisoners for no good reason. Zasulich was put on trial but the jury found her not guilty as her actions were considered to be just. Many believed that was clear indication that the legal reforms of 1864 had created a climate that would allow revolutionary activity to flourish.

Virgin Land campaign   Khrushchev's plan to exploit the 'virgin' soils of Kazakhstan and Western Siberia.

Vyborg Manifesto   A set of demands from militant *Duma* MPs asking the people of Finland not to pay taxes or serve in the armed forces until the *Duma* was restored.

War Bonds   Government savings certificates issued during wartime to the public with a promised fixed rate of return after the war. They had the important psychological impact of making people feel that they were making a valid contribution to the war effort.

War Communism   A set of economic policies involving the centralised control of industry and commerce (nationalisation) by the communist government. Surpluses of goods, especially food, were requisitioned and redistributed among the population. It was considered to be a harsh but necessary measure to ensure that the people supporting the Reds were adequately fed, clothed and sheltered during a time of national crisis (the Civil War).

War indemnity   A sum of money paid by one nation to another as a result of losing a war.

Westernisers   Those who wanted to modernise Russia in the same way as Western Europe.

Whites   A general term for those who actively opposed the Bolsheviks during the Civil War.

Winter Palace   Official residence of the tsars in St Petersburg.

Workers' insurance system   Insurance against being injured in the workplace. Other schemes, against ill-health, old age and unemployment, were also introduced through the 1924 and 1936 constitutions.

Working-class consciousness   An awareness among workers that they were experiencing similar living and working conditions and therefore belonged to a single class of worker.

Index